Way of the Wanderers

JESS SMITH

one of Scotland's Travelling People, was raised on the road until she met and married her husband Dave, a non-Traveller. She left her old ways behind but always yearned for the freedom of the past. Her writing career did not begin until her three children left home to build their own nests. It was then she took the decision to return to her old life, by way of writing about her culture. *Jessie's Journey* was the first book in her autobiographical trilogy, which continued with *Tales from the Tent* and concluded with *Tears for a Tinker*. She has also written a novel, *Bruar's Rest,* and a collection of stories for young readers, *Sookin' Berries*. This book stems from a promise she made to her father.

Way of the Wanderers

The Story of Travellers in Scotland

Jess Smith

BIRLINN

First published in 2012 by
Birlinn Limited
West Newington House
10 Newington Road
Edinburgh
EH9 1QS

www.birlinn.co.uk

Reprinted in 2015

The author gratefully acknowledges the Estate of Athole Cameron for *The Gaun-Aboot Bairn*; Mamie Carson for Keith McPherson's *The Muckle Stane*; Robert Dawson for quotations from *Empty Lands* and unpublished documents; Mary McKay for *A Life Long Gone*; Andrew Sinclair for the quotations from *Rosslyn: The Story of Rosslyn Chapel and the True Story Behind the Da Vinci Code*; and Sheila Stewart for Belle Stewart's *The Berryfields o' Blair* and *Glen Isla*.

ISBN: 978 1 78027 334 1

British Library Cataloguing-in-Publication Data
A catalogue record for this book is available from the British
Library

Set in Bembo and Adobe Jenson at Birlinn

Printed and bound by Grafica Veneta
www.graficaveneta.com

CONTENTS

ILLUSTRATIONS

ACKNOWLEDGEMENTS

To my dear friend Anne for her belief in all I do.

To Robert Dawson, for uncovering the plight of the Scottish Travellers following on from the 1895 report prepared for the then Secretary of State for Scotland on 'The Vagrants, Itinerants, Beggars and Inebriates of Scotland'.

To Jim Caird for providing *A History, or Notes upon the Family of Caird, plus the Clan from Very Early Times* by Rennie Alexander Caird (1915).

To The National Archives of Scotland for *Educating of Scottish Tinkers and Vagrants*.

To the A.K.Bell library for copies of the Aldour Tinker School log book and letters.

To Seamus Macphee for allowing me to ransack his collected papers on the Perth and Kinross housing experiment for Tinkers.

To the Orkney archives.

To the late Sheila Stewart MBE and to Donald, John, George and Alistair for their sharing of family stories and filling blanks in the narrative.

To the late Belle Stewart BEM.

To Mary Mackay for her information on Irish Pavee (Irish Travellers).

To Mary Hendry for allowing me access to her prized collection of Andrew McCormack's Gypsy and Tinkler books.

To David Cowan for his expert advice on standing stones and to Colin Mayall who helped me understand a little of the Pictish and Roman history.

To Macainsh Brown for transporting me back in time to the day of a powerful battle over illicit stills.

When I was researching and compiling this book a 'sea of souls' closed ranks to help me make sense of a huge quantity of material. I want to shout out their names from a high point, but they wish for no recognition. You know who you are, so from my heart – a million thanks.

I dedicate this book to the ancestors of the Travelling People

The Inspiration

'There can be no greater enjoyment to the inquisitive mind
than to find light where there was till then darkness.'
From William Forbes Skene, *The Highlanders of Scotland*

It was early 1982 and there we were: him at death's door and me
crying my eyes out over the linen-sheeted bed, watching his life
ebbing away. Gripped by the sheer helplessness of knowing that
at any moment his sun would dip for the final time, I made him a
silent promise: to discover as much information about the Scottish
Travellers as it was possible to find, and to write a book, a simple,
easy-to-read book.

Yet, walking away from the hospital as the linen sheet was being
pulled across his face I knew there was no way I could write as much
as a goodbye note, let alone a book, in memory of that good man,
my father, Charles Riley. I had no proper education apart from the
usual basics. We were Travellers of the road, and we would leave
school in April, re-entering the classroom in October. Our ways
were travelling and had always been so.

Twenty years went by and my own family had flown their nests.
Totally convinced that writing a book was far beyond my abilities, I'd
decided instead to go where I could feel the breath of my ancestors
and walk in their hardy footsteps, traversing Scotland's remote paths
and climbing her formidable mountains. I found peace and happi-
ness in the sky above and the rock beneath, and I wished nothing
better for the future.

But life is an unpredictable mistress, guided by blind circumstance.
My father had a favourite saying: 'What's before you will not go by

you'. He wasn't a religious man, and he allowed blind fate to guide him rather than any holy text. I believe that is exactly how this book has come about, because in the summer of 2000 fate began to map out a new path for me.

I had just traversed across Buachaille Etive Mor and the neighbouring peaks of Glen Coe, the mountains glowing red and brown with autumn hues. It had been one of those days that all hill-walkers and mountaineers experience at some time: next to perfect, just enough warmth of sunshine on the climb and the bluest clarity all round on the summit where the eye can see for miles.

As I trudged back to the car park I was suddenly aware of something missing; there was a haunting silence. Why was there no busking piper? Standing on a narrow strip of tarmac in Macdonald's glen I strained my ears for that familiar sound, a sound that had always been part of me and my past. Where was the piper resplendent in full Highland regalia – the towering giant, Wullie MacPhee, or sturdy John Macdonald, the auld weaver, the handsome Townsleys or those stirring masters of the bagpipe, the Stewart boys?

The tourists who flocked to the Pass of Glencoe would eagerly take photographs of the Scottish piper, surrounded by the glens and mountains of their forebears, the heartland of the Diaspora, to display proudly back home. To many this moment was the highlight of their Scottish tour. At Edinburgh Castle pipers resplendent in their tartan kilts made excellent subjects for a camera lens, but they were nothing in comparison to a lone piper, his face brooding on the past, with the haunting shape of the Aonach Eagath ridge on his right and the Lost Valley on his left, the deep notes stirring the ghosts of Macdonalds' children massacred centuries ago by those who ruled Scotland.

Standing in the vacant circle of silence, legs weary with the day's climbing, my heart ached. I was mourning the loss of those giants of Traveller culture who piped through thunderstorms and fierce gales. They did it because they needed their summer busking money; without it they'd see a lean winter, but it was more than that, much more. Piping at the Pass was a way of honouring those Macdonald clansmen.

My career as a writer was seeded that day. Somewhere deep inside a quiet voice was urging me to write about our kind, those who were the pipers of the pass, to write about our lives, our paths and campsites.

I have told the story of my first steps in writing in my earlier books, the *Jessie's Journey* trilogy. I decided my lack of English grammar would not stop me, and with that in mind, when I began to write, I didn't write to be read, I wrote to be heard! This approach proved highly successful, and I now have five published books to my credit. My journey as a writer began ten years ago. Since then I've met many people and have never stopped sharing my own story and the tales of my culture with an eager readership.

I'd carved my niche and was ready to carry on writing my books about life on the road. Then a totally unexpected thing happened. I was signing my books at a book festival in the north of Scotland. An elderly lady approached, grabbed my arm and spoke to me seriously. 'I'm a keen fan of your books and those by other wandering folk who've penned their personal stories. I like nothing better than to sit and read them with a cup of tea. I'm an old woman now, but I was raised on tales about all you wanderers of the road. My granny and her granny before her swore by the skills of the tinsmiths who went from place to place. But as a matter of fact we didn't know them as "travellers", they were our Tinker folk who mended pots and pans. There's an untold history about all these people, your people. Why don't you find it and write it down? Now that you're a popular writer, why don't you tell Scotland what the schools ignore, the complete history of the Tinker folk? Forget kings and queens, concentrate on that!'

I was totally dumbstruck. Was this my wake-up call, fate guiding my pen? Perhaps this elderly lady had the uncanny power to see into my mind, or was my father using her as a gentle reminder that I'd made a deathbed promise?

I was worried. Insurmountable obstacles troubled me. How was it possible to write a book about a culture that was always on the move? About a people steeped in secrecy? Just because someone wants to capture it in book form, how can a hidden history suddenly be uncovered? Previously written material about my culture was preserved in the realms of academia, and dealt over and over again with a small number of characters who didn't even seem real to me. Where could I find a thread to guide me, to help me start my journey? Where would I find my sources?

There's an old saying, 'If you look hard enough and search long enough you'll find what you've lost.' I began an in-depth reading of

Scottish clan history. Throughout my life I'd been told tales, some of them dating back to biblical times, and all supposedly fictitious, about lost tribes of Israel. There were later stories about Irish kings with tinsmiths in the midst of their courts, of the break-up of the Jacobite clans and much more. I linked these to myths and legends about ancient smiths and the Roman occupation of Britain. In national and local archives I searched out government documents dealing with tinkers, vagrants and itinerants. Other clues were to be found in stories of tribal peoples found in the Bible, and finally, and most importantly, in the tales of the Travellers themselves, keepers and carriers of my culture. I'd found my sources.

Yet even before I began, another problem presented itself. What should I call my Travellers? In the past they were identified in many forms: as the olive-skinned gypsy with an eye for romance; the tinker/tynker/tinkler with his hammer and nail; the chapmen who not only sold their wares from village to village but brought story and song along with them; the vagabond tramp with nowhere but heather and glen to lay his head; the strolling minstrel and guising actor; bargee sailors of canal and river; the circus clown with painted tears; Romany folki; didiki; barrow boys, whispering horsemen and the gift-of-the-gab hawker. There are countless more names and identities. Even in histories and academic literature authors go from using the words Gypsy to Tinker while describing the same groups. Yet though the variations are innumerable we are really all people from the same seed. From this point on, when referring to historical accounts of my wandering people, I will revert from the name Traveller to that of Tinker, since this is the name that is used in most early books and documents.

This book is by no means an exact account of what really happened in history, but for those still travelling and those long settled it may help to point them in the right direction for a deeper search. I lighten the historical facts with stories of life on the road. As with my previous books, part of this history unfolds as we journey across the countryside, sharing myths, legends and customs as we travel on.

I

The Lochgilphead Tinker

My maiden name was Jessie Riley. I was born in 1948, fifth daughter to Charlie Riley and Jeannie Power. Although described on census records as Tinkers, my parents and relations would be referred to as Gypsies in modern academic studies. Our mobile home was a neatly converted Bedford bus. I shared my travelling days with a sharp-witted father, petite fortune-telling mother and seven sisters; our lives were not blessed with brothers. Our only other companion was a stubby-legged fox terrier affectionately referred to as Tiny, the stud!

Apart from putting food in our bellies it was my father's job to drive us wherever he felt the urge to go. He guided us through childhood and in my case made me conscious of our great culture and heritage. We shared our wanderings with wily foxes, rutting stags and snared rabbits, lived on mashed tatties, Scotch broth, soda scones and game. In winter, for a hundred days, our education was in the hands of the State. To me this was a prison, but we were taught to read, write and count, a priceless gift for every child though I was unaware of it at the time. In summer our education came from my father. His motto was 'respect the earth and commonsense', and it has moulded me into the writer I am today. He enrolled me into his 'organic university', without a lectern or a single red brick.

I was the proverbial question-everything child. I also had my ears open for every scrap of old knowledge or tale of the past. Once a wise old Tinsmith made my head reel with a historical account so vivid and yet so fantastic I hardly dared share it with anyone else until this day. I didn't believe his story at the time and for most of my life gave little thought to it. It's true he was a fantastic storyteller; but what I heard that day, I decided, could be nothing more than a Tinker's tale. Let me share it with you . . .

It was a balmy summer's afternoon in the late fifties. I was skipping about amongst shale on a calm beach near Lochgilphead in finger-shored Argyllshire, Scotland's most spectacular county. The Tinker man was working at his craft and making a colander for a minister's wife. She, like the man of metal, was of the old ways. Throughout her lifetime she had ordered baskets, heather pot-scourers, besom brooms and washing pegs from the passing tinker folk.

He sat at the open tent door of his tiny one-man abode, a lean figure dressed in a baggy jacket with leather-patched elbows and trousers frayed at the bottom. He wore a grey waistcoat with slit pockets buttoned over a collarless shirt. From one pocket hung a chunky gate chain, attached to a silver watch. Apart from his tools, these were all his worldly goods of any value. At an angle on an almost hairless scalp he wore an old army cap sporting an array of fishing hooks round the crown. Intermittent puffs of greyish smoke came from a clay pipe with a yellowed stem; only ever leaving his lips to allow him to spit on the ground. With a short-handled hammer in his blackened hand, he clinked gently on a masterpiece of shiny tin.

He seemed ancient, steeped in wisdom. I can't remember why, but I had a question burning within me that needed answering, and who better to ask.

'Tinker man, will you stop hammering for a minute and tell me something?'

I stared into his crinkled eyes as I quizzed him further: 'Where do we come from? And why is there always a fat boy who picks on me at school? And why are there people who stare at me with devil eyes? Why?'

'Folk don't like us, lassie, for this reason. Long, long ago, Romies brought us away from our tents in the desert. They stuck rings in our ears, chained us up, and made slaves o' us; turned us into human tools. Some of us ended up in Scotland. But don't call me a Tinker – I'm a Caird.'

'What are Romies and Cairds?'

He didn't answer, just pushed me to one side and chucked a log onto the embers of his near-dead fire. Then he continued. 'It's ingrained in folk to hate us, and they don't even know why. But I do. My father, his father and all their fathers before them knew.'

A spiral of blue smoke curled around my shoulders and with the help of a brisk wind blew into my eyes and up my nose. I twisted my head to one side and then the other in a fit of coughing.

He pulled on my sleeve and pointed at a log seat beside him. I sat at his command and got ready to listen to the wisdom of an elder of the Tinsmith trade. He spoke again.

'Greedy conquerors, with a hunger to control the entire known world, that's who the Romies were. The true folk o' this land of Scotland were called Picts, and they tried hard to keep the Romies away from their forts and weem tunnels, but were beaten in battle by the very swords our people had forged. Aye, nobody made the double-edgers like the Caird blacksmiths. Somewhere in that struggle of olden times you'll find the reasons why we'll never be accepted.'

He rubbed his large nose with the back of a hand and said, 'Get away with you now and leave me in peace.'

My mind was racing with a million questions, but as I turned on my heel to run off he tugged my sleeve again and said, 'Wait a minute lassie before you slope off.' I sat down once more on my seat. He laid his hammer and the piece of tin down on the ring of burnt grass at the fire's edge, and showed me his brown hands. 'See the colour o' this skin? These hands are not from this land. African deserts is where you'll see the likes of these. There are other tribes of our kind came out of India over fifteen hundred years ago. They even come here to this country but their tongue is different from ours.' He picked up his hammer again and added, 'Keep all this quiet, my girl. No one likes a brainy Tinker.'

He muttered something in our cant language about the 'manging tongue' of the Gaul, and added, 'There never was such a tongue among us folks, our language was Hebrew! Where do you think the name Hebridean Isles comes from?' I shrugged my shoulders; I was trapped in a maze with no way out. 'It comes from our people. We hear the call of the desert and are off to the wild places with our tents.'

My head was spinning, but it seemed to me this old man was one of the best storytellers who ever lived. He could take a tree's shadow and convince his listeners that there was a giant hiding behind the trunk. And at that moment I thought he was spinning me the tallest tale imaginable.

At the risk of trying his patience too far, I asked him why I should stay silent on the matter we were talking about. 'You're kidding me and making it all up. Anyway if it's true what you said, then why should I not shout it from the rooftops?'

'Because, lassie, folk only believe what they read in books. We keep everything in our heads, and always have. But because there's no books written about our olden days, when people hear our stories they call us liars and fools.'

My history master lowered his eyes and stared into the depths of the fire. I'll never forget the look on his deeply lined face as he touched my hand and slowly nodded his head. Yes, what he was saying was the truth – perhaps not my truth that day when I heard it, but certainly he really believed it. It would be another forty years before I discovered for myself that this history had been recorded, and read the name of the Caird in a printed book.

I stood up and stamped my foot on the ground. A million particles of ash rose into the air and eddied back down to earth. Waving my arms I cried out, 'A Traveller should find the truth about this and write a book about it. They'll believe it then!'

Fixing me with his eye, he hissed, 'The worst thing that ever happened to our kinchin was putting them to schools!' He laid down his hammer again. An incoming tide was creeping nearer to our fire. His bones cracked as he rose to his feet and recited a poem, which I later learned was written by the Scottish poet Andrew Lang.

> 'Ye wanderers that were my sires,
> Who read men's fortunes in their hand,
> Who voyaged with your smithy fires,
> From waste to waste across the land,
> Why did you leave for garth and town,
> Your life by heath and river's brink,
> Why lay your Gypsy freedom down,
> And doom your child to pen and ink?'

With this our conversation stopped dead. The old man closed his teeth around the pipe and said no more. It was as if he'd swallowed hot coals and and was robbed of the power of speech. Perhaps he thought he had already stepped over the line, sharing secrets long held, never uttered, especially to a blabbermouthed teenager. He waved a half-burnt stick at me, as if he was shooing a pup away.

A few minutes later I was breathlessly relating what I'd just heard to my father. Like me, he had a passion for the history of our people. He knew of the slave and Roman connection, but shook his head at the void of time that separated us from those days. He reminded me that King Edward Longshanks burnt every Scottish library he could lay his torch to after his fight with Wallace in the wars between England and Scotland. Cromwell the witch-hunter finished the job when he torched Catholic abbeys and their collections of books and manuscripts. If there were books mentioning Rome and its Scottish slaves then they would have been lost. Academics wouldn't allow this version of history to be taught in schools. He also reminded me that many Travellers had long since given up their old ways and would take no pleasure hearing of an historical account making out that they were different from normal people.

'There's a fear among some of their own Traveller identity. It is woven into the tapestry of history, but the scattered threads of our story have been unpicked by years of persecution. Maybe one day when I am an old man and you have grown into a woman, changes will come.'

Because we shared a passion for history and respect for our Traveller identity, our father and daughter relationship was tested many times after this. We had serious arguments about whether he should write about his experiences. He had lived through hard times in his early years and I wanted him to tell the world about it, but he didn't seem willing to do that.

Many years later when his travelling days were behind him, and old age had brought ill health and the usual wear and tear, he sprang a surprise on me. He opened a drawer in the small bureau by his fireside chair and took out a large notebook. Smiling from ear to ear, he said, 'Well, Jess, I've started that book!'

I was at his side in an instant, but he slammed the drawer shut. 'When it's finished I'll surprise you, Jess.'

Two years later he'd still not shared the writings in his notebook, and to be honest I didn't think there was much of them to share. My mother said she thought he'd given up the idea. The opposite was the case. He'd scrapped his volumes of handwritten material and hired a typist to work on an autobiography with no holds barred.

He called the book *The White Nigger*, a shocking title, but one that described how he felt he had been treated all his life. Although my enthusiasm to read what he'd written was overwhelming I stayed out of his space and waited until he'd finished.

But there was an enemy creeping into his body; emphysema, like a nagging wife, dominated his every waking minute. To try to get relief he woke early, went over his handwritten notes, and then slept most of the rest of the day, getting up for a few hours to dictate the text of his book to the lady who typed for him.

Two different coloured inhalers which never left his side kept his airways clear, and without them he would have suffered a fatal seizure. To be honest it was touch and go whether he would finish his masterpiece, but he was no quitter. He remained adamant however that I shouldn't read it until the time came when he thought it was ready for my eyes. I was sorely disappointed not to be able to read it, but he said it would look much better as a proper book with a nice cover, a personal signed copy from father to daughter.

One day he completed his task and sent the finished typescript to a renowned folklorist. An answer came by return: 'I shall be happy to read *The White Nigger* over the festive period.'

I remember holding his feeble body and feeling the emotion and sense of achievement running through his weakened frame – at long last he'd written that book! He had climbed an unconquered mountain, touched a star – his life would now be worth something.

His masterpiece was destined never to be published. It lay amongst the learned volumes in the late Mr Henderson's library. Twelve years later it was found by a keen-eyed researcher, who kindly sent it back to me. One day I shall let the world see his book as he would have wanted.

2

THE BEGINNING OF THE JOURNEY

Although I never forgot the revelations of the Lochgilphead Tinsmith, I found that searching for the origins of Travellers was an almost impossible task. It was like asking a palaeontologist to recreate the body of an ancient dinosaur of the largest size from a few bones, in minute detail!

I did come across a tale told by Spanish Gypsies about the beginnings of our kind.

Once upon a time when the first man and woman were moulded, the god of the earth breathed his perfection onto a handful of seeds. He planted the seeds in a small bag beneath the tree of knowledge. When the original couple, Adam and Eve, had disobeyed his command and eaten of the forbidden fruit, he turned them out of the Garden of Eden, blaming himself for allowing them the gift of free will.

The many gods scattered throughout the heavens laughed at the god of the earth and said, 'It was a mistake to sprinkle the seeds with perfection when there is no such a thing.'

The serpent of the underworld, which existed to tempt all living creatures, thought differently. She knew of the bag of seeds, and thinking the earth god would try to populate his world once more, but on his second attempt remove free will from men and women, she stole the seeds and scattered them from a mountain top. From there the wind blew each seed to every corner of the world.

When the earth god discovered her cunning plan, he sent an angel to whisper to his seeds that they must never settle anywhere or else the serpent would find them. He further instructed the angel to tell them that they must set off on a journey, and when the time was right he would guide them home to the Garden of Eden. He blew breath through the angel into each seed, so that they would resemble his first children, Adam and Eve. He gave them many skills so that through the power of their hands they would survive. They were told they must not follow any king, accept any false book of instructions and that they should live by two laws: 'Nothing in excess' and 'Know yourself'.

As we are on the subject of the mythical origins of Travellers, let me share another tale from ancient times. There are several versions of this story which mainly come from Eastern Europe.

The Fourth Nail and Ruth's Seed

Jerusalem was in a terrible state! The Messiah was to be crucified, had been judged and sentenced. Pontius Pilate, the governor of the city, had delivered him to a prison cell to await his death the following day upon the rugged cross.

It was midday, and two of Pilate's young soldiers were given a large sum of money to pay for four nails. They were to be forged by the hand of a Jew. Those were the orders, and the young recruits were to be back with the nails by curfew. The city was at boiling point, and after dark a roman soldier outside the security of his garrison walls would not have stood a chance.

Beneath their uniforms of thick leather and metal armour the sweating flesh of the two men overheated. With the additional burden of swords, shields and spears, they were fit to melt. As they stepped out into the streets of Jerusalem, a delicious aroma of rich wine wafted from one of the many inns along the way. They looked at each other, both thinking the same thing. We had better replenish our flagging energies before crossing town to the quarter where blacksmiths worked their forges. It was an easy decision to take: they would slink in and take a few pennies' worth of wine.

Once they were inside and their weighty helmets and weaponry laid aside, one drink soon led to another, and then another. Lowly foot soldiers seldom had so much freedom, or so much money in their hands. In no time the amount of money they had been given was halved.

Only when they saw how little was left of the money did they come to their senses. Aware that their decision to waste on drink the money given for a specific purpose would lead to a nasty end on the cedarwood cross like other thieves and murderers, they rushed outside into the dusty streets. Where had the time gone? It was almost five, and the curfew bells rang at six!

It was not two disciplined soldiers of the mighty imperial army, but a couple of drink-sodden, dishevelled, angry individuals who stood in front of the big Jewish blacksmith with the hammer in his hand. When they ordered him to forge the nails and be quick about it, he asked for payment. When they offered only half the regular amount, he refused. They were in no mood to tolerate disobedience to the might of Rome from a subject Jew. After demands came threats. When, however, the frightened blacksmith asked why they wanted four large nails, the soldiers angrily retorted that they were to be used to crucify the prophet.

The smith laid down his hammer and refused to do the job. Defying furious soldiers with so much alcohol in them could only have one result. In a matter of moments the poor smith lay in a pool of blood and the soldiers pushed on. Three more times they were refused, first by a Samarian, then by a Carpathian, and then by another Jew. However often they asked, no hand would forge those nails. Soon each of the obstinate blacksmiths lay dead.

As the soldiers, now beginning to sober up, reached the city wall and found no more blacksmiths they began to panic. There was only one more chance. The Egyptians who lived outside the walls of Jerusalem had blacksmiths. As the curfew was fast approaching they broke with the usual protocol and went outside to find a blacksmith. The soldiers found a man called Cyrus working at his forge. He was a poor man with a pregnant wife to support and had never heard of the son of Joseph Bin Miriam. However there was a problem – Cyrus had no iron with which to cast the nails.

None, that is, apart from a precious gift he had received two nights ago from Seth, the Egyptian God of storms. In countless prayers he had asked for a blessed piece of heaven-rock, as the Egyptians called meteorites, from which to forge the fingers of Seth. Also known as the 'Bia', the fingers of Seth were a delicate set of tongs and were considered the greatest gift an Egyptian father of the blacksmith craft could give his first-born. The High Priest of the Egyptian religion would use the tongs to open the mouth of the dead person in a ceremony performed on the 'mummy' at a funeral. The 'opening of the mouth' enabled the soul to give the correct answers to the doorkeepers of the underworld and to gain admittance to the underworld. The blacksmith who was the keeper of such an instrument was held in great honour by the High Priest. Just two nights previously Cyrus's prayers had been answered: a meteorite fell from the sky. Believing that the God of storm had indeed blessed his new-born child, he kept this heaven-rock made of precious metal out of sight, keeping it in a small casket beneath his forge.

As the soldiers grew angrier he lowered his head and apologised to them for having no iron or any other metal with which to make the nails. In blind panic they began to trash the man's small workshop and soon found the casket with the blackish lump of metal inside. 'Here,' one said, thrusting it at the blacksmith, 'use this.'

Cyrus had no choice: the soldiers had their swords in their hands. So taking the mysterious lump of planetary metal, he piled more charcoal into his brazier, use the bellows to create a fierce heat and forged three stout nails. Before he could finish the fourth, the first chime of the curfew bell rang within the city. Grabbing the three nails that were ready the men rushed off. What lies they were going to tell as an excuse for their lateness, was their business.

Cyrus's heart was heavy. The heavenly metal Seth had sent him was now in the hands of the Romans, and was to be used to crucify a strange Jew! That night, as a full moon rose over Jerusalem, the worried blacksmith, tired and hungry, went home to the arms of Ruth, his lovely wife, a daughter of the ancient Hebrew tribe of Dan. Against her tribe's laws and customs Ruth had married an Egyptian; just another curse to add to those already weighing on the shoulders of her tribespeople, who were now scattered far and wide through the world.

Many centuries ago the tribe of Dan was among the multitudes of other Hebrew slaves who left Egypt and followed Moses to the Promised Land. Half-way there, however, as their holy leader was on Mount Sinai receiving the Ten Commandments from God, the tribe of Dan melted down all their gold and formed a statue to the God Baal. He, the god of all earthly pleasures, offered them a way out of their miserable wanderings in the desert: a new world. When Moses discovered their blasphemous idolatry he sent them out of the Hebrew encampment. He said he was separating goats from the sheep. He kept the sheep who followed the true God and laid a curse on the goats to wander the world forever.

So, unaware of the cataclysmic event that was to take place at dawn the coming day, Ruth and her husband slept peacefully in each other's arms. When they awoke the next morning there was a strange darkness, and it rained all day.

On the following day, before breakfast, the sound of an angry mob was to be heard outside the house of Cyrus and Ruth. The two soldiers who had broken the curfew and returned with only three nails, when they had been sent for four, were awaiting deportation to the island of barbarians, Britannia, as a punishment. Word had got out that they were helped by an Egyptian, who had forged the nails that crucified Christ.

Within minutes Ruth stood, tears streaming down her cheeks, as they dragged off her beloved husband, who she knew to be an innocent man, to be interviewed by the authorities. Next day she visited the governor. He'd let her husband go free if she would pay for their passage aboard a slave galley, along with those accursed soldiers, heading to Britannia. This she did willingly. Not long after, they set sail for a new life in a faraway land where their fate awaited them.

They disembarked at last on the shores of the north of Britannia, the land which in ages to come was to become Scotland. Although they were free people, because of Cyrus's skills they were both put into chains on arrival. They worked as slaves in the fortified home of a Roman general: he as a forger of weapons, and she, after the birth of her baby son which took place soon after they landed, was employed as a hairdresser and hairbraider of Roman ladies.

Their son grew strong, into a handsome and pleasant-natured youth. His master became so fond of him he gave him his freedom. And there the story peters out, but it has a mysterious sequel.

The fourth nail, according to a tradition among European Romanies, was given into the care of Ruth by her husband Cyrus. When he died she asked the authorities for permission to allow her and her son to bury her husband in a special sacred place. Permission was granted. They lowered him into the ground along with a small, narrow box. His grave was ten feet deep and filled in with stone rather than earth. I was informed by those who told me the story that the place where he was buried remains a sacred site, and there is a chapel there. Nowhere else in Scotland, they say, stands its like. I tried to find out from my informants the exact location, but they refused to say, apart from indicating that it was somewhere near Edinburgh. They visited the place annually.

I found a very interesting story which might shed light on this mystery while scanning through Robert Chambers' *Domestic Annals of Scotland from the Reformation to the Rebellion*. He writes: 'While Egyptians [i.e. Gypsies] were looked upon as a proscribed race, and often the victims of indiscriminate severity, there was a man who believed that every one deserved mercy. This was Sir William Sinclair of Roslin Castle, Lord Justice-General under Queen Mary, and while riding home one day from Edinburgh, found a poor Egyptian about to be hanged on the gibbet at the Burgh-moor.

"Why are you hanging this fellow?" he asked the Sheriff.

"Sire, this is a Gypsy and as you know his very existence is an abomination against God."'

Sinclair lied and said that the man was one of his stable hands and had nothing to do with Egyptians. Instantly the rope was removed from his neck and he was set free.

He wasted no time in warning the young Gypsy that he and his people were in danger, and to avoid capture they should come and winter around the stanks [marshes] of the castle were he would give them sanctuary. That winter was the severest it had been for many a year, the poor Gypsies were freezing to death in their thin canvas tents, and if Sir William hadn't offered them shelter in two towers of his castle they surely would have perished. From that kind act they named the towers 'Robin Hood and Little John', and every year, to honour their kindly saviour, they acted a play of the same name.

It may be more than a coincidence that close by Roslin Castle is the famous Rosslyn Chapel, where reputedly the Holy Grail is concealed.

At Roslin there's another Roman connection. I'm told that to be found there is the grave of a great outlaw called Salamantes, who at every opportunity fought and harassed the occupying Romans. It's believed that he hid slaves who were considered too old to work, or ones who became ill or injured, before their masters ended their lives. Had Salamantes himself been a slave from Egypt, perhaps going on to be one of the forefathers of a strong Highland clan?

3
The Greens

None of us knew why generations of Travellers chose the same camping grounds, but year after year familiar faces and stories followed one another, like dog nose on cat tail, to the same spots. Those were our private holiday places, and every year my people returned to relive the joyful traditions within our own society; to speak our language, share stories and sing songs. There were many places – coastal inlets with caverns, tussocky moorlands, ancient areas with standing stones and burial mounds that belonged to the once mighty ancestors of Scottish people called the Picts. I can only guess that these were places that no man of authority could put his stamp on. But perhaps there were deeper reasons behind the choice of such peaceful campsites.

These common camping places, along with many others, were known simply as 'the greens'. When it was time to uproot and take to the road after a long cold winter, my father could be heard repeating his itinerary of 'greens', our safe havens where law could not touch us and no one would trouble our peaceful existence.

For this part of the journey to enlightenment I shall concentrate on the campsites of Perthshire, especially the ones that no longer exist. Some of them now lie under widened roads, housing schemes and supermarkets.

Beginning around the 1930s, Perthshire was flourishing as an agricultural area. Farmers and Travellers needed each other. Our favourite summer greens were ones prepared for us by eager Perthshire fruit growers seeking a hardy workforce to gather berries, strawberries and peas. For the travellers to make a decent enough income to see them through the coming winter, this was an important part of their year. Hard-earned harvest money helped pay the winter rent, bought the 'tug' for hawking and, for the children, paid for our school uniforms.

It was also the final chance to live as a complete society again. As we gathered at the days end around a welcome camp-fire, we sang ballads and shared our tales. For a few weeks of the year the old tribes of Scotland lived again! Later in the year we converged on the fields to gather up the nation's potatoes. Sadly, all these jobs are no longer viable for Travellers and Scotland's agricultural work is now mainly undertaken by Eastern Europeans.

Life came and went on the greens: in one tent an old person lay flat out on a straw mattress, taking his final breath; in another, a new life began, a baby punching the air for the first time. Elsewhere on the green, deals were made. Hands slapped to seal the deal for a new lorry, a good hound and, on the rare occasion, a good woman!

On the greens of Blairgowrie at berry-picking time, folklore revivalists in the mid-fifties discovered the wealth of our songs and ballads, the music of the pipes and stories that seemed to flow from the Travelling folk like streams of gold. They came from all over the world to record our music, riddles and songs, which they then introduced to a waiting world. The famous travelling family, the Stewarts of Blair – mother Belle and husband Alex with his bagpipes, daughters Sheila and Cathy along with songbirds Jeannie Robertson and Lizzie Higgins – had no idea what heights of fame the folklorists would elevate them to. Matriarch Belle, for her contribution to the world of traditional music, was awarded the BEM; her daughter Sheila, the sole survivor of the Stewarts of Blair, who now carries the wealth of traditions on her own, was given an MBE.

Jeannie Robertson's famous nephew, the late Stanley Robertson, was an expert on the Tinker folk of the north east, a brilliant balladeer, storyteller and acclaimed author. Before his death in 2008 he was made a Fellow of Aberdeen University.

All the folklorists were held in high regard by the travelling folk, especially Hamish Henderson, affectionately referred to as 'Him wi' the box', the box being his recording equipment (battery-powered, of course). I remember late one evening, when he arrived at our campsite to set up his 'box', he asked if anyone had a stool to sit it on. My father dutifully pointed at my own three-legged contraption, which he had made for me to sit on after I had broken my leg, but I point-blank refused to give it to Hamish because I thought he would sit on it. If he had done, with the size of his behind, the stool would have ended in bits on the fire. Everybody burst out laughing when Hamish said he only wanted it to put his box on.

Other familiar faces at our campsites were the collectors of folk-song and folklore, Ewan McColl and American Peggy Seeger who, like Hamish, sat around the campfire at night, recording the musicians and songsters. Daddy was impressed by the visiting collectors, and remembered one or two of them in later years, but thought most were on the make. He thought they were stealing the old songs, and for this reason refused at the time to approach them and let them record his traditional knowledge. In this he wasn't alone among Travellers. It was considered taboo to let outsiders in. No one should know our words, songs or riddles apart from our own kind.

Personally, I am glad this work of collection continued over the years. Who would know about us in the future, if the recordings hadn't been made and kept safe in Edinburgh University's School of Scottish studies? But in hindsight I feel the collectors only got the tip of the iceberg. Waiting in the wings were many more talented Travellers who would have liked to be heard, but when the folklorists ended their studies, they stepped back into the shadows and gave up on the dream of showing off their abilities.

During tattie-picking time, other greens near Crieff in Perthshire saw the gathering of many travelling folk. Crieff is set in a great stretch of fertile land which, through the famous Perthshire tattie, brought wealth aplenty to scores of farmers, who all provided greens during the season for large numbers of 'tattie howkers'. Duncan Williamson, who once told me he thought his people were descended all the way from the Picts, met his pretty young wife-to-be, Linda, at one of these. She was there in her capacity as a field-worker in the area of folklore, and she went on to introduce Duncan as Scotland's master storyteller to the world.

Another Traveller writer, the late Betsy White, who gave the world those wonderful classic books *Yellow on the Broom* and *Red Rowans and Wild Honey*, spent many summers on her favourite greens and later shared her experience with a world of eager readers. During berry-picking time our family and hers camped side by side on a green called Marshall's Field, a mile from a quaint little town called Alyth. In those early years neither of us had the slightest notion that one day we would both write extensively about our cultural journeys on the roads.

4
MANSION ON WHEELS

We travelled the length and breadth of Britain in our bus-home, and I gathered every memory like a magpie collecting coloured baubles. In our mobile dwelling a twelve-inch wide woollen carpet, stretching from underneath the driver's seat to our parents' boudoir at the rear kept our feet warm. A cupboard for pots, pans and dishes was bolted to the floor, the luggage racks above our heads accommodated our undies, there was a table where we shared our family meals and a wee Queenie stove for heating and for cooking during the winter. In summer a campfire did the same job.

When springtime approached, my excitement knew no bounds. The road called and there was nothing to hold us back. I think there could be no creature in the entire world more ecstatic than me at leaving our winter campsite behind. I was acutely aware that all across the land other Travellers were stirring from their hibernation, eager to smell the reek from the camp fire and to taste fresh air once more. The winter of hard frost and snow with its burden of flu and coughs was gone. Vivid memories of the big bully boy of the classroom would drift away like the smoke of town chimneys as we headed for the countryside.

The schools officially closed in July, but Travellers were able to leave in April before the settled kids. To do this we needed a certificate authorising our release, and once we had got this there was no holding us back. Honestly, it was like getting out of prison. Until that vital certificate allowing me and my siblings to leave in springtime was secured in our mother's brown leather handbag, I didn't sleep soundly. If she had lost or misplaced it she'd have incurred the wrath of us all. The laws relating to Travellers' education were tight, and later in this book we shall discover why.

Before we could set off, however, that old blue Bedford bus had to be given a service. Sometimes a coating of rust had curled around every nut and bolt, but this didn't matter because my father could fix anything. During the war he had been trained as a mechanical engineer, and now he cared affectionately and skilfully for his mobile home. The bus had to be completely mechanically sound – Scotland's country roads could throw unforeseen potholes in our way, or the police in certain areas who had an intolerant attitude to Travellers would keep us on the move. So he'd don a baggy pair of oily over-alls and live in them until the repairs were complete and the engine whipped into prime condition.

We were known among the Travelling community as Charlie and Jeannie's family of frocks. Our paternal Granny had another name for us – sardines on wheels. An old auntie called us premenstrual succubuses! My father was quite vocal about how Mother Nature had cheated him by never producing a male child for the family, but when we were left to our own devices we females could stack tons of corn, plant fields of potatoes, gather mountains of red fruit, clear acres of brock wool, dig deep ditches and work alongside the strongest men, equalling their strength. And we had brains too!

Our winter green for most of my teenage years was Lennie's Yard, a redundant pottery built in red brick in the Gallatown, a district in Kirkcaldy famous for coal mines. Mr Andrews, who lived next to the yard, was a coal merchant who lived in a spacious Edwardian house next door. Many a day, over his old green gate, we shared a crack.

When everything was ready and my father revved up the engine I would stand by his shoulder behind the driver's seat like Queen Boadicea, eyes scanning the horizon. Mr Andrew always positioned himself by the green gate and called out to me, 'Mind, now, come home with plenty stories for me!'

Through the open window of the door I'd answer, 'Do you want fairy or kelpy ones?'

'Just keep all your adventures stored up in your head and we'll share them when you come back.'

In my eagerness to see the back of our settled existence I would lean out the door with the wind in my hair. My mother would forcibly drag me back inside and shut the window tight, saying, 'I'm in two minds about renaming you Mindy's Monkey!'

Mindy was a Traveller from Aberdeen way. She used to stand up on her cart when her horse tackled a bend and shout out, 'Gaun tae yer richt-haun side, cuddy, an mind an no wallop yon tree tae yer left!' She was famous among Travellers for her companion of over thirty years – a wide-eyed monkey who, it was believed, knew every word of the Doric cant language. One day the horse got spooked by a noise from the undergrowth at the side of the road and began to gallop blindly out of control. Trying to stop the animal, Mindy grabbed the first thing to hand, which was her beloved pet monkey, and threw it at the horse. It fell into the road and hurt its leg. She swore blind that after that it refused to sit near her or eat from her hand. She said it was in the huff, and after its limp disappeared it ran away and she never saw it again. Within six months she died of a broken heart. Sadly, as a monkey is believed by Travellers to be a bad omen, not many other Travellers would have anything to do with her.

＊

When we drove out of Fife with an east wind to our back, our usual route was to Perth, via Thornton, Glenrothes and on through ancient Falkland with its fairytale castle. Many kings and queens stayed in this ancient palace, but I want to mention King James V in particular, because of an incident that involved him and one of the first mentions in historical sources of the elusive Scottish Tinker.

King James was basically a decent kind of man and often wondered about his peasants and what their lives were really like. To find out he would sometimes disguise himself as a poor man, putting on the blue cloak worn by a beggar-man, or Gaberlunzie, as they were called. According to this story, which as far as I know is true, one day when he was in disguise he met a band of Tinkers. Unaware that he was of royal blood, they invited him back to their home, which was a cave near Wemyss in Fife. They had a party with singing, dancing and drinking. Being a jolly lad, His Majesty decided to join in, and soon became intoxicated with the drink. Inevitably a fight broke out. Jimmy found himself in the midst of the Tinkers' brawl. Though born with a silver spoon in his mouth, he was outclassed in the art of bone-rattling, and thought he was going to be severely injured.

His shouts and screams in his normal accent made it immediately apparent to the Tinkers that he wasn't one of them. If this stranger wasn't a true blue Tinker then he must surely be a spy.

Unsure whether they should kill him for his treachery or not, they decided to dump all their bundles on his back and use him like a donkey to carry them along the road. After several miles his legs buckled, so they left him lying exhausted by the roadside.

Back home in Falkland Castle, relieved to have escaped with his life, the king put his blue Gaberlunzie cloak away in a cupboard and never ventured out in disguise again. Despite, or perhaps because of, his experience, James V was generally well-disposed to Tinkers and Gypsies and they were not persecuted during his reign. However if the Wemyss tinkers had realised how his grandson, James VI, would treat them, they should have tried him for spying and stretched his bonny white neck when they had the opportunity.

James VI, who also had a boiling hatred against witches and caused many harmless wise women to be burned at the stake, loathed Gypsies and set out to exterminate them. Even before he came to the throne the authorities had issued a proclamation that Gypsies had to be treated like thieves and driven out of the country. This proclamation of 1573 stated that all Gypsies were 'to be scurgit throughout the toun or parrochyn; and swa to be impresonit and scurgit fra parrochyn to parrochyn quhill thay be utterlie removit furth of this realme.'

When James came to the throne of England he wasted no time in passing further acts against Gypsies, or Egiptians as he called them, until just being a Gypsy or Tinker became a crime to be punished by death. His act of 1609 was passed:

'Commanding the vagabounds, sorners, and common thiefes commonlie called Egiptians, to passe forth of this Kingdome, and remaine perpetuallie forth therof, and never to returne within the samin, under the paine of death, and that the samin have force and execution after the first day of August next to come. After the whilk tyme if any of the saids vagabounds, called Egiptians, als well wemen as men, shal be found within this Kingdome or any part thereof; it shall be lesome to all his Majesties good subjects, or any ane of them, to cause take, apprehend, imprison, and execute to death the saids Egiptians, either men or wemen, as common, notorious and condemned theifes, by ane assyse onely to be tryed, that they are called, knawn, reput and halden Egiptians.'

From then on there was no mercy. The genocide of Gypsies and Tinkers – women, children and the elderly – became official government policy, and no one was spared.

5
PERTH AND THE ROMANS

As you head to Perth you come to the winding pass of Glen Balvaird, which Tinkers call 'the twisted whip' and say is haunted by a horseman. They tell stories of how, in the darkest night as families lay asleep in their tents, a sudden crack of a whip was occasionally heard above their sleepy heads. In terror they'd pack up and move on.

This place held a memory for me too. Big Wullie McPhee (last of the tinsmiths) told me the story of how once he played his pipes at a castle ruin there for two Americans who paid him a princely sum. He swore to me that, at the back of the place, a ghostly hand came out of the wall and tried to steal his pipes. I was very young at the time I heard this, but even to this day I rush by the place, never lingering.

I'll head into Perth now, where I believe, if my Lochgilphead tinsmith's tale of our origins was correct, our seed first came to Scotland via Rome.

Most history books agree that it was Agricola who first sailed up the Tay to establish a Roman outpost. He was under orders from Hadrian to find a way into the barbarians' land and to take control of their wild tribes. Agricola searched every watery inlet on the Scottish coast without luck until he came across the estuary of the Tay. Aware, no doubt, of the presence of many Picts and Pictish fortresses in the area, he probably brought his fleet slowly up the river's tidal sweep under the cloak of darkness to avoid being seen. Latin authors wrote that the Picts were the fiercest warriors ever encountered by the conquering Romans. The Romans must have been more than relieved to find somewhere to land at the end of such a mighty stretch of water and to be able to disembark without being attacked by the barbarians.

Roman coins and earthenware unearthed in Orkney indicate that the invaders sailed further north than Perth, but all the evidence confirms that ancient Perthshire was their preferred base where they landed and began building their forts, towers, and signal stations. Experts in ancient history say the name Perth is a version of the Pictish name Bertha, but there is another story that the Romans may have named the town after the first centurion who stepped on land there, who was called Perticus. When the Romans first came to Perth it was a small port by the estuary of the silvery Tay. Later it was extensively rebuilt, the conquerers using their architectural genius to repel, not just Pictish warriors, but the rising waters of a river prone to serious flooding.

There is another story that, in the early years of Christianity, John the disciple visited Scotland. As Scone, which is joined to Perth, was where the kings had their seat, it was called John's Town, and when he was made a saint it became St Johnstone. Several Roman Catholic monasteries were built and flourished for centuries, before a new protestant religion rose up, demolishing every stone and burning every beam to hasten their demise.

No place is more important in the history of the kings and queens of Scotland than Perth and her castle of Scone, where monarchs would sit upon the sacred 'Stone of Destiny'. The story goes that, after being blessed by the hand of God, the Stone was brought from the deserts of Egypt by Scota, the daughter of a Pharaoh, to Ireland, and then to Scotland. One of the tales about its journey from the east is that the Egyptian Princess had chosen seven bodyguards to accompany her. Such was the secrecy surrounding their mission their tongues had been removed to render them mute. These brave soldiers without tongues guarded the Stone and never let it out of their sight when it arrived in Scotland. The site of Scone Palace, Moot (Mute) Hill, is named after them. The people of Scotland revered the Stone, believing it showed that our birthright was to remain an independent country with our own monarch, since the God of the desert lion had decreed it so.

King Edward I of England, who battled to take control of Scotland in medieval times, had the Stone transported to London in 1296. I have no idea why the honourable men of the south would steal our God-given Stone, but no other relic of ancient times has so much life in it as this mysterious object. Because Scots regard it as their national treasure, in 1950 a group of Scottish students stole it from Westminster Abbey, took it back to Scotland and refused to disclose its whereabouts. A year or so later a stone was left in Arbroath Abbey and taken back to Westminster, but many doubted its authenticity and said it was a replica. This was the stone that was brought back to Edinburgh Castle in 1996. Even as I write, there are those who are spending their lives trying to find the true whereabouts of the original mystical Stone. If you happen to know where it is, reader, you possess an important secret, because I tell you this – Tinker folk believe that, until the original Stone is returned to Scone, Scotland shall never flourish.

In old days travelling Tinkers didn't refer to the town as Perth, preferring the old name of St Johnstone instead. Among Perthshire travellers there are more named Johnstone than any other surname. This may tie in with my Lochgilphead tinsmith's slave theory, since this part of Perthshire was the main point where slaves were disembarked.

Another coincidence: when archaeologists were excavating the mouth of the River Almond near Perth, they discovered great quantities of Roman weaponry of the type produced by the slave tinsmiths. Today, in exactly the same vicinity, a state-of-the-art Travellers' site called the Double Dykes is situated.

In the Tinkers' domain, history is kept alive in the head and shared with the tongue. I was always made aware of this important fact as I grew into adulthood. Children were instructed to sit in a circle with the *shanechy* (tale-teller) in the centre. It was his or her job to fill our heads with stories, truths about life and any important knowledge relating to campsites or people. We were told which greens should be avoided and why, who was dead and who had a new addition to their family. There were never divorces among travellers, so it was always couples who were referred to, for example, Cherlie and Jeannie, or Dykes and Peesie, Big Wullie and Bella, Mat and Peg, Brochie and the Heilan' Chief, etc, etc. This was the way information was passed around, in such a way that we never forgot it.

This is an ancient practice among Travellers, and it's my belief that, because of our nomadic lifestyles, it was the only way we could remain a culture. Further back in the mists of time people employed Tinker balladeers whose only duties were to gather news, convert it into lyrics and music, and to make certain it was remembered. In the form of ballads, historical stories, whether they be of sudden death, battle, childbirth or any other information the balladeer's employer was interested in, were preserved and passed on. Payment would depend on the accuracy and skill of the balladeer. Tinker kids' heads were filled with stories of other people's business, because all these news stories would also be shared with the families of the balladeer. This is how we have a wealth of songs and stories. Rabbie Burns openly acknowledged how much material for his poems and songs he collected from wandering folk, as did Sir Walter Scott and later writers like George Borrow and the American poet, Longfellow.

6

THE WANDERING TRAIL

As we follow the trail of the scattered seed of the wanderers through this book, we'll uncover evidence that, just as the tinsmith said, the earliest Travellers in Scotland were indeed skilled armourers to the clans, and yes, they were indeed called Cairds as he maintained. In both England and Scotland, masons, coppersmiths, goldsmiths, blacksmiths and other metalworkers owe their origins to the slaves who were brought to the country by the ancient Romans. Metalworkers are some of the oldest tradesmen of all. In old Norse and German mythology, the weapons of the gods were made by a character called Wayland the Smith. Today Smith, along with Brown, is the commonest surname throughout the country.

There are two names of travelling Tinkers which have an ancient pedigree, Townsley and MacPhee. These names have been passed down through the centuries. Here's a story of the origins of Macphee according to the old cave-dwellers of Wick.

Many years ago during the rule of Picts, after the Romans had left these shores, a king of Ireland sent for 100 slaves. The King had visited personally and chosen each to his specification: they were of mixed crafts – blacksmiths for his horses, goldsmiths for his jewellery and that of his lady fair, weapon-makers to forge mighty double-edged swords, potters to replace his cracked earthenware, silversmiths to design new goblets of the finest metal for his new wines, tailors to sew a fine set of clothes. After much discussion of payment a price was set. For the slaves a ship of the same weight in gold was offered and accepted. Now in those days there were a great many superstitions about the ocean. It was believed by the old Picts and

Irish Celts that the earth was at one time ruled by the sea. Beneath the waves there existed a kingdom, and to appease the creatures of the deep, sacrifices of bullocks and lambs had to be offered. But by the time this deal was struck a form of Christianity was in place, and although believers in the ancient gods warned both the Pictish ruler and the Irish king to appease the old gods, they laughed off the warnings and the ships set sail.

To everyone's terror, when they were half-way across, a mighty storm broke out. Waves as high as a hundred Caledonian pine trees towered over the ships. At the first onslaught of the huge swell both vessels were lifted, rolled and thrown around at the ocean's mercy. Watchers on each shore held their breath as the sea claimed the ships for the deep. The slaves went down first, swiftly followed by the ship laden with gold. It was pointless to attempt a rescue; nothing could be saved or salvaged from the angry sea!

Both rulers saw that they had upset the sea gods and went home to lick their wounds. No sooner had the sea vented her fury on the ships when, like a baby, she fell asleep and her waves rolled gently onto the shoreline. On an uninhabited island off the west coast, named Colonsay, as the waves softly swept ashore, with them were washed up many of the shipwrecked slaves. Scattered along the coast, around half of the human cargo survived.

Without masters or soldiers holding weapons to their throats, for the first time in their lives these slave craftsmen smelt sweet freedom. Soon, on the mainland, gossip began to spread about a race of sea creatures who had taken over the island. No fishermen dared venture there, in case they should be attacked, or worse still, eaten by the monsters. Rumours abounded about the angry sea gods who swallowed up ships of man and gold. Those who had appeared so mysteriously on the island must be creatures of the deep. Not even the bravest or strongest would venture near Colonsay. So the slaves lived out their free lives without hindrance. Colonsay waters had a plentiful supply of fish, so they'd not starve. It had sufficient wood for fires, and as they had all the necessary skills for making things, survival was easy. Generations were born and died in relative peace and tranquillity.

One day a small fishing vessel from the island suffered damage on rocks. With its cargo of two men and some fish it floated aimlessly until it came to land on the mainland. There were people there who helped them to fix the boat. When they were ready to set off again they asked them where they had sailed from and what was their name.

'We come from over there,' they answered, pointing to Colonsay, 'and we are named "Nilfee".'

From that chance meeting came the surname of MacFee or MacPhee, which means 'the men who were bought from serfdom by the sea fairies'.

In a book of surnames the name is explained thus: 'Mac Dhuibhshith, from Gaelic dhubh, "dark" and sith, "peace", dark one of peace, but has also been linked to sidh, "fairy". A very old name, originating on Colonsay and found later in Lochaber. One of the names of Scotland's Travelling People. Also spelt MacFee, MacHaffie, MacAfee.' I have many friends among MacPhees.

The second oldest name indicating Traveller pedigree is Townsley. I was originally told this meant the ones who live next to a town, but this was a red herring. The name has changed over the years from Touchler or Toughler, which means leather-softener – another nomadic skill. A similar name is Tranter, which means a 'carrier or hawker'. Hawkins, Nawkens, Narken and Nachin are also names associated with Tinker culture.

These names have the rather unpleasant link with knackers – men of the old horse trade, men who slaughtered horses, but if we go far back into Biblical times we can find mention of a tribe of Natrons who were from the land of Cush, located some place between Ethiopia and Libya. They sold sodium carbonate, a natural substance found in that area and used as carbolic soap for washing. The Hebrew name for these people was Neter, the Egyptian was Nitiru, and in Spanish and French it has become Nawrins.

I mentioned earlier that Ruth was of the 'accursed tribe of Dan'; and her husband was a blacksmith. In a book by F.W. Robins called *The Smiths: Traditions and Lore of an Ancient Craft*, there is a fascinating description of the Egyptian origins of those mysterious craftsmen in metal. Later chapters tell of the close involvement of their descendents in carrying folklore and traditions between Ireland and Scotland.

Despite the importance of metal-working and the skills of the craftsman to society, these manual workers were generally considered to be 'low-caste' persons throughout the ancient east, and in various regions this remains the case. In Malabar, for example, blacksmiths must not come within twenty-four feet of a member of the Brahmin caste. The Tuareg tribesmen of North Africa not only look down upon blacksmiths, but, since they are men who live by fire, they believe them to be destined for hell!

No doubt the separation of men of the craft from society is, as with witches in earlier times, partly the deliberate creation of the smiths themselves. They preserved their power by turning their profession into a closely guarded mystery and by handing down trade secrets only to close family members. The Bantu people of Lake Nyasa in Africa fear and honour the smith. They believe he and his ancestors are in touch with mysterious, potent powers. Robins writes:

'In the Eastern world, except in the case of aboriginal races, smith status is noticeably different. There are several reasons, but the main one is that the smiths are generally not merely of a separate clan, but actually of a different race.' Their profession alone signals them as men apart, not to be approached without respect for their powers. It should always be borne in mind that they are to be valued and feared at the same time.

The North African Haddad are blacksmiths, weavers, potters and doctors, but especially known for their smithing skills. They are a separate tribe from the Arabic peoples around them. Under threat of death in the far-off past they were forced to convert to Islam, but failed to follow the practice of the religion diligently. Some Muslims were hostile to smiths and regarded them as cursed because they believed that it was a blacksmith who betrayed the Prophet to his enemies. 'There is a marked analogy here to the position of Gypsies, whose Christianity is still half pagan and who were, not very long ago, regarded as heathens in parts of Europe. Like the Gypsies there are legends woven around them. The Prophet himself tried to convert them, but without success. Frightened for their safety after that, they left and sought refuge south-westwards, passing through the Nile Valley and on to Nigeria. Another legend told among the Haddad themselves relates how, when Adam left the earthly paradise, he and his offspring wandered in the country of Cham, suffering grievously, until God, taking pity, sent them an angel to furnish them with the instruments they needed. Calling together the children of Adam, the angel made an axe, a spade, a knife and a needle; the implements of peace and cultivation. But the sons of Adam, growing bold, demanded to be shown how to protect themselves against their enemies, the Suleiman. The son of the angel made the iron malleable like wet clay and with his divine hands forged a helmet, a cuirass and a sword. The men then understood that iron was a gift of God and could make tools for working and weapons for hunting and fighting; when they knew how to work the iron, the angel, Mahomet, called the Riguebets, in the wadi near Medina, blacksmiths. We see again the mysterious craft is given a divine origin.

The legend of the Haddad goes on:

"When Moussa went up the mountain to speak with God, he took with him the chief of the blacksmiths, all of whom are descended from Lalouale. God then dictated the Law and Lalouale wrote it down on brazen tablets. He also wrote down the method of working metals in a book of iron pages. He gave it to the blacksmiths, descended from Lalouale, but the sons of the blacksmith of Moussa lost the book. They rewrote it imperfectly from memory on thin parchment, and that is why blacksmiths of today are ignorant of the processes of their forefathers.'"

Wandering as a separate clan, the Haddad joined the cursed tribe of Dan. In a variation on the other stories about the Stone of Destiny, there is a tradition that a Jewish princess of this tribe was given the divine mission to take a sacred stone, blessed by the breath of God, to a holy place where monarchs one day would use it as a throne for their coronation.

All these stories have some elements in common. Smiths and Gypsies have similar origins in the middle east, among the wandering tribes of Israel. They have often been enslaved, have sometimes been shunned by the general population and live apart from them. They came from Egypt to Scotland in ancient times as slaves of the Romans, but have no fixed home.

In the Book of Ezekiel in the Old Testament of the Bible there is a prophecy which has sometimes been interpreted as a reference to Gypsies:

'I will trouble the hearts of many peoples, when I carry you captive among the nations, into the countries which you have not known. I will make many people appalled at you.' (Chapter 32, verse 9.)

I really don't believe that when the prophet wrote this he was meaning harm to Gypsies, but ever since, for some ignorant members of the godfearing population this has been seen as divine justification for their hatred of Gypsies.

7
Closing-Down Sale

When guns began to be introduced, the mighty sword-maker found that his sought-after trade was no longer in demand. From then on his main work was shoeing horses and forging tools. In order to provide for his family the travelling smith would also turn his hand to other crafts and produce items such as baskets and wicker seats. In the Travellers' camps a variety of mainly kitchen and household goods, such as pots, pans and pottery, would be hand-made and then hawked to local householders. People in far-flung houses and villages looked forward anxiously to the nomadic merchants knocking their doors.

As we come up to modern times, many who found the road becoming less friendly settled down and gave up their wandering for good. Only those who were unable to ignore the call of the wild continued to roam.

Just as the sword passed into the history books, the basket-weavers too saw their wares decline in popularity. In the 1950s a retail giant had its stores in every town in the land, opening its doors and swallowing up the pennies of the ordinary man and woman in the street. Woolworths, which had been around since the early years of the century, began to stock cheap plastic merchandise, household goods mass-produced in huge factories. This new stock, sold on every high street, sounded the death knell of Chapman Billy's baskets and all things handcrafted.

Wherever the mighty Woolworths opened its doors it sent a chill down the spines of the older Tinker folk. Tools that had been dutifully handed down from father to son became redundant overnight.

Rams' horns were no longer curled into the handles of shepherds' crooks and horn spoons were no longer dipped delicately into boiled eggs. Instead of being turned into something beautiful and useful, animal horns were discarded in piles at the rear of abattoirs waiting to be disposed of as rubbish by the slaughter men. It was the birth of the throwaway society. Woollies led the way, and soon there were thousands of plastic items piled up in every high street supermarket and every corner shop.

Although our handmade goods were fast losing their appeal, Woolworth's had no way of taking over the arts of reading palms, tea-cups or simply dukkering (fortune-telling). My mother would go from door to door with her basket of hawking 'tug' – bundles of needles, threads, darning wools, buttons, hooks and eyes and whatever else thrifty housewives needed for their days of mending. She'd continue to sit with the woman of the house after showing her the goods and while away a few minutes over a cup of tea and a reading, and in this way would always raise a wing or two.

Traveller women in my day were always known for selling fabrics – tweed cloth, Irish linen and handmade lace. My aunt sold small fireside rugs. They were cheap runners easily afforded by young wives struggling to feed growing families with only a small purse to dip into. I remember a funny story about the time when she went to buy her tug rugs from the wholesaler but he only had expensive ones in stock. Knowing that the lassies who lived in the tenements couldn't afford pure wool rugs, she headed to the more affluent streets. Smelling fresh paint she approached a house with big bay windows and plush blue velvet drapes. Pulling from her bundle a blue fireside rug, she knocked on the door. As soon as the lady of the house saw the rug, auntie was invited in. The lady was obviously keen, and brought her into a newly decorated lounge where she laid the rug in front of the fireplace. She was so impressed that she bent down to feel the thickness of the pile, and as she did so, let off a corker of a fart!

'Oh dear me,' she exclaimed, 'I'm so very sorry – it must be the pea soup!'

Auntie, an honest woman who said what she thought, smiled and replied, 'Wife, don't worry about that, when I tell you the price of the carpet you'll shit yourself!'

All things come to an end, even Woolworths. The old Travellers hadn't forgotten the damage the shops had done to their culture, so when an elderly travelling man heard of the demise of Woollies he felt compelled to visit his local branch. Seeing the giant glass doors and windows covered with For Sale signs and Closing-Down banners, he folded his arms, smiled broadly and said to a passer-by, 'Great funeral, eh?'

8

THE BROXDEN CURSE

Here's another tale from Perth.

Routes to Dundee, Edinburgh, Glasgow, Perth and Inverness all converge at a big roundabout named Broxden. This is one of the most notorious circles of tarmac anywhere in the British Isles and an ongoing headache for road managers. It does provide a few coppers for repair garages however. Why? Because the road holds a secret – it nurses a curse!

If in this modern day you find such an announcement hard to swallow, then speak to any of the many drivers who have had to be rescued from their cabs after their lorries were thrown onto their sides. It is a mystery as to why this happens and as yet no expert has provided an reason or solution for the problem. Yet if any of these road-engineers had consulted a Perthshire Traveller they'd have been met with a smile and the reply, 'You don't know? I thought everyone knew about old Annie's stone.'

Well now, folks, let's journey back two hundred years to the spot before there ever was a roundabout there, and see what happened. It might be that when I've told you this tale a clearer picture will emerge.

In a strip of woodland between Lamberkine path and Tinkers Loan, a worried and desperate father-to-be, Bobby Naismith, was holding his young wife's hand. As he wiped the sweat beads from her forehead she whispered through clenched teeth, 'Go get the herb-wife, she'll know what to do.'

Poor women unable to pay for a 'proper' midwife would send for the herb-wife to help with the delivery of their babies. This was only thought necessary when mothers-to-be were having their first babies or were in dire need. This was Alison's first child, and it was causing her no end of distress. Our young innocents were pedlars, of the kind referred to in Burns's poem *Tam o' Shanter* as Chapman Billies. For a living they made and sold pot-scourers from heather roots, clothes-pegs of alder and besom brooms.

Leaving Alison as comfortable as possible in her bow-tent home of hazel sticks and animal skins he set off to fetch old Annie Milady, the nearest herb-wife, who lived three miles away over a hillock in a tiny cottar house near the village of Craigend, on the outskirts of Perth.

He had hardly gone a mile when a nasty-looking band of men, uncouth and fierce-mouthed with drink, barred his way. He knew by their appearance they were army deserters; they wore torn plaidies and Glengarry bonnets with a crest of wildfowl feathers, and some of them had bare feet.

It was clear to see that their purpose was robbery, so he dropped his guard, smiled and stretched out a hand. 'Let me go unhindered, lads,' he said, 'for I have a wife who needs help to bear her baby, and I am in haste to fetch the herb-wife.' He spread his hands to show he carried nothing, neither a purse nor a weapon.

One of the band, a bushy-bearded, red-nosed fellow with massive forearms and not a hair on his head, stepped forward and for a few moments stared at Bobby through menacing eyes like slits. Then, without a word, he turned Bobby around and whipped off his leather belt. At once his shirt loosened and his plaid fell to the ground. 'This is a nightmare,' he heard a voice whisper deep inside.

As the reality of fear crept over his body in a cold sweat he shivered and silently answered the voice. 'Of all the times to be met by soulless villains.'

He prayed and pleaded with the men for an ounce of compassion in the midst of violence. 'Oh God almighty, whatever you men have done and whoever hounds you for it, my eyes will not witness your presence on this path, and my words will never tell of it. Let me pass. My sweet sixteen-year-old wife is in fear this very minute. Allow me to go in peace to fetch the old woman.'

One half-witted ruffian pushed his bulky frame against Bobby, almost knocking him over, snuffling and giggling and snorting like a pig. Another ill-natured brute, slightly hunched over and weatherbeaten, prodded Bobby's ribs with a sharp stick, mocking him in a shrill voice, 'Oh, yer wee wife's haein a wean. Yer wee wife canna dae it herself. Oh shame – ivverybody cry, shame!' Raucous laughter rent the damp air.

Bobby, though usually brave and resolute, began to lose hope. He bit his lip so as not to provoke them with an angry answer. Alison's predicament helped him to remain strong, and the last thing he needed was to show his anguish. They were looking to play with him, like a cat trapping and terrorising a mouse. Like the mouse he was way out of his depth – it would take an army of lawful soldiers or a miracle to save him.

And praise be, help came from none other than the bushy-bearded one who seemed to hold more authority than the rest. He rapped an order. 'Shut up! I'll see if this intruder has the guts to put me back.' The ruffian scanned his cohorts and said, 'What have ye, men? Shall we let him pass or will we charge him a mighty penny for toll, or will I teach him not to come running past our hollow without permission?'

A roar of laughter rose in the darkening air, followed by 'Charge the fool!'

Fingering an empty tobacco pouch, he was obviously itching for a smoke and had nothing to feed the pipe clenched between his filthy teeth. The leader sniffed, ran the back of his hand across his dripping nose and said, 'Did you hear them, lad? We want a florin from you.'

Bobby winced. The last thing his pride wanted to do was to pay homage in money to such a villain, but the vital thing was to get away. In his desperate state he would have promised the earth just to be given leave to go.

'I have not a farthing, let alone two shillings, but if you let me pass I'll borrow the money from the herb-wife.'

Lowering his menacing gaze, the leader leaned over, laid a grimy hand on Bobby's shoulder and handed back his belt, saying, 'Here, laddie, stop fretting, put on your plaid.' He pointed at the plaid and snarled, 'We don't want your pennies.' He patted a fat pouch tied to his belt and continued, 'We got lucky in a cock fight yesterday. We don't want yer money, but I'm dreeling on a smoke; are you damn sure there's no baccy hidden in that bonnie white sark?'

Bobby, grateful that the whole thing was simply an ill-natured jest, shook his head at the question. He could smell the foul breath as his companion leaned closer, and trembled at words spat in a low whisper through yellow, clenched teeth,

'You must know, laddie, we canna let you go free, don't you? There's a troop searching for us. We deserted Fort Geordy and have been on the run six months now. We keep clear o' the law by silencing witnesses. So, sorry, laddie, but it's time to finish you off. Want to go clean with a stroke of the knife or take on me boys one by one?'

Bobby wasn't sure if the man, like the torturing cat, was still playing mind-games with him, or whether at a whim he would truly relish cutting his throat. But Alison's predicament, not his own safety, was all that mattered. 'If this is my last journey,' he thought, 'at least I'll die wearing my family tartan?'

A heavy silence hung in the air with the moorland mist as Bobby bent down to pull on his plaid. Surreptitiously he glanced around, looking for an opening through which he could escape the band of mindless murderers. It would probably be death to make a run for it, but he was desperate.

Reading his mind the red-faced leader kicked out, knocking Bobby flat, then stood hard upon his hand. 'You're going nowhere laddie!' From a leather scabbard, lying close by, he pulled out a short, broken-bladed sword, and began to hack wildly at Bobby's clothing. At the mercy of this evil deserter and thief, Bobby had no choice. In his mind's eye he saw his wife screaming in pain – left all alone and without help she would certainly die. Lunging at the brigand about to end his life, he put all his strength behind a heavy tackle. Down and over a craggy outcrop they tumbled, rolling further from the other outlaws who were still laughing and drinking. 'You die this night,' they called out, thinking their leader was cutting poor undefended Bobby to pieces.

At any other time or place the outcome would have been different, but in the heart of the laddie was a precious image – his lassie, in child. What better reason for fighting back with desperation like that of a cornered rat? With a fierce swing of the arm he caught his opponent a jagging uppercut which sent him down like a sack full of stones. In blind panic Bobby's legs seemed to make a decision on their own and made off in a homeward direction. Yet as he went the young man had enough spunk to shout out, 'The barrack at Fort George will hear about you lot. I'd scatter if I were you. This miserable excuse for a man is clay dead in the grass – if you want to check!'

His heart beat louder than thunder claps as he bounded back over the moor.

Alison had had her own battle while he was gone, but as he neared their tent he heard the most heavenly sound: a baby's cries.

Inside he embraced his wife, and after a storm of weeping they decided it was no longer safe to stay in their quiet corner of Lamberkine wood. Alison was far too weak to walk, so Bobby, constantly scanning the horizon for any sign of the deserters seeking revenge, harnessed up his old horse and made a comfortable bed for his wife and their baby son in the cart.

Half a mile from the path barred by the deserters there was a lesser-known drover's route which would take them around their camp and onto a cottage owned by a candlemaker. Bobby knew the candlemaker and his wife fairly well; they were a decent couple who had always bought his long-lasting washing pegs and other pedlar wares.

Providence must have been asleep that day, because the moor's unwelcome band of thieves were not finished with young Bobby. On either side of the winding track those demons were waiting for them. The pedlar felt like a fly in a spider's web. They surrounded them on all sides. He stood aghast. Where could he turn to now with his wife and new-born child?

Bobby drew breath. 'They'll kill us, Alison. Take the baby and get into the bushes. I love you, Alison. Kiss my son for me, lassie.'

Bobby was no hero, but on this day he fought with a passion that none of those outlaws had seen before. Before the club was raised which delivered the fatal blow, he'd taken three of his enemies with him.

Fortune was not for the brave on that fateful day, because, apart from those who ripped into the flesh of Alison and left her lying in her own blood, no eye survived to tell what happened next.

The outlaws spared the life of the baby as beneath their contempt. When the candlemakers chanced upon the horrific scene, they found Alison still clinging onto life. With her dying breath she was able to tell her neighbours what happened, and they reassured her they would look after the tiny boy.

When the terrible news reached old Annie Milady, the herb-wife, she covered her head in a black shawl and went up to the grisly scene. Carefully she and several local folks cleared a plot in the gorse bushes and buried the young couple there.

The pedlar's old horse hadn't escaped the clutches of death either, and it too lay twisted in the heather by the path. The animal was sent for butchering and the upturned cart with its improvised bed was burnt.

When the mourners left, old Annie unearthed a large stone and rolled it to the spot where the young couple had been killed. She knelt down and uttered a few ancient incantations over the stone and the place of death.

'On this stone I put a curse.

> *Wheel rolls and rim over,*
> *Watch now ye wild rover,*
> *Earth ripple and rumble,*
> *Cart coup and load tumble.'*

In the present time, according to Tayside Police, in one year alone there were 71 accidents reported on the Broxden roundabout. This is proof that it deserves its reputation as one of the most notorious circles of road in the entire country. And yes, I reckon if my calculations are correct, the roundabout is situated on the exact spot where the curse was made by the old herb-wife.

If you are driving round this bit of road, I'd advise slowing down and being extra careful. Remember the curse and the pedlars' fate with respect, and no harm should come to you. Speed on that spot and I can't guarantee you a safe journey.

A well-travelled lorry driver who has spent twenty-five years of his life on the road and knows the moods of every road in Britain is well aware of the hazards of this route. He doesn't believe in a curse, but puts the accidents down to the fact that a road shouldn't exist in this place. Some areas are just not happy with roads on them, and Broxden is one of them. It might be down to the presence of ley lines or some other phenonomen. In these disturbed places, flyovers and slip roads avoiding contact with the affected area should be built to guide drivers safely to their destinations. Most drivers who use the roundabout frequently agree that there are too many routes too close together going in different directions, and this is the cause of the problems

Confusion reigns! I'll let you think for a while on this one, reader. Yes, it's only a simple folk tale and has several versions.

9
AND ON WE GO

Three miles outside the town of Crieff, which lies 17 miles from Perth, there's a turn-off to the Sma' Glen. The glen has given birth to a wealth of stories from the one about a green lady floating over the moors to that of a tiny mythical settlement. Tinker folk had over ten secluded greens on this stretch of moorland, courtesy of the landowners who in days gone by employed them to burn heather, beat grouse, trap rabbits, pull flax and many more country chores. I recently made a tour of the glen and not a single green remains.

This next story about the Sma' Glen is no myth, but it did help to put off anyone who was considering setting a thriving whisky business.

The Sma' Glen leads over to Aberfeldy in one direction, Dunkeld in the other. The river Bran meanders through it, and was one of the main thoroughfares for whisky smuggling. Crieff at one end, a busy centre for cattle droving and with her wide River Earn, was a gold mine for smugglers. Needless to say the place was full of soldiers run off their feet trying to keep abreast of all things illegal. I have little doubt my Tinker lot were up to their wee brown necks in this outlaw trade, and I've discovered narrow deer tracks over the breadth of the Sma' Glen leading past standing stones and old campsites that suggest I'm right. It wouldn't be right to pen an account of the area without popping in a tale of the golden nectar.

Wars and battles were fought right across Scotland between the moonshine boys and the gadgers (police). Here's my favourite, with thanks to Mr MacAinsh Brown, who found this story in a booklet about bonny Strathearn written in 1860, which was one of the earliest tourist guides for the area.

'Amulree is the scene of a great annual market for cattle, driven from the northern counties. In its solitude, separated as it is by lofty mountains, too bleak even for the labours of the husbandsman, it seems to afford a perfect retreat to summer visitors, either for the pleasure of solitary angling or of undisturbed meditation.

Here in days of yore every surrounding nook had its whisky still. To suppress such contraband traffic, a troop of cavalry was at times quartered at Crieff, to aid the revenue officer named McPhee (known as the gauger), who, it is whispered, was unpopular in every glen in the Highlands of Perthshire where the smell of whisky was wafted on the air. There had been far too much smuggling as far as the authorities were concerned, and McPhee decided to make a raid into Glenquaich. So backed by a party of Scots Greys, "the gauger loon" penetrated the Sma' Glen and climbed up to the moor of Corrymuckloch. About twenty smugglers, unaware of the approaching soldiers and not counting on such a visit, were on the move southwards. Every other man was on horseback, each with a couple of ankers of whisky swinging from his saddle crupper. When the soldiers attacked, the wily smugglers fought hard and with mighty ferocity won their battle.

The Battle of Corrymuckloch

December on the twenty-first,
A party o' our Scottish Greys,
Gaed up among our mountaineers
Some whisky from them for to seize.

Wi' sword and pistol by their side,
They thocht to mak a grand attack;
And a' they wanted was to seize
Pair Donald wi' his smuggled drap.

Chorus:
Dirim dye a dow a dee,
Dirim dye a dow a daddie.

An a' they wanted there to find,
Was Donald wi' his smuggled drappie.

The Gauger an' the Greys cam' on,
And they poor Donald did surrroun'
He says, "Your whisky I maun seize
By virtue of the British crown."

"Hoot, hoot," quo' Donald, "no sae fast,
Ye ken the whisky is her nain;
She fearna you, nor your grey horse,
Nor yet yer muckle bearded men."

Chorus

Then Donald and his men drew up,
And Donald he did gie command;
And a' the arms pair Donald had
Was just a stick in ilka hand,

An' where puir Donald's men drew up,
A guid stane dyke was at their back;
Sae, when the sticks to pronnach went,
Wi' stance they made a bold attack.

Chorus

Or ere the action it was o'er,
There fell a horseman on the plain,
Quo' Sandy unto Donald syne,
"Ye've killed one o' the bearded men."

But up he gat and left his horse,
And straight to Amulree he flew,
And left the rest to do their best,
As they were left at Waterloo.

Chorus

But Donald and his men stuck fast,
An' garr'd the beardies left the field;
The gauger he wis thump'd weel,
Afore his pride would let him yield.

Then Donald's men they a' cried oot,
"Ye, nasty, filthy gauger loon,
If ye come back, ye'll ne'er win hame,
Tae see yer Ouchterarder toon."

Chorus

And when the battle it was o'er,
And not a horseman to be seen,
Quo' Donald syne unto his men,
"Ye'll a' sit doon upon the green.

For noo, my lads, we'll hae a look
Shust o' the gear sic likes we hae."
"Aye, that's richt," quo' Dougal, "but a'm sure
They got a filthy hurry doon the brae.'"

—

My gentle parents had special places that now and again prompted a dip into past recollections as Tinkers of the road. I have my own memories of several nooks and crannies. One in particular was of a burn where we were washing our feet. When our parents took off their shoes they asked us to judge who between them had the most perfect feet!

As a child this meant little to me, and only when I became an adult, and as the Bible says, I put away my childish ways, did I realise the ritual significance of this act. What my beloved mother and father were doing was proudly displaying, and comparing, feet that had for most of their young lives walked over untold miles, sometimes leading a horse pulling a cart and sometimes, when there was no horse, with their young spines loaded with the family's worldly goods. This was not such a difficult task by the standards of the lifestyle, but when those feet were bare without the protection of shoes, and had to traverse hill road and heather moorland, then you can see the importance they would attach to being able proudly to hold them up and ask the question, 'Whose feet are best?'

They spoke often of Jacky Six Toes, who'd lost the other four while taking a shortcut through a field and stepping on a scythe-blade left by a harvester. They'd say, 'Aye, man – in the blink o' an eye, four fat trotters for hungry crows.' Then they'd both snigger, remembering another sausage-shaped part of the male anatomy that caused a hell of a stir when someone found it on a farm road. The stories that went the rounds about that penis would have filled the *News of the World* for months! Its owner and its amputator were a complete mystery. The explanations ranging from an apprentice undertaker having a laugh, to a spurned lover, circulated like reek from a fire made with wet sticks.

Anyway, the barefoot years left many a young Tinker with injury to limbs and crippled body. There was no end to the possible mishaps from fire, hidden sharp objects and the river, which was always a potential death trap with flooded pools that concealed broken bottles, jagged metals and God alone knew what else. So I now realise to be at the age they were with a grown family and have unblemished feet was as near to miraculous as one could get.

Come to think of it, they had healthy hands too. Hands that had shot guns, set snares, skinned rabbits, whittled wands for tent pegs and heather scourers, and woven baskets. That they had come through all that unscathed, says a lot. My mother had the most beautiful hands. Washing for a family of ten people, using hard carbolic soap and wringing the heaviest bundles of bed linen, back bent over river banks, should have turned her hands into shrivelled, hag-like, warty things, but they were perfect. At night, when we were all storied and bedded, she would open the Pandora's box in which she kept cures and a repair kit for all ills, and would work her magic with a well worn nailfile on any ragged edges, followed by a complete rub with olive oil before applying a thin layer of her favourite nail polish.

Looking her best for my father was paramount. Oft times as we grew into teenagers, her watch words to us were 'Be a barry deekin' wee manishi. Always run a comb through the fez and lippy the moi for him comin' hame. Even if ye're half dead with work and worry, he has to see the beauty he married. Don't let yerself go with fat and sags, keep the back straight and the ankles slender. If he leaves you for another, remember it takes two to make a perfect couple.'

Once, while examining her toes and reciting 'Ten little piggies went to market', I found a tiny red corn on the side of her little toe. She instantly insisted that it was the fault of a shan manishi with narrow feet who had given her a pair of shoes one day while out hawking. She thought they were beautiful, and though they were a size too small, forced them on anyway. My father made her even more keen to wear them by telling her that Hollywood belle Barbara Stanwyck wore the identical pair in a recent film, but couldn't hold a candle to his beloved for the way she swung up the tobber in the peerie heels. Even although her feet were in agony, she kept the shoes on because he had paid her a genuine compliment. I can't remember seeing those shoes again, however, after the discovery of the corn.

My father, on the other hand, never had any such problem. To him the foot, the transporter of the body, was to be treated like royalty and never taken for granted. He wore perfectly fitting size eight leather brogues over pure wool socks. These had proper leather laces, not plastic cloth or string rubbish. As I say, it was not until later that I realised what lay behind their pride in good strong feet. Feet crippled by sores or any other injury meant lost miles. Lost miles might mean the difference between a trouble-free journey and getting stopped by bigoted policemen or sadistic factors hell-bent on making certain that Tinkers didn't travel through their patch again. This was not just a minor inconvenience. I was once told by Dougall Macgregor; late of Taynuilt, that a few Tinker men who fell foul of a certain policeman keeping his patch free of 'undesirables' met a watery end in Inveraray Harbour.

My father had a superstitious belief that only the dead should sleep with their socks on. In the middle of winter, when all the rest of us bedded down in woollies and two pairs of thick socks, he refused to keep his feet covered. During the war he'd seen his fair share of corpses scattered around the field of battle. I remember asking him, 'What difference would wearing a pair of socks make to you if you're dead?' For answer I got a rolled-up newspaper across my legs.

10

THE CRIEFF CONNECTION

It's my pleasure now to take you to Crieff, which is a Pictish name meaning 'people of the strong back'. The Romans avoided Crieff and took a detour round it instead; all records state that they settled in the Broich lands below Crieff. I wonder if in those old days there was widespread belief in superstitious stories about the wee town on the hill and its strong-backed people.

Tinkers loved the town and were constantly drawn to it. We, along with other families we knew, wintered there on several occasions. The initial reason for Tinkers coming to Crieff was that during the Irish famine a strong young priest fought for a Catholic Church and school to be built to take in the many hundreds of Irish refugees who flooded Scotland after the nineteenth-century failure of the potato crop. Many of these Irish immigrants lived side by side in tents with Tinkers until such time as they found houses.

Crieff used its Irish incomers, with their knowledge of agriculture, as labourers to grow and cultivate a vast acreage of root vegetables in the surrounding land. Census records show that my paternal grandparents lived in North Bridge Street; years later they returned and moved into a house in the High Street. Quite a large number of relatives moved there, many from Ireland. My parents and other family members are buried in the cemetery in Ford Road.

Crieff had more 'greens' than any other town in Scotland apart from Blairgowrie, whose produce was fruit. Wanderers found not only employment in each place, but fine places to settle. The old folks were the first to make their homes there, and in time the younger families joined them. Many left the old travelling ways behind them.

Mary Thomson, a genealogist from Dundee, has worked extensively on our family tree. She has discovered that in Ireland my great, great, great-grandmother Sally Malloy (a widow at the time) married Richard Mackay (known as the bard) from Armagh. During the Irish famine of 1847 they escaped death by herding their eleven children on a cattle boat. To pay their passage he sold his collection of songs and music. Mary tells me that today traditional performers sing his work unaware of who the original writer was. One such tune is 'The Road and the Miles to Dundee'. Originally it would have had a different title relating to Ireland.

One of their children, the daughter of Sally's first husband Charles McManus, was called Catherine. Charles had died after the birth of their third child. Young Catherine was my great, great-granny on my mother's father's side.

British authorities refused to refer to the new arrivals as Irish Tinkers (Pavee) listing them instead in official documents as 'vagrants'. They faced a long hard battle for respect and recognition.

The consequences of the Irish potato famine sent some of my forebears to spread their wings throughout Britain and abroad. Some settled in Bradford and other areas of Yorkshire, Lancashire and other English counties. More relatives are in Canada, America and Australia.

Both sides of my family were extremely close-knit units, who seldom married outside their local area. This devotion to family ties would serve them well in the turbulent period that awaited them.

＊

Braidhaugh, down next to the river Earn on the back road to Comrie, was our favourite summer green. Others were Halley's Barrow and the Crow's Wood on the low Comrie road. Three Tinker greens by the Muthill road were in sight of standing stones. At the other end of the town there's a place called Tomaknock (mentioned in my previous books) which served for a few years as our winter green. Other greens in this area were around the Monzie area, at Gilmerton, Cultoquy, Madderty, Fowlis with its ancient pictish barrow and standing stones (an area where there is a burial site for Tinkers), in the Sma' Glen, several places on the banks of the Earn, Innerpeffray, and the scattered woods on either side of the road between Crieff and Auchterarder at Mauchnie.

Big roomy greens were North Fore and South Fore on the Broich Road, where Mammy first pierced my ears with a large darning needle! (There's a burial site here too). Then there was Pittentain where local children reported seeing a ghost of an elderly woman wearing a tartan shawl. Other greens were Culcrieff, Curlews Moor, Highlandman's Loan, Bantry, Knock Earn and Knock Mary, where the so-called witch Kate Macniven was burned and rolled down the hill. It's believed she cursed the entire family line of the landed gentry who were responsible for her demise.

Between Braco and Muthill at the crossroads several tinker encampments were dotted around. It was here, during the time of horse-drawn haulage wagons, that local men from Auchterarder killed a Tinker man and stole his horse and money. Near the crossroads there's a site called the Suicides' Graveyard, and it was here the murderers buried him. From a Braco man I received a fragment of a poem penned by Tinkers about this barbaric act:

> 'Whistle ower the moon lads,
> Steadfast on yer course.
> A'm trevelling frae the Deevil's den,
> Tae claim ma bonny horse.'

Tradition says the 'ghost o' suicide crossroads' haunted anyone who stepped on his resting place and further adds, 'more than one has heard a blood-curdling scream, then seen a fiery horse with a terrified man strapped on its back.'

People tell me that before the Reformation these little crossroad graveyards for suicides were commonplace and deliberately chosen. If someone took their own life or died under mysterious circumstances they had to be buried where the roads crossed, so that their souls wouldn't know which way led to peace. Seemingly such sacred places were scattered throughout the Highlands of Scotland.

Braidhaugh was, during the Second World War, a POW camp. After the war military men dismantled the barracks, but thankfully left the concrete bases of the huts, which served as perfect pulling on stances for caravans, and in particular our old Bedford bus home. Those concrete bases would have been perfect for erecting bowdie tents on, but by then Tinkers were progressing into more modern mobile homes, abandoning the old hazel wattles and carts. (It's a shame, that, because there was no better atmosphere than to be crowded inside the bowdie while a fierce thunderstorm raged outside. If erected properly by an expert, my father said they resembled 'the skin around a rib cage'. I heard my best ghost tales while sitting inside one of these old humped abodes.)

Braidhaugh road is a straight stretch of three miles, and is believed to be another gift left to us by the genius for construction of the Romans, who seem to have been exceedingly active in that area, with a network of roads not just on the coast but also zigzagging the countryside. Pictish barrows and standing stones are a prominent feature along this road, for example a standing stone to the left heading out of Crieff. On the right of the road is an area frequented by dozens of Tinker folk who lived around nearby.

Faint, almost invisible Tinker bridle paths criss-cross the entire area. The Tinkers when deciding what route these tracks should take were well aware of the alignment of ley lines underlying the landscape. Throughout Europe ley lines feature very strongly, taking the form of electrical energies driven by underground streams. It is believed spiritual powers abound around them. They are said to link up ancient monuments and pathways and provide routes for unsettled spirits to travel along. At certain points underwater streams can meet in a vortex and cause havoc above ground. Unholy spirits emerge as black spirals and battle to find ways upwards through the bodies of the living. Some people not gifted with the Tinker's second sight and ability in fortune-telling have pitched their tents on top of a black spiral. As a result they become seriously ill, are unable to eat or drink, and then fall into a coma which is seldom survived. Others have had to run for it in the night when their bedcovers rose in the air and voices could be heard whispering through trees. An English Gypsy told me that in certain Gypsy families there were people who knew the powers of the leylines. When travellers wished to make a journey, but were uncertain of the route through bogs and dangerous cliffs etc, they could for a few pennies pay the Lees (Leys) who would guide them safely on their way. The Lees also used water dowsing and cloud reading as well as the ley lines. With their extensive knowledge of these mysteries they knew where to set camp and what wood to burn.

I performed a small experiment in wellie boots, trekking over the Braidhaugh area, and found that although Roman roads were close to ley lines they did not cross them; evidence that the Picts, Romans and Tinkers shared the same understanding of the ley network and knowledge of the land.

When I was in the Muthill area I was told the story of a woman with child who had passed her confinement time. When, after 43 weeks, the baby finally came, she was of the belief that her healthy baby had taken too long to be born, and therefore did not belong to the earth but rather the Devil. She killed her child and buried its body in a field between two pointed standing stones. At that spot I had an overwhelming sense of fear and anguish. With the local farmer's permission, I was allowed to bury a tiny cross there. What compelled me to do this I cannot say, but for some reason it seemed proper and necessary. Later, when I returned to visit the place, a feeling of serenity replaced my earlier fear and alarm.

II

COMRIE AND BEYOND

Comrie, to the north, was another place that the Romans knew well. The ancient Pictish name for the strath in which it sits was the Kingdom of Fortren. Driving along the A85 it's easy to spot some of the settlements dating from that period, but not so easy to make out if they were Roman or Pictish. Between Comrie and St Fillans there's a prominent hill, named Dundurn Hill, with a circle of stones which in 1970 was discovered to be a Pictish fort. Right on the crest of it are rocks in the form of a throne, and surveying the area from this vantage-point it is easy to see where sacrifices might have taken place. In a straight line from the fort's gravel circle is an old church. In its graveyard are several Pictish stones with symbols of death and mystical rebirth, and representations of what seem to have been tools. Sadly, not too many of the right people see the importance of conserving this ancient area, so the Pictish remains head rapidly into disrepair. Cows and sheep use the crumbling walls of the church shelter. Shame on Scottish Natural Heritage for ignoring this time-worn relic. I'd recommend a visit before it disappears completely.

There are also nearby two old campsites and a Tinkers' burial ground. I'm sworn to secrecy as to the burial spot's exact location; however it does not take an Einstein to work out just how secluded and protected by woodland the wanderers' resting place is.

One lovely autumn afternoon I visited the area to take pictures of the rutting stags of a nearby braeside. The colours of gold, orange and yellow swirled around. After a while I sat down feeling quite light-headed and as I did so I could swear I heard singing from a patch of undergrowth. I investigated and found an old lady wearing a crown of fallen leaves and not much else. She smiled and asked me in to a little bower of branches. I wondered if perhaps she was suffering from dementia but I thought I'd better humour her. Crawling into her leafy den I sat and listened to her performing the most beautiful words and music. When I then asked her if she needed help getting home, she answered by saying, 'My dear girl, I am home.'

I said my goodbyes and set off back to the car, but halfway there I felt guilty at leaving her, so I turned back to find the little den again, only to discover she had vanished! Wherever to, I had no idea. This was enough to reassure me, however, that my nature-loving companion was in good health.

Three weeks later I met her in Comrie Post Office, perfectly healthy and wearing the clothes of a grand lady. She recognised me immediately, and enquired if I'd been back to her little home of autumn leaves and soft ferns.

Comrie has a strange title, The Shaky Toon; so called because it lies on a geological fault line which has created many a small earthquake; in some cases it has tumbled sleeping bodies from their beds. There have been quite strong tremors that have broken crockery and caused noticeable shifting of bricks and mortar.

I met a lady called Mamie Carson while out on a walk one day who was the first to tell me about the history of Comrie. We were destined to meet again thirty years later and become firm friends, and it was then she presented me with a book of poems by her late father, Keith McPherson. Historians write extensively about Roman occupation in Strathearn, and like many a bard in the area this inspired Keith to weave them into his verses.

Keith ran a local garage. This poem centres on the night Comrie man Andra MacLeod was beaten at the bowls for the first time by the local blacksmith, Mr Crerar. It all took place in the late 1950s. Not that long ago to be seeing ancient Romans, but many are the tall tales told by Comrie worthies of ghostly appearances. These always happen at night, and, may I add, often after a dram or two has been shared around the big stone in Andra's garden.

The Muckle Stane

Oh ken ye MacLeod frae the muckle big stane,
It stands in the field at the fit o' his lane,
A link wi' the Romans wi' cup an' wi' mark.

Their ghosts gaither roond every night efter dark,
And Andra, guid man, makes it one o' his rules
Tae join in their crack on his way fae the bools.

But ae' nicht this winter, no many weeks gane,
He passed without stopping at the muckle big stane,
Wi' his chin on his chest, and sae doon at the mou'
The ghosts thocht at first sicht that Andra wis fou,
And they agreed that strong drink makes the best o' men fools,
Then they heard Andra mutter, 'I'm bate at the bools'.

So they bade him come ower jist like one o' their ain,
And they sat themselves doon by the muckle big stane.
Andra spoke oot —and his heart it grew sairer,
He jist couldna thole bein' lickit by Crerar,
A buddie gey handy wi' blacksmithing tools,
But no in a class wi' himself at the bools.

Noo the ghosts made a ring, each the ither hand taen,
And they swore by the marks in the muckle big stane,
That Crerar the smith they would visit that night,
And leave the puir buddie half dein' wi' fright.
They swore by the elves wha bide under toadstools,
He'd never again beat their man at the bools.

Noo Andra Macleod, be it sleet, snow or rain,
Aye stops when he's passin' the muckle big stane,
Since that fearful nicht, when he gi'ed them his crack,
The whole Roman Empire he's had at his back.
So long as the Stane, Andra's destiny rules,
He'll no lose tae Crerar again at the bools.

Mamie Carson remained my friend until her recent demise, and
with hand on heart I can honestly say that no nicer human being
walked this earth. She rests in a beautiful spot on the low Comrie
road with woodland to her head and the river to her feet.

So let's resume our journey.

Comrie can claim two beautiful rivers which cross at the northern
end of the town – the Ruchil and the Earn. It was at this crossing

that a vast Tinkers' campsite was situated. Locals called it 'the white city'. Every winter, dozens of families, my ancestors included, made their weary way there to live in relative peace and harmony. And yes, a few hundred yards up the road was their talisman, a large and prominent standing stone as clearly visible today as it would have been for hundreds of years.

For unknown reasons the people of Comrie had an affinity with the Tinkers like that to be found in Blairgowrie and Crieff. This wasn't shared in any other place in Perthshire apart from close-knit rural villages where the appearance of Tinkers was thought to bring good luck. Pitlochry and Aberfeldy would eventually embrace us, but it would take a lot of suffering on the Tinkers' part and a process of educating the worthy folk of those areas before anything like harmony would emerge. (We shall dip into this subject later in the book.)

12
The Dreaded Humpies

Here's a personal story of something that happened in Comrie.

Three miles north of the town, on the Dalchonzie bend, our Bedford gave a deep gurgle and juddered to a halt on the longest corner in Scotland. Ploughing was in full swing which meant it didn't take long for a line of greasy Fergies to form in a queue behind us. One irate ploughman pulled out in his tractor, not seeing the oncoming lorry which hit him full on. The road was blocked, and my goodness was the air not blue!

My father was in no mood to argue with the ploughmen, so tried enlisting their expertise in engines. This amounted to one old boy with an inflamed boil on the nape of his neck who knew plenty about horses and ploughs of old, but precious little about bus engines.

The lorry driver, who told us to call him Big Brogues on account of the size of his feet, was more interested in a mouthful of tea than fixing a breakdown. My mother too was dying for a cuppy, so while I skipped over the hedge to build and light a fire she prepared some food. In no time the aroma of strong tea and fresh baked flat cake was drifting across to the farm lads who were in the middle of trying to convince my father to scrap the Bedford bus and go back on the road with a faithful horse and cart like real Tinkers! I thought this argument might end in fists, so called out over the hedge that my mother had tea and scones ready. She gave me a look as if to say, 'Shut up, there are too many mouths out there.'

Unable to resist the tantalising smells, the ploughmen came over and helped finish off her fresh bakes. Thankfully she had made enough. Once he was refreshed to his own satisfaction, Big Brogues set to work with my father to fix our bus.

Thinking that the road-block would take a while to clear, I went for a wander in the woods to explore. As I meandered on, something about the terrain puzzled me; for as far as the eye could see through the trees, small mounds of earth were everywhere. These little hillocks measuring about six feet high and perhaps twenty feet circumference didn't look like the work of mother nature; they were surely man-made. It was then I remembered being told years ago that around Comrie and neighbouring Dundurn a Pictish village (also a favourite stopping ground for Travellers) along with a burial site, had been discovered by archaeologists. Maybe I was walking on sacred ground. A feeling of dread seized me, as I pictured the skeletal creatures beneath my feet. This soon put a stop to my exploration as I rushed back to the company of living people.

By this time more vehicles had joined the melée, including a midwife driving a baby Austin. She was on an emergency dash to assist at the birth of a baby, and was in no mood to eat scones, crack about boils on necks, big feet or bus engines.

With all this commotion on a main road I wondered when the police would appear. No Traveller likes to see them, but as sure as day turns to night, who should come cycling up to the back of the queue but none other than flat-footed Sergeant Smith – or, to those who knew him well – Smudger. 'What in blue bleezes is this pile o' reeking engines?' he shouted out, face redder than beetroot.

'Yon Tinker wi' the bus has broken doon,' called someone.

'Aye, and I canna get tae Maggie Ford's tae deliver her seventh,' added the small round-faced midwife, panic making her eyeballs bulge like bubbles.

'Come on now, boys,' said the Sergeant, 'Let's push some of this stuff out of the way to let Aggie get tae the wean. Number seven, ye say? My God, yon woman's a bairn factory. Her and Tam huv only been married six year.'

A cheeky grin spread across the policeman's face as he began ordering every able-bodied man to push Aggie's miniature vehicle onto the grass verge and down past the line of vehicles blocking the main road. Today there would be so many vehicles that this would have been impossible, but few people owned cars in those days so it was feasible to do it.

Soon Aggie was speeding off to deliver another baby to add to what sounded like a love nest somewhere in the hills beyond Dundurn.

Sergeant Smith approached my father and asked what the problem was.

His previous informant pointed a finger at my father and called out, 'He's broke doon, a' telt ye.'

'It is our bus home that's broken down,' I called out in my poshest accent, adding, 'not our faither!'

Smudger plodded through a throng of blethering folk standing with arms folded on their chests, shaking their heads and muttering under their breath about Tinkers deserting the faithful horse and cart and now going to drive every broken-down vehicle in Scotland.

At that moment the Bedford burst into life with a puff of black smoke. Big Brogues slapped my father on the back and as they straightened up from the engine to display smiles of white teeth in blackened faces everyone clapped in unison. Within a couple of minutes the Bedford was driven off the road into a field.

It took a while for the tractors, cars and lorries to roll by, leaving father and his new mate Big Brogues chatting with Smudger. Smudger's pride and joy was his Raleigh bicycle that never gave him the slightest worry. He'd heard that the polis in Glasgow used vehicles, but in the Shaky Toon two wheels upon a frame were enough for him. I started to ask him what he'd do if criminals drove off in a car having robbed the bank, but my mother interrupted me by offering to mix more flour, eggs and milk into another batch of flat cake. I was handed the kettle to refill.

For the best part of the afternoon there was more tea and more crack, and then the man with the sore neck came back and asked my mother if she could suggest a poultice for his boil. She obliged and off he went looking greatly relieved. Travelling people have natural cures for hundreds of illnesses and the rural folk knew this. It seems that when he went home and told his wife who had broken down she had sent him back to get the necessary medical instructions from my mother. She sternly instructed him to 'take a big dollop of treacle; mix with Epsom salts and heat; then apply to the boil and cover with brown paper soaked in vinegar. The mixture has to be almost unbearably hot when applied, the hotter the better. Put it on at night. In the morning it should be gone. If it isn't, find someone with a sharp knife and lance the bugger.' Mammy had an air of authority whenever she was doing her doctoring role.

Not wanting to tax the Bedford's engine, my father drove it down a drove track and insisted we stay the night. The thought of the grisly skeletons all around filled me with dread on hearing this, and I asked if we could move further up the road. It was to no avail, we were staying put.

Big Brogues had a load of lime to deliver, so he said his farewells. As he was about to leave I did a terrible thing – I asked him to take off his boots and let us see just how big his feet were. He smiled and happily showed his flippers. I was shocked by what I saw – when he peeled off his socks his toes fanned out like piglets escaping from a sty. His feet were long, but those toes were something else, once seen, never forgotten. He wished us a safe journey, but before climbing into his cab he said, with a meaty fist resting on my father's shoulder and a tear in his eye, 'My old mother had a saying, "If ifs and ands were pots and pans, there'd be no need for Tinkers!"'

To us that was an old-fashioned remark, because we had to go back three generations before we came across Tinker craftsmen. Apart from the odd hammer we'd not handled a tool in our lives. But I, for one, felt my chest swell by another inch or two – not with the curves of breesties, but with a sense of pride that the settled folk had looked upon our kind as important people in the pots and pans world. My tinsmith friend in Lochgilphead, who had given me a lesson in Tinker origins, sprang to mind.

Smudger, after giving my father a new copy of the Highway Code, straddled his bike and left us to the night. As far as I was concerned he was abandoning us to the mercies of glimmering Pictish ghouls! For most of the day my younger sisters had stayed inside Bedford reading Enid Blyton's Famous Five books and were oblivious to the events going on around them, and to a group of characters who would stay in my mind forever. My older sisters no longer took to the roads with us in the bus, so hectic activity of the day gave way to peace and quiet.

While we were eating supper I shared my fears of what lay in wait for us out there in the ever increasing, creeping shadows. I got a clout from my mother for trying to put the frighteners into her wee lambs, my younger sisters. The night and Dalchonzie corner were not, however, finished with us!

My father and I spent ages by the dying fire discussing the events of the day and listening as the landscape came alive with night sounds. My eyes were strained with scanning every movement on the darkening horizon. Mother washed her hands in the basin on its stand before whispering that the young ones were snoring and it was time I did the same. Even Tiny had made a last visit to the birch tree he had claimed, where for ever more a slightly yellowish patch would signify to all creatures how he'd used it!

Reluctantly I went to bed, where the big toe on Mary's left foot was going up my nose and Babsy's elbow sticking in my right ear. Renie, although she never said so, must have harboured dreams of being a ballet dancer, because she used our small cramped bed as a place to practise her pirouette. Some nights when I'd had enough I'd give her a dig, but this usually resulted in screams which woke our mother. Half asleep, she didn't believe in administering justice to just one offender, and would give us all a skelp on which ever hip was nearest her hand.

In no time my father had tied his belt around the inside handle of the door to our bus home and slipped quietly beneath the blankets and cuddled into my mother's back. She whispered a few sweet nothings, he replied and in no time they were sleeping soundly.

Gently shifting the feet and elbows out of my face and rolling spider-legged Renie onto her side to give me more room, I curled up, but sleep evaded me. Putting my bare feet onto the strip of Axminster carpet that ran up the aisle of the bus I tiptoed down to the empty seat at the front of the bus, the carpet muffling any sound. Whenever I had tummy pains or something bothered me during the night, this comfy cushioned seat was large enough for me to curl up on. A tartan rug was draped over it, so wrapping my feet in a fold of it I sat staring out at the night.

It took quite a time before my eyes adjusted to the shadows. I know that many a strange phenonomen can be dismissed as the wild imaginings of an over-active teenage mind, but with hand on pounding heart I can assure you that the sight of a moving creature like the walking trees of Macbeth's Dunsinane wood was real enough. It was shaped like one of the Pictish burial mounds and was flailing two long arms about in an erratic fashion.

'Daaaaaa,' I screamed, 'a live monster! Quick, get behind the wheel of the bus and shift!'

My entire family shot from their beds and in seconds were staring out at the creature.

'What the hell is that?' choked my father. Tiny was at his heel with a ridge of stiff hair raised down his back. His mouth wide open, he was slavering and growling like a wolf.

My mother had already grabbed a brush handle with one hand, with the other she gathered her girls. She rushed to prevent our father, pale and grim, from opening the door and facing whatever demon was outside. He told her, 'Bide where you are, stay inside and do not leave this bus!'

Too late to stop him, she watched helplessly as her husband, without a pair of trousers on, went to face the monster. I called out that it was a Pict and we couldn't speak its language, but to offer it a cup of tea and it might spare our lives.

He looked back at me over his shoulder and said, 'Jess, you definitely need that head examined, there's a few screws missing.'

'You'll think twice when that fossil chops off your goolies with those pincers hanging from his dinosaur shell.'

Without pausing for any more conversation he headed towards the creature and hit it over the head with a stick. There was an ear-piercing clanging sound before the monster fell over and stuck four legs in the air like an upturned hedgehog.

I ran the door, ignoring my mother's instructions through clenched teeth to get back inside, and rushed to my father's defence. 'Two warriors are stronger than one,' I shouted, only to find him helping a sorry-looking man who was lying on his back in an upside down coracle with two pearlfishing twangs (pincers for picking the oysters from the river bed) in his hands.

It was a regular traveller of the road, old Sandy Sutherland. My father was not too pleased by my behaviour and gave me what for.

'Don't fret the bairn, Charlie,' said Sandy in my defence, 'you were the one who ran and clouted me.'

'Aye, but not because I thought you were a bloody two-thousand-year-old skeleton shaped like a neep!'

My mother had already dressed and was raking up the fire's embers and adding sticks under the always full kettle. My sisters were back under the bedclothes, unperturbed by the incident and snoring peacefully.

When the tea was poured and all was calm, Sandy told us what had led him to our woodland site. Earlier while fishing for trout at the mouth of the Earn, he met an Irish Tinker fellow who had a pearl-fishing boat for sale. Sandy had always used a glass-bottomed milk jug to look for freshwater oysters and was excited at the thought of a vessel specially designed for the job – he wanted to see it. The fellow took him back to his tent and right enough, there it was – a perfectly round coracle with a glass window in the bottom.

Now Sandy (and every travelling person will tell you the same thing) is a man who, once he gets his eye on a thing, has to own it. Seemingly it took a damn lot of haggling before a price was set and the purchase settled, and Sandy became the owner of the boat. That might have been his view, but then the son of Erin informed him that he'd stolen it from a cousin. It was decided rather than take the road, Sandy would head off along the river path to avoid the rightful owner of the coracle who no doubt would be searching for his property.

'You should have left that thing and got your money back,' said my mother, throwing another stick into the flames and adding, 'God turns his hand against thieves. You should have left the boat and trekked home to Sadie. How is she these days anyway? I've not seen hide nor hair o' her for years.'

'Oh my dearest wee wife has never been healthier. A little grey at the temples but wearing well, she is. She still gives the tonsils an airing from time to time.'

The river was rolling a mist of wet smir against our faces, cold and damp, so it was decided that rather than let Sandy bundle home to wherever he and Sadie were camped he'd sleep on a horsehair mattress on the bus floor. Every inch of his clothes had a pungent aroma of Boggy Roll tobacco, and with the two slabs of gorgonzola cheese that he called feet he made doubly certain sleep was a luxury denied me that night. Perhaps exhaustion allowed me a few minutes of slumber, I don't know, but when my mother slipped past me on all fours and whispered something in Sandy's ear, I was wide awake.

'Sandy,' she said, nudging him, 'there's somebody raking around your wee boatie. Might be thon Irishman come for revenge. Charlie's asleep, so you get out and sort your own mess!'

Pulling back his jacket sleeve and displaying a wrist watch, he shoved it in my face. 'What time is that, Jess, I canna read it?'

'Stupid having a watch and not knowing the time. It's five o'clock.'

Mother added that it was dawn, because she'd heard a cockerel in a nearby farm gaining his hens' attention. 'There's enough light to face whoever is out there. Now, my bold lad, out you go,' she ordered.

Sandy was no hero and didn't care who knew it, so sliding his hand inside his jacket and retrieving a solid oak salmon priest (club) he pulled open the door and threw himself blindly at the culprit, who just so happened to be none other than Smudger, the policeman. And if that wasn't bad enough, Tiny who'd been denied a go at Sandy, dived and sank every gnasher into the policeman's goolies! Have you ever seen a dog fly?

Knowing Sandy very well and also because his aim was somewhat inaccurate, the big policeman was able to grasp the weapon and wrestle Sandy to the ground,

By now my father had risen and was pulling leather braces over his shoulders. 'Sergeant, whit seems tae be the problem?'

'Apart from this eejit attempting to knock ma brains out and your nippit dog trying to bite off one o' ma balls; nothing at all,' he said. He seemed a wee bit embarrassed as he added, 'I can't seem to find my bicycle pump and thought maybe I lost it here, yesterday.'

'Oh,' said my father, 'I thought the two wheels upon a frame was road-proof.'

Smudger looked down at Sandy who was still crumpled at his feet and said, 'Aye, Charlie, but when the winds out o' the tyres it's a bloody useless contraption for sure.'

We moved on after breakfast in the morning, and as is the way of the road never found out if Sandy and his coracle parted company or not, or if the real owner got the money from his Irish friend.

As the old folk used to mutter, 'Aye, gossip for the Gods.'

13
CLOOTY AND THE GHOST OF ARDVORLICH

Loch Earn with her basin of gentle water slowly trickling over into the River Earn is breathtakingly beautiful at sunset. It has a small crannog several hundred metres from the shore; another relic of the ancient ones who preferred living on stilts in the middle of the water rather than on land. Did they fear wolves and bears, or did they just like to be separated from landlubbers? A colourful flock of mallard ducks have taken up residence there now – or should I say, squat!

St Fillans is the name of the village where visitors from the north arrive at the loch. I, for one, always thought the houses in the village looked rather grand to be homes of local lochside dwellers, and I suspected that at one time Victorian toffs had come on holiday or for hunting, liked the place, and decided to take it over. But my suspicions were unfounded because it turns out the houses were built by the owners of local weaving mills. In the eighteenth and nineteenth centuries, all round the loch was a thriving weaving area.

Old postcards show a picturesque row of old thatched roof cotter homes as typical of the place. It's obvious, though, that the weaver bosses were very well off, and obviously weren't prepared to live in such lowly abodes. They got in London architects and up went the mansions. Still, they are beautiful homes and what a view they have! Their location meant it was nice and easy to travel back and forth to Glasgow and Edinburgh too.

Further up on the south side is Lochearnhead village, once another scant little row of thatched cottages where the inhabitants probably eked out a living from fishing. Now it's a lively haven for speedboats. All of the land from Stirling to this point belonged to the Drummond family, and even today the lochside and its lands is still under the control of the present owner Lady Jane Willoughby (granddaughter of Lord Drummond.) That is, of course, another story.

Every time we approached the T-junction where the road joins the Strathyre one, we always turned our heads in unison like lemmings to look across to the hillside where once stood the regal Lochearnhead Hotel, run by a grand host called Ewan Cameron. He was a kilted giant of a man, with more than a few tales to share.

Sadly he passed away a while back and the hotel burned to the ground, but we had many memories of him. One day, while we were visiting Lochearnhead to send a few letters to my mother's relatives before hawking the village houses, he sat down at our roadside fire for a crack. My mother knew Ewan fairly well, so his presence was always welcome. He was a lover of fine whisky, and although my father hardly touched the stuff he would take a wee glass with Ewan, with just enough whisky to leave a taste on the tongue. I was about fourteen at the time and big Ewan shared this story with me . . .

—

Although he was raised in a house, Peter was a travelling man right through to the bone. He'd no recollection when his parents gave up the gravel track in favour of carpet but he enjoyed his summers by taking to the road as his ancestors had done before him. At the first sign of lambs bleating, he was off. With little more than a few necessities strapped on his back, he traversed the country from Stirling to Callendar, the Trossachs, Balquhidder and over into Lochearnhead, and there he stayed until the first cold breezes of autumn sent him back home to Bruce's royal town to complete the circle.

While walking through the noted places he'd knock on doors, and for a meal, cut grass, trim hedges or do a bit of gardening. Not having a tent or any kind of portable abode he had a strange habit of begging for old rags which were usually handed over without question. Now if anyone gave us any tuggery (old clothes or cast-offs) it was bagged and away to the rag-merchant to be sold. Peter had a different use for the discarded clothing; his accumulated fragments were expertly sown together and became his colourful summer abode. This practice led to his nickname, Clooty, and for the duration of our tale that is what I shall call him.

Now, that might conjure up a strange picture in your head, a Tinker's tent of many colours. It made me think of rainbows, but in more practical terms it would be seen miles away by the police, who, knowing it belonged to a Tinker, would come to search it for stolen goods. However Clooty covered his rag tent with a roll of waterproof army camouflage, draping it over the patchwork to keep out the weather, and blended into the wild greenery of the moss and fern growing around the loch's mouth. Nowhere in Scotland could there be found a happier man, fishing in the loch, living the old ways and enjoying his peaceful existence than Clooty!

Ewan had no idea how long Clooty Peter had been coming to the place, because he was wrinkled and old when he met him for the first time. However time or date are irrelevant to this tale, so we'll not bother with them.

There had been heavy rain which fell relentlessly all day and into the night. Clooty was hungry; the wet weather had put paid to the fire and he was in need of a bellyfull of sustenance. Not until two in the morning did the rain decide to stop. Clooty wasted no time in crawling out of his bed and setting light to the fire. Soon the glow of its flame could be seen all across the water and halfway up Ben Vorlich. Warmth spread through him as a gulp of tea joined with a lump of bread and cheese and disappeared down his thrapple.

It was July, and in no time an army of hungry midges were nipping at the back of his neck. 'Bugger aff, ye bisoms,' he exclaimed, annoyed by the tiny warriors which would no doubt have sent him back into his tent if he'd not been able to light up his clay pipe. It took a while, though, to puff up enough smoke to see them off.

Eventually, as quiet returned to the night, and feeling satisfied and comfortable at last, he leaned back in a tattered armchair that an elderly lady who lived nearby had given him in payment for a summer of grass cutting. His eyelids grew heavier as a broad log crackled on a bed of burning ash when suddenly someone ran past. Startled, he rose swiftly and called out, 'Wha wid bother an' auld cratur at this time o' nicht?'

The figure stopped running and turned towards him. It was a woman, in drenched clothing. Her eyes bulged in pale grey sockets. He walked over and put an arm around her shivering shoulders. 'God help us lassie, yer drookit through. Where in heaven's name huv ye bin tae git as weet as this?'

He guided the silent woman over to his seat and saw immediately that she was heavily pregnant. 'Oh, poor wee thing, sit doon an' ah'll git a cover frae the tent.'

Covering her with a woollen blanket, he asked her if she was alone, and did she have kin?

'Did ye see Macgregor's men?' was all she would say. 'Speak quickly now, did they pass this way?' Her eyes darted into every area of darkness the flames failed to reveal.

Staring all around her like a frightened deer, she repeated the question several times until Clooty himself felt a dread run up his spine.

'Now, lassie, every year I come here and pitch the tent onto this boggy strip of ground, and the closest I get to crowds is at the Lochearnhead Games. Not many come by here until then. I ken auld Jeannie Macgregor, but she's crippled wi' bandy legs and couldnae walk the length o' herself. The only man she iver had was Tam, wha lies unner the grun in yon auld graveyard roon aside the broken church.'

He asked her again if she had any friends or family, well aware that soon this lassie would need a nurse or doctor, but all she answered was, 'Macgregor's men are coming!'

At that time of night, however, it was the darkness that proved the biggest stumbling block. He decided to keep her quiet until the welcome coming of dawn. Then he'd settle her in the tent and go fetch a woman to help with the birth. He himself had never had a woman or fathered a bairn. After a while her agitation grew less and she began to chant, gently rocking back and forth. With warmth from the fire, his full belly and her rhythmic chanting he gradually nodded off.

There was a hazel tree with spreading branches above his head, and when a tawny owl landed there and hooted loudly it brought his slumber to an abrupt end.

'Shut yer mooth, hoolit,' he cried, grabbing a stick and shaking it at the bird. Indignant at being disturbed the feathered creature of the night slowly lifted off into the dawn sky and drifted away to find a dark barn where it could wink away the day.

'Oh lassie, I'm richt vexed by yon hoolit, did he waken ye?' Clooty's words trailed off, as he realised his pregnant visitor had gone, where and to whom he had no idea.

He made his way down to the village, positive that news of a new baby would be heard there. He asked at every door, but no one knew anything of a baby. His companion of the night remained a complete mystery.

Autumn came fast that year, and before he left for Stirling he went to gather nuts around the south side of the loch. He'd walked and gathered quite a few pounds on the way, stopping to rest at Ardvorlich. Waves gently rolled onto the shore as he sat admiring the early reds and browns tipping the leaves on the tree-lined waterfront.

When he felt rested enough, he got up to go back the way he had come when he heard the sound of sobbing from the field behind him. When he looked he saw it was a young woman – and not just any young woman. Hardly able to believe his eyes he rubbed them both and stared again. She was heavily pregnant. It was the lassie who had shared his fireside over four months past! Surely this couldn't be. He called out, 'Lassie, are ye still with bairn?'

She looked at him with a tear-stained face and, without a single word, vanished – yes, completely disappeared!

Well, according to big Ewan, Clooty came into the hotel and was as white as snow. He left that year and never returned.

The mystery of the pregnant ghost became common knowledge, but it was not until a trio of Fortingall Tinker brothers, named Mackenzie, came over the following year for the games, that the mysterious lady's identity become known.

Perthshire's travelling pipers came from families of Macarthurs, Stewarts, Macgregors, Mackenzies, Reids, Townsleys, McDonalds, Williamsons, Johnstones and Macphees. Highland Gatherings would never be complete without one or more of these gifted musicians in attendance. The music was never written down and most of the pipers were illiterate, but many a star pupil, once taught by means of the *cantarach* (mouth music) never forgot it.

Well, as I said, onto the field marched the trio of Mackenzies playing a fine pibroch in perfect harmony. It was a glorious day, and when they had finished playing they shared a drink in the hospitality tent with big Ewan. After a few fistfuls of drams the crack swung like a dancer's kilt. Eventually Clooty and his apparition were mentioned.

'Och, yon will be the lady wha saw the head of her dear brother sat upon a plate,' commented Duncan, the oldest brother, who turned to John, his younger brother, and said, 'You ken that tale, Jock, tell it tae the hantle.' (The hantle is the word Perthshire Tinkers use for non-Travellers.)

At that point a thunderous downpour of rain descended, and half the field of runners, kilted lassie dancers and villagers headed for cover. The big marquee of the hospitality tent was near bursting at its seams with droves of people. So, according to big Ewan Cameron, as Jock Mackenzie lowered his eyes and laid down his airless pipes, the tale of Lady Ardvorlich was heard by a fine gathering of listeners.

'You all know that on the south side o' the water near Coillemhor sits a stone marking the last resting place of Jamie Stewart, he of Ardvorlich.

Well, a dark night it was when me and my mother were heading home after a busy day hawking our baskets among the crofters scattered thereabout, when we heard a mort [woman] sobbing. As we turned the bend in the narrow road we saw her; a heavy pregnant lassie lying on the very spot. Mammy made over and bade the lass sit up, and as she did so draped a shawl around her. "Now, bairn," said Mammy, "what are ye daeing without a body to assist you in this time of dire need?"

My mother meant that the lassie shouldn't have been on her own, her reaching full time with child, that is. I would now like to add that the staring eyes and terror on that creature's face was turning the warm dinner we had not long before shared with an elderly lady into frost in my belly. "Come on, Mammy," I pleaded, "let's leave this mort and move on from here. I feel that something is not of this world."

"Och, son, this poor deserted lassie needs a hand, not you and your rubbish talk of unearthly things."'

Jock then turned to the listeners, and as the rain pelted on the canvas of the marquee, he said, 'I was always seeing things that no other person did, even as a wee laddie. I even remember hearing voices in the wind. According to the auld yins, I had the sixth sense. My great granny from Ireland called it *Nawchen Shanna*, which is Irish cant for "Travellers' spirit". Well, I'll tell you no lie, it was strong that night. Several times I tried to convince Mammy to leave the pregnant mort, but she refused.

Just as we were getting the mort quietened down, she jumped to her feet, stared into my face and said, "The Macgregors cut aff my brother Drummond Earnoch's head and put it on a plate. Now they are coming for me and my baby. Tell them you have not seen me!" With that said, she tore off up the side o' Ben Vorlich and disappeared. My poor auld mother's legs were so weak I near had to carry her home.

It was next day when the sun shone bright in the westerly sky, crofter Sandy Graham told me that the Stewarts were always fighting with the MacDonalds and their cousins the Macgregors. One day a group of Macgregors were caught feasting on Stewart pheasants which had been poached from land around Ardvorlich. Drummond Earnoch, a bright young bullyboy, had been appointed factor to the lands of Stewart and had made a vow he'd get rid of the enemy once and for all. So he had the Macgregors on that occasion tied to a tree and their ears cut off. Revenge was sweet when, several months later, the earless lads captured Drummond Earnoch and decapitated him. They marched proudly down to Ardvorlich House, home of his pregnant sister, who was the laird's wife, and asked for sustenance. As was the way of Highlanders in those days, she dutifully went off to fetch bread and cheese for them. She bade them sit while she went into the kitchen to prepare some meat. When she came back her brother's head was dripping on a plate with the bread and cheese stuffed in his mouth. The lassie, who was almost near her time, ran off screaming and hid in some broom on the hillside. When her husband came home, it took four days before they eventually found her. Her son James was born that night and it is said she had a vision of the Macgregors coming for him too.

From then on the feud between the Macgregors and their cousins the Macdonalds against the Stewarts intensified, and when James died in 1660 his body was buried in a secret place. Some say it was at Dundurn near St Fillan's, others say it was further down the lochside, but most believe it lies at Coillemhor, the very spot where Clooty, Jock and Mrs Mackenzie, aye, and no doubt many a fellow swaying home from Ewan's hotel bar, may have seen the ghost of Stewart of Ardvorlich's pregnant wife.'

Jock was in such a fine storytelling mood that day and by the time he'd finished his tale, had many a drop o' the cratur. Just as well his brothers Duncan and Donald had broad shoulders, as he had to be carted off to Fortingall on them.

A witness later told Ewan that the trio ended up arguing violently about the tale of the ghost of Ardvorlich. According to the other

brothers it wasn't the Macgregors (children of the mist) who cut off
the Stewart's head, but the MacDonalds.

The clans of auld Scotia were a right lot of warmongers, that's
all I can add to the matter.

I knew these lads, and heard many a tale of Jock's telling where the
hair rose on the nape of my neck. I wonder what became of Clooty?

Before we move on, I remember hearing that the Glencoe Mac-
Donalds who were slaughtered by the Campbells were considered
by certain people to be thieving Tinkers. I searched far and wide
for evidence of this, sifting through books galore, then came across
this wee bit of Scottish history in Chambers' *Domestic Annals of
Scotland*. In the entry for 13 February, 1692, it describes how
King William was growing impatient at the rebelliousness of the
Jacobite clans, chiefly the MacDonalds of Glengarry, Keppoch,
and Glencoe, the Grants of Glenmoriston and the Camerons of
Lochiel. Their unrest meant that troops had to be kept in Scotland,
which he needed for his army in Flanders. His Scottish ministers,
and particularly Sir John Dalrymple, Master of Stair, Secretary of
State, nursed a hatred of those clans, feeling that they were a threat
to the new order of things.

In August 1691, the King issued a proclamation of indemnity,
promising pardon to those that had been in arms against him before
the first of June that year, provided that they came into the main
towns by 1 January 1692 to sign the oath of allegiance. Dalrymple
grudged the generosity of these terms to the Jacobites, and secretly
hoped that they would refuse so he could adopt harsher measures
against them. It suited him that the time of grace expired in the
depth of winter, for as he wrote in a letter to Colonel Hamilton,
'that will be the right season to maul them, in the cold long nights'.
In another letter to Sir Thomas Livingstone, commander-in-chief of
the Scottish forces, he says, 'Just now my Lord Argyll tells me that
Glencoe hath not taken the oaths; at which I rejoice – it's a great
work of charity to be exact in rooting out that damnable sect, the
worst in all the Highlands.'

Certain orders signed by the King followed on the sixteenth,
permitting terms to be offered to Glengarry, whose house was
strong enough to give trouble, but adding, 'If McIan of Glencoe

and that tribe can be well separated from the rest, it will be a proper vindication of the public justice to extirpate that sect of thieves.' On the same day Dalrymple wrote to Colonel Hill, Governor of Inverlochy: 'I shall entreat you that, for a just vengeance and public example, the thieving tribe of Glencoe are rooted out. The Earls of Argyll and Breadalbane have promised they shall have no retreat in their bounds.' He felt however it must be 'quietly' done, otherwise they would shift both their cattle and themselves into the mists. There can be no doubt what he meant – to harry them, while leaving them alive, would make them worse thieves than before. 'They must,' he says, 'be rooted out and cut off.'

Meantime the old Chief of Glencoe had set off, under a snow-filled sky, with honest heart, to sign the oath at Inverlochy, Fort William, but it was the wrong place. When he arrived, frozen and exhausted, he was instructed to go to Inveraray. The tired old man toiled his way through the wild winter gales to Inveraray, where he found that the sheriff who had to witness his signature, was to be away for two days. It was not until 6 January that he was able to take his oath. But when the register of oaths was sent to the Privy Council in Edinburgh, the name of MacDonald of Glencoe was conveniently missing from it.

On 12 February, the Massacre of Glencoe saw 38 members of his clan slaughtered. There are those to this day who state that at the spot, after a snowstorm, small pools of blood appear upon the ground.

Was this sect of thieves and undesirables that the Crown wanted rid of indeed a group of Tinkers?

14
EAST OF LOCHEARNHEAD

East of Lochearnhead are many places where at one time you'd see the signs of campsites. These were mainly occupied by Tinker folk from the Stirling area. This is Rob Roy Macgregor land, and because of his portrayal as an outlaw by Sir Walter Scott's pen, was adopted as the hero of the Tinkers from that area. His mother being a Campbell clinched their belief that perhaps he was more of a wanderer than the clan folks let on.

Yet Campbell is a well-known name across the land. Walter Campbell from Argyllshire was the great-great-grandfather of Robert Burns, who changed his name to Burnhouse. His son took the name Burnett, which was changed in turn by his son to Burness. The father of the bard when he moved to Ayrshire would change the spelling to Burns. I find this a wee bit strange. Why should the family lineage go from Campbell to Burns in three generations without a scholar giving a reason for it? There is a lot of mystery about our Scottish bard and to be honest I like it that way.

I'll briefly list some greens used by Tinkers in Macgregor country and the Trossachs. There's Callander, Brig' o' Turk, Glenfinlas and Balquhidder with its famous burial ground of Rob Roy and his family. They share the site with ancient slabs of no known date, including Clach Aonghais (the stone of St Angus) whose figure is sculpted into the slab. Angus was a disciple of Columba, one of the earliest Christian missionaries to the area. Another green is found at Balvaig Stream, where a teenage Tinker girl drowned her newborn infant rather than let her father kill it on account of its bastardry, before she herself committed suicide in the nearby Loch Voil. I mustn't forget the Invertrossachs road with its 'little spoon' campsites, so called because this country of small fields and wooded inlets was where the Horners lived. These Tinkers were regular visitors to local farms, where they were allowed to gather rams' horns. All manner of spoons, handles for walking sticks and umbrellas and a variety of useful implements were produced by the Horner Tinkers. I'm told there is no clear information about the date when they arrived in the area, but a visit by Queen Victoria to inspect a newly built Glasgow waterworks at Loch Venachar put an end to their annual visits. Ahead of her visit the campsites were closed down and were no more to be seen in the area.

Near the Horners' camping ground is a wee mountain named Ben Ledi (Mount of God). At 2875 feet it is a medium to difficult climb, and I'm told that the Horners always climbed it when they arrived at their usual sites and planted a flower on the summit. In the year when their camps had been cleared and they never appeared the locals noticed that a mist descended on the top of Ben Ledi and didn't shift the whole summer. A clear path winds its way up the mountain, and sometimes if you're very quiet you'll hear a lassie singing at the cairn at the top. Now this is creepy, because although many walkers have heard her, no one has seen her. According to tradition, the ancient Beltane mysteries were celebrated on the summit. Worth a visit!

15

STORIES FROM KILLIN

Many trips in our bus took us up Glen Ogle (the 'glen of terrors'). This is a hazardous brute of a road with the jerky gear stick dropping to its lowest point of the gearbox. It caused my mother to grab her sewing bag and rapidly crochet anything that came to hand, as long as it kept her eyes from straying onto the bends and climbs that certainly put our grumpy old Bedford through his paces.

Every time we took this route my father would point across at the viaduct spanning the sheer drop over which the northern train trundled and say, 'Your Uncle Purney was on the building of that engineering masterpiece.'

Uncle Purney, or, to give him his Sunday name, Bernard, was my paternal grandfather's younger brother, and he was married to my mother's sister, Margaret. This made him not just my father's uncle but his brother-in-law as well! Does that not tell you, reader, that we Travellers are as linked by blood to others of our own kind as the Queen herself to other royals?

Lots of my Tinker relatives gave up their wandering lives to stay and raise their family among the settled population. Uncle Purney seemed to gel with Aberfeldy and it was there he put down roots. He and Auntie Maggie were the most gentle of folk, and lived quietly in the bonny town where, incidentally, I was born. They are buried over at Logerait Cemetery, as are many Perthshire Travellers.

When my father had successfully reached the top of the road my mother always bundled up her coloured mass of crocheted squares and insisted that the kettle should be put on the boil. Our first stop was usually a lay-by near where a little loch hides the biggest trout imaginable. While we'd set up our fire, my father would wander off to his favourite inlet. Here he would break off a hazel branch, roll out a length of cat gut and attach to it a bent safety pin. After lifting a few large boulders he would find the fattest worm and soon have it attached to the pin and dangling juicily above an unsuspecting trout. Our trout was always eaten with gratitude and went down well. I remember one year a farmer gave us a big box of tatties and neeps to have with it, along with fresh butter and milk. This was for allowing him the use of Tiny to eradicate some rats which had laid claim to his barn. To us our family pet was an adorable cuddly little dog, but to farmyard vermin he was a murderous wolf.

As you leave Glen Ogle, you pass a place called Lix Toll, before the road forks to Glen Dochart and Killin. My father told us the name meant it was 59 miles from Glasgow. Lix is the Roman numeral for 59, so some folk reckoned that must be the distance to the biggest city in the west. He didn't know for certain because he'd heard the name had several meanings. The explanation for the second part of the name was that here cattle drovers heading south had to pay a toll before being allowed to take their animals further on; it was like bridge and road tolls of today, I suppose. My mother suggested that it was called Lix because the cattle might have been friendly and licked the hand of the tollkeeper. Father's response was, 'Keep the day job, Jeannie.' The truth turns out to be that Lix is a very old Gaelic word describing the lay of the land, as in middle lic, lower lic, upper lic, or wester and easter lic.

The road meandering to the right leads to Killin, a happy stopping green for Tinkers of bygone days. The River Dochart, famous the world over for its waters cascading over rocky outcrops and tourists come for miles to enjoy her spectacular falls. A broad road bridge spans the tumbling waters, and from its narrow pavement the Dochart Falls are photographed by cameras from every corner of the world.

Tinker folk from Perthshire were always tuned into the myths and legends of the area. Across the road from the war memorial in Killin there's an opening which takes one on a lovely walk. It leads onto several criss-crossing paths in dense controlled forestry. If you fancy a walk then get a map from the tourist office, because the forest is like a natural maze and it is easy to lose yourself among the pine smells, the sound of foxes barking, and, depending on the season, the chorus of cuckoos and cooing pigeons. I have met walkers in the woods who have been reduced to sweating wrecks. They had left their cars at the top of Glen Ogle and now would ask plaintively how they came to be facing Killin. 'It's not a problem to locals,' I told them, 'get the map!'

Like the local folk, Tinkers knew the place like the back of their hands. Because it was my natural childhood playground I too remember lots of wee greens, though not the royal palace of the Breadalbane fairies (*sithichean*), which can never, ever be found because it lies far beneath the waters of Loch Tay. No way, I hear you say, how can a green be underwater?

'Because the fairies can do what they want; it's all to do with magic.'

Back in the old days, Killin folk believed that fairies, witches and warlocks really did exist, and would be offended if anyone said that was not the case.

———

Here's a bit of folklore from the area.

Nature's moods can be wild at times, with dark brooding skies and stormy waters. It was on such a night that Maradun, a dairy maid who herded her cows on the hillocks near the fountain which rises in the Corrie of Carie near the south-west side of Ben Lawers, heard a loud rumble beneath the earth. All the fairy folk had heard it too, and called to the dairy maid to move her animals to higher ground. When she asked what was wrong, they told her it was her fault, because the previous night, after she'd watered the animals, she had forgotten to lock the door which held back the waters of the fountain. The silly young lass had been singing and dancing fantastically with the forest goblins, and although she knew she was always to lock the fountain door, had neglected her duties. Out of the hillside poured the water, fast and furious. It poured and poured without ending, until Fionn, the Celtic warrior giant, and his hounds damned up the waterway and locked the door. It took many months before this was done, and when the task was completed the glen below was filled with water. All the fairies cried and called from the mountain tops that Maradun had let the water out and made a 'Loch Tatha', which is Gaelic for 'it is a loch'. That's where the name Loch Tay originated from. Beneath the loch lived the fairies in their original home which once was in the glen. So to get a bit of fresh air they can sometimes be seen in the forest sitting in a circle, enjoying a bit of fire and crack with the imps and goblins. This gathering nearly always ends in a punch-up for obvious reasons. Granny Power told us if we were to get married and have a girl, we shouldn't call her Maradun. If any of us decide to ignore that advice, then we should stay clear of Loch Tay!

16
FINN AND ST FILLAN

I once purchased an old book in an Oxfam shop called *In Famed Breadalbane*, by William A. Gillies. I love this book, and though I don't speak a word of Gaelic I'd happily sit for hours turning over its pages and slowly pronouncing the music of the Erse tongue in my head.

Here's another couple of snippets about the famous Fionn from this lovely book, and a wee drop of Gaelic.

Fionn used to stand with one foot on Cioch Na Maighdean and the other on Cist Buille a Chlaidheimh, two hills a mile apart, above Ardtalnaig. In this position he was able to stoop towards Glenlednock, wash his hands in Lochan nan Lamh,* stand up, turn around and quench his thirst in Loch Tay.

Now another wee gem which tells of Fionn's demise:

In the midst of Loch Dochart there is an isle called Eilean Iubhar where Taileachd, a friend of Fionn lived, who had a fairy lover. Fionn got to know her and soon found that he enjoyed her company. The more they met they closer they became.

When Taileachd realised his friend's visits had more to do with his beloved than himself he decided to question them both. Jealousy can be an evil thing. Both men decided that it should be the lady who chose between them, but when asked, she found this too difficult a decision because she loved them both.

'I want you to stop this anger. I have a task for you. The man who wins the victory in a "leap" shall win my affection with pleasure.'

The two giants then went outside and leapt. Taileachd leapt from the island onto the shore and Fionn leaped after him. Then

Lochan nan Lamh, the little loch of the hands.

Taileachd said, 'I would leap the channels backwards, and if you cannot do the same then I have the hand of the lady.' They both leapt backwards, but Taileachd leapt first, and landed on dry land. But when Fionn leapt he sank down so far that only his head was above water. Taileachd saw his chance to get rid of his opponent, and before Fionn could wriggle free, Taileachd cut off his head.

Now Fionn was leader of the dreaded Fiann warriors, and no doubt they'd be after Taileachd when the news reached them. He knew this, so taking the head he fled the spot. At the top of Loch Laidon his steps grew heavy with the weight of the head, and there he decided to put it on a pole on a black knoll, at a ford of the river, which thereafter bore the name of Ath Chinn.★

Now, when the warriors found the headless body of their ruler they raised him up and buried him behind the knoll, in a grave which has ever since been called Cill Fhinn★ (Killin).

But justice had not been done, so the Fiann warriors set off to find Taileachd and their master's head. Thoroughly they scoured the land, and at last found the head upon the pole where Taileachd left it. One put his finger under Fionn's tooth of knowledge (the wisdom tooth) and it was revealed that Taileachd was hiding in a cave on Ben Alder. He was soon found. 'Do you repent of slaying the great Fionn?' he was asked. He replied, 'No!'

The Fiann cut off his right hand and then his left. Again he was asked, 'Do you repent of such evil?'

Taileachd would not change his mind and stayed true to his crime. His heart was pierced many times, and there on the spot he died.

That was a small introduction, my friends, to the old tales of the Gael and the ancient tongue – I hope you enjoyed it.

From this area, here's another tale that I was raised on.

Before Christianity had come to Scotland, when the ancient Celts ruled the land, news of a strange man, dressed in a long grey garment of sackcloth, circulated through the country. He was very tall and went from place to place talking to anyone who would listen of a powerful invisible god. Now, this was a dangerous thing to do in an age when people were convinced of the existence of many gods, each more powerful than the next. The priests of these gods

★*Ath Chinn*, the ford of the head, *Cill Fhinn*, the cell of Fionn.

usually reigned like kings in places of worship, being idolised by an ignorant people, mainly poor and easily led.

One day the tall stranger was walking towards Killin when a woman approached him from the forest, screaming that her baby had been taken by the water. She rushed by him and ran off towards a place of worship where she desperately hoped the priests would help her get the child back. The tall man followed her. She ran down and under the bridge, along the river embankment and fell at the mouth of a cave set among rocks, where hazel trees spead their boughs thickly across the entrance. 'Help me,' she cried, stooping down before going into the cave. 'Oh, please help me find my beloved son!'

Her follower stood outside, hiding among the trees and listening. 'Woman, what is this you say of a son lost to the water?' one of the priests asked. 'If the child was plucked from the bank and swallowed, then the river god Rollo has desired a sacrifice. Do not quarrel with the water, it shall not give your baby back.'

Another man said, 'Be happy, woman, not everybody is chosen. You will drink of your child's spirit. Here, take this cup and lower it into the river. Bring it back and we shall bring forth your child's voice of peace. The great Rollo will be pleased.'

The broken-hearted mother came out of the cave, knelt down at the riverside and gathered a cupful of water.

The tall man touched her shoulder and said, 'Do you believe that the river god Rollo has your child?'

Her eyes swollen and red with crying, she answered his question, yes indeed she did.

'Will you believe that my God is far more powerful than any of yours,' he told her, 'will you let me bring back your little one?' She went pale and began to shiver, so much so the cup fell from her shaking hand.

He picked up the cup and refilled it. 'Come with me,' he said. She followed him into the cave, where three hooded men with long white beards sat in a row. He told the mother to sit at the cave mouth and say nothing.

'I am thirsty for a drink of water,' he said, 'but in this river there is a captured kidnapped baby, therefore I cannot drink this.' The priests looked at each other as he poured the water from the cup into the dim embers of a fire and said nothing.

He sat down and pulled out a knife, then cut a small piece of cloth from the hem of his garment, which he laid on the ground.

'Woman, if you want to see your child once more, to hold him and feed him from your warm milk, take this knife and cut off my finger.' He laid his index finger upon the cloth.

'Sir, I shall die without my babe, I know in my heart. You have no part in his loss, you are no enemy of mine, so how can I violate you in such a way?'

He raised his voice as the three men stayed silent. 'If you love your child, then do as I say and cut off my finger!'

She took hold of the knife, closed her eyes and hacked the index finger from the man's hand. Quickly he rolled it up in the cloth and handed it to her.

For a moment she could say nothing, then to her absolute astonishment and that of the three priests, a little hand punched the air. The severed finger disappeared, and there in its place lay the tiny infant, very much alive.

In no time the mother was rushing off to tell everyone that the tall man dressed in simple sackcloth had the powers of all the gods on earth.

The man was St Fillan, and from that day people gathered within his tiny house in Glen Dochart to listen like innocent babies to tales of the great Jesus and how he was brought back to life. The saint told them he was no powerful lord with great wealth, but he promised more than gold or finery; he spoke in simple words about a great and wonderful spirit who was always there.

It was believed that St Fillan gathered twelve men to spread the word of the Gospel. He named them Stewards, that is, keepers of the holy word. It is thought that these important figures were the forebears of a great Scottish name – Stewart. Incidentally, in the Tinker world there are more Stewarts than people of any other name.

As far as the Tinker folk were concerned, Jesus was the first Traveller. Born in a lowly stable, he never had a proper home and even from birth was being moved on. Some things never change. Loch Tayside today has several state-of-the-art caravan sites but they don't allow travellers on, sad to say.

Historians have recorded that a relic of immense holiness was set at the foot of Robert the Bruce on the eve of the battle of Bannockburn: St Fillan's forearm in a glass casket.

17

DERMOT O'RILEY

My cousin Charlie lived in Killin, a lovely gentleman. His lovely couthy wife, who made every visitor feel like royalty, could conjure up a feast or spread a table and fill it with home bakes at the drop of a hat.

It was during a visit to Charlie's that I found out a few home truths about the Rileys of old, my forebears.

The auld country, Erin's green isle, is a place of mystical glens, deep lochs and stories from the mists of time. From her blood came most of our people. It is the O'Riley line Charlie refers to in sharing this supposedly true story.

It seems that in the eighteenth century the O'Rileys lived some place between Kilkenny and Waterford, and here many of the family worked with horse and hound. The men were of tall and muscular stature while the women were small, jet-black-haired specimens.

What made them stand out from other Pavee (Traveller folk) were their beautiful singing voices and natural love of music and verse. This inherited gift for songwriting and music gained them respect, and many were the invitations that came requesting their presence at upper-crust weddings and balls. Their work for the gentry looking after their horses and hounds meant that they enjoyed a higher standing of living than most of their impoverished neighbours. Pulled by healthy shires, their wagons would set off to travel peacefully through Ireland's leafy lanes. The pleasant O'Rileys were a welcome sight to people dwelling in their small crofts along the way. At night, when fires were lit and bellies filled, local folk would wander onto the green to listen to their music and songs, which once heard were spoken of for years to come. Yes, the O'Riley tribe were thought to be as a grand a bunch as ever wandered in the countryside of Erin's green isle.

All, however, was not as it seemed to be. In this idyllic setting a seed of devilish corruption was growing into manhood. Dermot O'Riley had the heart of an adder, and he would have been driven out of the family by his father had it not been for his mother's intervention. His slithering, spiteful ways would have been tolerated to a degree had his wayward eye not begun to burn with desire for colleens; as many as he could entice into his clutches and force his will upon. His parents, at their wits' end, had paid a fortune to hush up a number of scandals, but it all became too much at last. The 18-year-old Dermot took the wife of a captain in the army and after spending a roaring night with the woman left her tied to a tree, injured and terribly distressed. Fearing her husband would have bloodhounds on his tail he fled the tribe of O'Rileys, but not before he had relieved every man and woman of their entire fortunes. This could not be forgiven. An old woman spat into the bones, scattered them and, to the sound of his poor mother's wails, cursed Dermot O'Riley to hell.

As he scoured his wicked way through Ireland, many were the songs written of his criminal exploits. Travelling only by twilight, taking what was not his, he soon gathered a following of vagabonds and outlaws. By the time he'd reached twenty years of age, a beleaguered Ireland breathed a sigh of relief as Dermot O'Riley and his band of disciples set sail to find another place to plunder. It was England's turn. The English law officers were soon to find that keeping track of the wily O'Riley was no easy task. Within a year he'd stolen horses, burgled houses, stolen from churches and brothels, villages and towns. After several very close calls when the authorities had nearly captured him, he and his rogues raged over the border and headed north.

After many misdeeds, he and his men happened to be running away from a band of dragoons who were enlisting recruits with more force than persuasion for some far or near battle (Scotland was always battling someone or other in the eighteenth century). Dermot found himself at the northern point of Loch Tay, where, in its secluded glen, was Killin. In summer its inhabitants climbed the hills to stay for a while in their sheilings and raise their cattle. In winter they returned to the firesides of their thatch-roofed crofts, and never bothered a soul, just got on with the business of living. It was deep in the winter when Dermot came upon this haven of tranquillity and immediately thought, 'what better place for me to set up as lord and master?'

Like a hurricane, dagger in hand, he tore through the village, shouting and swearing at the top of his voice, his cohorts following at his heel. Never having heard anything louder in the place than the roar of a rutting stag, the terrified residents scurried to the nearest hidey-hole in fear of their lives.

A grand granite building sat upon a heathery knowe, home to Mr Stewart, the local minister. He was a shambling wimp of a man, fonder of his whisky bottle than saving souls. In two minutes Dermot had thrown Stewart out on to the street and moved into the glebe house himself.

It is now that a tale of love begins.

Dermot gave orders to Gavin, his right-hand man. 'Go and get me a broad-horn, slaughter it and we'll have ourselves a feast!'

To his other henchmen he rapped, 'Find the holy man's whisky store and fill the table with his bottles!' Draping a velvet cover which he found on a brocaded armchair across his shoulders, he laughed loudly. 'This place is a goldmine, we'll stay as long as our luck runs smoothly, boys,' and with that he tossed his curly mane of hair and slapped his thigh.

His men, without respect for furniture or furnishings, soft or otherwise, began to trash the house. But at that moment a fiery lassie was striding to meet them without fear or hesitation. The minister's housekeeper, Kirsten MacPhee, who'd been toiling over the week's laundry with damp sleeves rolled up over her elbows, had heard the shouting and commotion. Her hackles were immediately up – and she was in no mood to banter with Irish outlaws or their leader either.

No one saw her until she kicked open the kitchen door and strode boldly towards Dermot, brandishing a heavy axe. Before he could defend himself she had hacked at him, and without doubt would have severed his arm if he hadn't thrown himself to the floor and grappled with her legs. She went over backwards and dropped the axe, and as she tried to retrieve it he seized her in a vice-like grip.

'Well now,' said he, getting back to his feet, 'what manner of creature is this who was going to sever my lifeline from the earth?'

Kirsten spat into his face and hissed, 'and what kind of snake throws an old man from his home, a God fearing minister of the cloth at that?'

Dermot was taken aback by the defiance of the lassie; never before had he seen fire like that in a wench, nor, come to think of it, such beauty – green eyes flashing with anger, red rosy cheeks inflamed with passion, and those breasts . . . my, oh my, what a woman! His heart beat like a drum as their eyes met, his burning with an instant flame of desire, hers returning pointblank hatred! He let her go, and in a flash she tossed her auburn hair, repeated her question, and without waiting for an answer, started to pick the scattered cushions from the floor and setting the small chairs and tables on their feet again.

Dermot smiled, lowered his eyelids (this usually melted the hardest female heart) and reached for her hand. Under his fingers he felt a clenched fist and thought, 'Here's a fiery bitch and no mistake. It will take the best o' me charms to melt this Scottish ice-maiden.'

'You take your filthy hands off me and move away from me or I'll have the skin off yer hand!'

Dermot was disconcerted: women never showed him anything other than weakness or subservience. Had he met his match or lost his touch at last?

'Woman, Dermot O'Riley at your service! The holy man is worth nothing to me, but you, now – you, on the other hand, present a better reason for meself to linger awhile in this carpeted house. How soft are the beds?'

If a woman had ever resisted the wild rover before, their efforts paled in comparison to Kirsten's next move. Breathing deeply, she stepped towards Dermot and kissed him full on the lips, drew back and waited. For the first time in his entire life the strength drained away from his legs which almost buckled under the wave of emotion surging through his body. It wasn't her passionate kiss that laid him down on the carpeted floor, however, it was the sudden uppercut she planted square on his chin!

It was hard to imagine what possessed her to take the feet from Dermot O'Riley; surely she knew his companions wouldn't stand by without giving her more of the same treatment. Kirsten squared her shoulders and held herself ready for the onslaught. Her feistiness was, however, no match for the group of hardy rogues who grabbed her like a rag doll, hurling her down onto the floor. In a flash Dermot was gathering her into his arms and apologising repeatedly, 'Colleen, are ye hurt? God in heaven, speak to me!' Abruptly he turned to his companions and said, 'Any man who touches this wench again will have me to answer to, clear?' It was a fool who'd not pay heed to the fire in his flashing eyes.

Gavin turned to the men next to him and said, 'When the wimmin is in, the wit is oot.' His companions nodded and they left Dermot and Kirsten alone in the room.

'Your actions in this place are enough to hang every one of you. If I were you I'd fill me belly and take myself off over the Ptarmigan Mountain out there.' Kirsten pointed to the high hills visible from the large window from which Dermot's men had unceremoniously ripped down the faded purple drapes. She picked up the curtains that were scattered on the floor and began to fold them up. The assault on her at the hands of his cruel followers had left her with a cut above her eye and a torn dress. He, without a word, kissed the nape of her neck where it was exposed by a tear. For reasons she didn't understand she found herself responding to his touch and smiling softly. Then, remembering how violent and insolent his intrusion had been she stepped back. Outside she heard shouts and mocking laughter; his gang was bullying and frightening the inhabitants of sleepy Killin, and this should have added to her abhorrence of the man. She found it hard to keep up her anger, however, and felt her resistance beginning to melt. The truth was that she'd been kept cooped up in the manse for years and seldom had the attention of any man, let alone this handsome braggart. So telling herself that a heart is blind she gave in, and guided him upstairs and into the minister's bed.

From that day on she turned a blind eye to the inexcusable treatment of her neighbours, going out only to buy food. Dermot ordered his men to take up residence in the small hamlet regarding as his the whole of the surrounding area. He even went as far as to change the name of Killin to Ballycoist, which is Irish for 'crossing of the roads'.

However, after six months of cruel treatment, the villagers decided enough was enough. One night, under cover of darkness, they met in secret up the river in the MacNab graveyard beneath the Dochart Bridge, and planned a once and for all overthrow of those Irish intruders. A fleet-footed youngster was given food, spare shoes and clothing to go to Perth and alert the army. It was summer time, and the long hours of daylight would speed his way.

He was gone for four weeks, and many thought the lad had fallen foul of a robber or come to some other nasty end. Then suddenly a man came rushing into the village to report that a troop of soldiers was heading towards them.

Dermot and his men made their escape into the Lawers hills and over the Ptarmigan, but Kirsten, being with child, was unable to go with them. Their time in Ballycoist had made the men soft and weakened their resolve, however, and the troops, ironically Irish Dragoons, found it a relatively easy task to round up the gang, including Dermot

At the far end of Killin, gallows were erected and, much to the joy and relief of the residents, Dermot O'Riley and his hell-raisers were hung until dead. Only one of them, Gavin, escaped. He cheated the scythe of death because the rope being used to hang him was tied without a proper knot. According to the law he was therefore free to leave, and that he did, never to return. It is believed that Gavin was the one who was later to spread tales of the exploits of Dermot throughout the land.

Kirsten was branded on the cheek as a collaborator and sent packing. Some say she had a boy who was brought up with stories of his wayward father, told to him by his sad and lonely mother.

It would take a famine and another hundred years before the O'Rileys set foot in Scotland again and more years would pass before they would gain respect for their hard and honest work in the Atholl forests as woodcutters. These O'Rileys are, of course, my family, and proud I am of them regardless. I also am proud to say that many of my folk are beautiful singers.

When Charlie shared this story with me he finished it by saying, 'Do you know that here in Killin there's a road named Ballycoist? He also pointed out that at one time there was a minister named Stewart in Killin. It seems he had to leave the area after steeping himself in alcohol and so paying no attention to his parishioners, who were at the time being harassed by a fierce group of army deserters and turned to him for help. I wonder if there is any connection between this incident and Charlie's tale?

18

From Kenmore to the Appalachians

So, my friends, let us meander further along the side of Loch Tay (and what a beautiful view) to where the village of Kenmore opens up another chapter for us in the tale of bygone days.

Many Tinker folk remembered Kenmore by its old name of Inchadney, but to the Gaels it is An Ceannmhor (the big-headed place). There have been times when the loch engulfed Kenmore in furious floods after severe winter snows, and kept voyagers from travelling on their weary way to Aberfeldy. The village is famous for the mighty Taymouth Castle, once home to many royals and some not so royal. Needless to say the history of Taymouth Castle is as turbulent as the waves of Loch Tay during a thunderstorm. It has housed warring religious fanatics, and in its catacomb-like cellars housemaids have given birth to many an aristocratic heir, who seldom saw its father or even a ray of sunshine at birth, being disposed of by a fatal blow after delivery.

For centuries Taymouth was synonymous with Campbell – that name again. Cousins of queens and kings, countesses, marchionesses and dukes, from east to west the Campbells ruled supreme.

In Kenmore another famous building is the Kenmore Hotel. I'm informed by a Gaelic friend that this old inn, which predates 1570, is called by Celts Tigh Mor a' Cheannmhoir (The Big House of Kenmore). Robert Burns in his travels through Perthshire frequented it. Near the chimney piece, the bard wrote one of his famous poems.

Admiring nature in her widest grace,
These northern scenes with weary feet I trace

O'er many a winding dale and painful steep,
Th' abodes of covey'd grouse and timid sheep.
My savage journey, curious, I pursue,
Till famed Breadalbane opens to my view.
The meeting cliffs each deep-sunk glen divides,
The woods, wild scattered, clothe their ample sides;
Th' outstretching lake, embosomed 'mong the hills,
The eye with wonder and amazement fills;
The Tay meandering sweet in infant pride,
The palace rising on his verdant side,
The lawns wood-fringed in nature's native taste,
The hillocks dropt in nature's careless haste,
The arches striding ore the newborn stream,
The village glittering in the noon-side beam-
Poetic ardours in my bosom swell,
Lone wandering by the hermit's mossy cell;
The sweeping theatre of hanging woods,
Th' incessant roar of headlong tumbling floods.
Here Poesy might wake her heav'n taught lyre,
And look through nature with creative fire;
Here, to the wrongs of Fate half-reconciled,
Misfortune's lightened steps might wander wild;
And disappointment, in these lonely bounds,
Find balm to soothe her bitter rankling wounds;
Here heart-struck Grief might heavenward stretch her scan,
And injured Worth forget and pardon man.

In mid-May one year, when we were staying near Kenmore, we had a trifling run-in with a local policeman who warned us not to light a fire in the area. We appealed to him to allow us a controlled fire because the bus stove had a hole in it. He agreed he didn't see the harm in it, so long as we used a bundle of firewood bought from the local store. Although the bus boot was stapped full with kindling, we did purchase a few bundles as we had said we would. On top of the fire we used a small oil drum, cut off at the top for cooking, and as this kept the flames from flaring up, it helped the policemen to turn a blind eye.

The great thing about travelling the country is that one meets many people who love to investigate the history of their area. The first bit of history I got when I went into Kenmore was when I eaves-dropped on the conversation a large chap was having as he lorded it over a busload of tourists by the Kenmore Hotel. He was puffing on a Sherlock Holmes pipe; spirals of blue-grey reek belched from it. I was searching for our wee dog Tiny, who had wandered away from our camp, at the time, but was attracted by the depth of this man's voice; he sounded like a Shakespearian actor, wide gestures echoing the rhythm of his monologue. He pointed to the castle and said, 'That was Balloch Castle long before it took the name of Taymouth, and then it was the Highland home of Clan Gregor.' He turned and pointed to the neighbouring hillside and continued, 'And that's the boundary line of Stewart and Menzies country. Bad deeds were done in a house that once stood where the hotel in which we are all about to partake of some delicious Scottish fare now stands, it was a place of blood and lies.'

Before I heard another word my mother called to tell me that they had found Tiny by the lochside. There was a man and woman petting him when I arrived. The chance meeting resulted in a far more interesting tale than the one force-fed to the visitors at Kenmore Hotel. Falkirk couple Harry and Elspeth Mackenzie had spent a few nights in a strange bubble-shaped caravan parked next to our bus. It wasn't unusual to meet friendly non-travellers when we were camped, and Harry and Elspeth got on well with us. Later that day we were listening to Harry Menzies share a grand story, which I am assured by his dear wife was without doubt-true.

We were sitting in their company by our oil drum fire. Rows of apple trees with their heavily scented blossom had generously coloured the waterside pink and white, with the fallen petals lying inches thick. Wild bluebells gathered at tree roots pushed aside the fading green and yellow of clumps of daffodils as if to say, move over, it's our time. Heaven itself could not surpass that moment, or inspire the feelings that stirred this Tinker lassie to give heartfelt thanks to Mother Nature for what she had given. I remember the scene vividly.

Flames began to shoot wildly up each side of the oil drum; the local policeman raised his eyebrows as he passed by, probably keeping a watchful eye on us. The roaring fire with kettle on the boil at the time was drawing attention, so Daddy handed me a jam jar and pointed to the water of the loch lapping gently at my feet. Instinctively I scooped some up and dripped it onto the flames. A hiss of steam filled the quiet air, and in a few moments the orange and yellow flames were tamed.

Mammy was away reading a local wife's palm. My sisters were, as always, stuck inside the bus gossiping or reading comics, while Daddy and I had Harry the taleteller and Elspeth for entertainment.

He began by saying that in the seventeenth century an ancestor of his had been a minister at Kenmore. If there was any more information about his lineage, or indeed any more stories about the minister, then he didn't share them.

Before we start, I should mention that if anything got my hackles up it was hearing about incidents of witch-burning. Just the thought of it got me into an awful state. Immediately it was clear that his story was about that very thing. I flared up and said that if I'd been alive in those days I'd have given them burning all right, and my face went bright red. Nothing was more infuriating to me even at that young age than the actions of religious fanatics burning herb wives and accusing them of supping with the devil. For no greater crime than having a knowledge of healing, they were burned at stakes across the length and breadth of Scotland. Only a minority of these terrible executions were ever recorded, and those that were noted were usually by churchmen.

Black-clothed fanatics in these times created a reign of terror in Scotland. Fearsome men on horseback, brandishing bibles, screamed hell and damnation through glens and over hilltops, putting fear and dread into the stoutest hearts. Catholics who refused to submit to the new faith were unceremoniously put to the sword. People were scared to close their eyes in case they were next. Tinker folk were targeted more than any other section of society. Very few escaped the clutches of hell's scourers.

I listened as Harry and Daddy cracked on for a while on how religion was the cause of wars and feuds among nations, until I interrupted to ask when he'd get round to the story in hand. Much to my relief, Harry at last got round to his story.

John and Margaret Loudon were basket-makers who came every year to Loch Tay, mainly for the rough grasses, perfect for weaving sturdy creels, that grew abundantly in a particular spot there. Their relatives had been regular campers there for many a year. However, they were alone without kith or kin and only their eleven-year-old son Neil for company that one night, while the moon shone bright in the sky, that they heard approaching through the bushes a terrifying sound of clashing swords and harsh voices. 'Come now, out ye be,' came a hoarse command. It was a press gang, scouring the country for young males over the age of twelve to force them to serve in the army. Behind the soldiers stretched a long line of shackled men who had been snatched from local roads and villages.

Margaret and young Neil were powerless against the heavily armed troopers, who in no time had tied John and added him to their human cargo. No matter how desperately she pleaded with them to let her man go free, her cries fell on deaf ears. Her distress was no different from that of dozens of wives and mothers they'd encountered across the land. The soldiers themselves had probably been recruited in the same brutal way, but now they were being paid as government troops. Faced with a choice of whether to keep a full belly or be court-martialled and shot the pressers continued to overpower helpless men and now a form of camaraderie united them. Any man attempting to escape his chains was left to rot with a lead bullet in his back or skewered through with a cold steel bayonet.

Once he arrived at the barracks the new enlisted man would be paid a shilling, and this meant he was now a defender of the realm. He'd wear a uniform and swear allegiance to the monarch of the day. No one could run away from this service without paying the penalty. Family and kin had to come second. One day they might meet again, but from the moment the soldier had signed or made his cross on the official document, any kind of absence was classed as desertion, a treasonable act for any soldier. Margaret knew all this and resigned herself to never seeing her John again. She at least was thankful for the time they had together, and of course for wee Neil.

John's distinctive red curls were the last she saw of him, as his shackled body disappeared into the mists over a black horizon. Poor wee Neil, he'd been left with a heavy burden. Now he had to care for his mother, herself a weak wee thing, and continue to gather and dry the grasses and reeds. One would imagine their lot couldn't get any harder. Not long after, however, Mr Menzies, the minister, and several aggressive parishioners, falsely accused them of plundering the poor box in the church. Overcome with shock and terror, Margaret began to choke and collapsed on the ground. Young Neil, within a week, had lost his other parent. Now he was left at the mercy of the state – that is, he was placed in the care of the parish. Menzies, who had little time for poor people of any kind, let alone Tinkers, after burying Margaret, ordered that Neil be sent to the nearest poor house at Logerait, not far from Pitlochry.

A lover of freedom since birth, this youngster had no intention of entering any house, rich or poor, so with the wind at his heels he took off, following a path which took him over Glen Quaich, down little Glen Shee and into Perth. The journey, travelling alone, took him two months. He found work in several places along the way, sometimes gathering nuts, at other times helping cottars with cattle and so on. Perhaps Menzies was glad to see the back of him. He had other things to concern him, as there was a lot of unrest in the countryside and he had trouble from interfering landowners, who were not at the church's bidding as they'd been in the past. An orphaned boy with itchy feet would only add to his problems. Neil therefore was free to traipse wherever he pleased.

From Perth, Neil, again working wherever he could to get food, set a steady pace for Aberdeen. There were many fishermen in the port there, and perhaps he'd find work mending creels. The best-laid plans go awry, however, and his fortunes took a turn for the worse when, at the busy dockside, he found lying in wait for him a fate similar to his father's.

Two islanders from Skye, Alex Macdonald from Sleat and Norman Macleod of Dunvegan had gone into the disgraceful business of kidnapping. They would abduct homeless and vulnerable people indiscriminately and sell them into slavery. Young Neil innocently disclosed his name and age to the pair, thinking he was being sent to work for a manufacturer of fishing nets and creel manufacturer, and then found himself bound and gagged and shipped on board a vessel headed for America.

Harry has no knowledge of how the lad fared on board, but he does know that on arrival in America he was sold to an English aristocrat, who had the lad branded like a horse with the letters HMS. This was done to all his workforce, and Harry speculated that it meant 'His Majesty's Slave'. Whatever the truth of this, Neil sent to work on one of his owner's many cotton plantations in the south.

Neil's desire to be free was perhaps stronger in him than in many of the other enslaved workers, and this could perhaps be put down to his wandering heritage, so he never stopped watching and waiting for a chance to escape. This didn't come until five years after his capture, and by then he was very familiar with the surrounding countryside.

He had fallen in love with a black girl called Ninny, and one dark night under cover of a storm the pair stole a horse and galloped away. They traversed Virginia, and eventually sold the horse to get money for food. Always travelling under cover of darkness because it was unlawful for slaves to be roaming free, they made their way through Carolina to the Appalachian mountain range. It was there that they settled and began to live as free people. Neil built a house and worked the soil. Between them they had twelve children, seven of whom died in infancy.

Neil himself died in 1789 and Ninny in 1807. In 1950 a descendant of theirs called Simon John Loudon came back to Scotland searching for his roots. He discovered that a Neil Loudon had sailed aboard a frigate bound for America full of slaves. Neil's name is recorded in Aberdeen. MacDonald and Macleod made meticulous lists of their shanghaied innocents which are still there for all to see.

Harry never told us how he came to know the details of this sad story, nor the source of his tale but it made me think. How many Americans, Canadians, Australians and New Zealanders are from Tinker stock? Anyway, I hope you enjoyed that story from Harry Menzies; a story my father and I brought to life again on many a long winter night. If any of you know where Harry is now I'd be delighted to hear from you.

As a postscript to this, it appears from the documents that a lad aged twelve (surname Williamson) was also kidnapped on Aberdeen docks. I have no details of this case, but I know an Aberdonian singer-songwriter called Bob Knight who has written a poignant version of this story in words and music.

19

The Picts of Kenmore

A few hundred yards up the way a bit from Kenmore, the road bends sharply and pikes into two; one fork takes the traveller back along the lower road of the loch, which Tinkers used to call Packman's March, the other leads on to Aberfeldy.

Today, by the road, a path leads over a bridge to a fine crannog in the loch. This is a replica of the original cone-shaped homestead of the ancient inhabitants of the area. It is a great tourist attraction and certainly worth a visit, but to me as a bairn, before the replica was built, it was simply known as 'the water hump' and was inaccessible from the land.

There was an air of menace about the place, however, when I was young. This stemmed from an incident when two children, on a warm summer day, swam over to explore the water hump. One got his foot stuck in an underwater branch and the other tried desperately to free him. This resulted in both boys drowning. Because of these deaths no Tinker folks ever stopped anywhere near the place. It was believed the boys had been stolen by a lonely water fairy. In some sad way the distraught parents believed this to be true, and that being the case found some consolation in the thought that in another world their children were happy and cared for.

The low road, which was supposedly built by the Picts and not the Romans, is a much more interesting route than the high road from Killin to Kenmore. The low road winds and undulates up and down. Many was the Tinker who, finding his days at a close, laid his tired limbs in some hidden spot between Kenmore and Ardeonaigh at the further end, never to raise his weary body again.

This poem from the gifted pen of Violet Jacobs captures that scene beautifully:

Last o' the Tinkler

Lay me in yon place, lad,
The gloamin's thick wi' nicht;
I canna see yer face, lad,
For my een's no richt.
But it's owre late for leein'
An' I ken fine I'm deein',
Like an auld craw fleein'
Tae the last o' the licht.

The kye gang tae the byre, lad,
The sheep tae the fauld,
Ye'll mak a spunk o' fire, lad,
For my he'rt's turned cauld;
And whaur the trees are meetin'
There's a soond like waters beatin',
An' the bird seems near tae greetin'
That was aye singin' bauld.

There's just the tent tae leave, lad,
I've gaither'd little gear,
There's just yersel' tae grieve, lad,
And the auld dog here;
But when the morn comes creepin'
And the waukin' birds are cheepin'
It'll find me lyin' sleepin'
As I've slept saxty year.

Ye'll rise tae meet the sun, lad,
And baith be trayv'lin' west,
But me that's auld an' done, lad,
I'll bide an' tak my rest;
For the grey heid is bendin'
And the auld shune's needin' mendin',
But the trayv'lin's near its endin',
An' the end's aye the best.

The above poem springs to mind whenever I think of a poignant find I made when I was a child. I may have been no more than seven or eight years old, and I was playing in the densely wooded area near to Loch Tay when I came across a complete skeleton propped up against a hazel tree. Picked clean it was! Daddy and his two brothers Joe and Eddy broke the bones into tiny pieces, before burying the remains exactly where they were found. I was in a right state and couldn't stop shaking, so to calm me they lied and said it was a kid-on – a puckle bones left there at Halloween by some tired weans on their way back from guising among the cottages that scatter themselves in quiet locations the length of the loch. But I know what I had seen, and those bones were real!

For weeks my teeth wouldn't stop rattling and my wee body shaking. To this day, when I am in the vicinity, I sometimes stop and pay homage to the unknown soul whose bones they were. But far be it from me to knock on the door of the lovely spacious house which now stands there, to disclose my well-kept secret to whoever dwells therein. The foundations of the house are built over the burial mound of that unknown soul. The poor people of the house might run to the hills if they knew that soil mixed with dead bones helps to keep the foundations of their house together!

As in many areas of Scotland, if you lace the boots up and the car remains behind in a car park, a wee jaunt onto the upper braes of Strathtay will reveal wonders that, once seen, will live in the memory forever. Two miles from Kenmore, the ancient Picts built one of the most elaborate stone circles in Scotland. Going further back into history the Bronze Age folk carved many cup and ring stones up and down the Strath. One brilliant example is the Braes o' Balloch Boulder on the road to Amulree, a stone's throw from Kenmore.

There is a tale that once, two lovers, one a Tinker lassie, the other a shepherd boy, when refused permission to wed, went in search of the sacred well on the hillside overlooking the stone circle. Once they had found it they held hands and called on the spirit of Queen Sybilla. The tradition was that she was a queen of Scotland who in 1122 saw blood in the well and could not sleep afterwards for worrying what it could mean. She spent days in the place until a voice from the well told her to prepare for her rest on Eilean nam Ban

Naomh, an island on the loch. There was a nunnery on the island and the name translates as Island of Holy Women. As she stepped off the boat that took her to the island, Queen Sybilla fell, banged her head and was fatally injured. Before she died she told the nuns that her body should be laid to rest there and not put on the mainland, following the instructions from the sacred well.

In my father's time, the road between Kenmore and Aberfeldy was heavily camped with Tinker families. They would pitch their tents along the river Tay, where there was an abundance of willow reeds for basket-weaving. It was in Aberfeldy, in March of 1948, at the Cottage Hospital, where I came into the world. My father was hoping for a boy, his first, but sadly that wasn't to be. I'm sad to say, though, that our family was blessed with a boy on one occasion, but sadly, due to a bout of measles, my mother miscarried at seven months. She never spoke of this unhappy episode afterwards, so I'll do the same.

20

Weem Tales

As there wasn't a proper Green at Aberfeldy, we usually drove over Marshall Wade's Bridge and headed to the outskirts of Weem for a couple of weeks, where we had a secluded wee coorie-in down next to the river. After we had settled in our favourite spot my parents and two youngest sisters usually scooted off to visit relatives over the bridge in Aberfeldy.

When I was old enough I was left to rake around for stones to build our fire. This was my regular task, just as skinning rabbits was my older sister's area of expertise. River stones were the best for this purpose, but if we weren't near a river I had to dig a few up. The rule was that when we moved away the stones had to be replaced where I had found them. Weem had the best stones in all of Scotland for making a fireplace – Tay paps; big shiny gurdy ones, that if placed properly in a circle would take four big pots and were great heat retainers. My sister Mary and I would gather a pile from the river's edge, then carry them to where I'd prepared a deep pit. This was marked out by measuring a circle in the grass. Using a trowel I dug down nine inches, and carefully lifted off the turf, making certain it was left in a safe place to be replaced when we were leaving. Mammy always said, 'Folks who live in a place won't remember us for our smiles or our curly hair, but for the mess we leave behind.' For this reason I always took care when building my masterpiece.

Even to this day, when I think about my fire-making skills I swell with pride. Maybe we Tinkers retain certain skills that are passed down through the genes, and it may be my ancestors were blacksmiths who made their living working over flames to forge metal; making swords, shields, daggers and horseshoes, an endless list of useful objects. I'm convinced that I'm from a long line of sturdy blackies.

Two years after my father came home from the last war, weary and peppered with shrapnel, he rented a small field on the green near the river Tay at Weem, several yards distant across the road from Menzies Castle. He built a basic wooden chalet which served as home for our growing family of four daughters. My appearance in March '48 made it five. That wee wooden chalet was my first home. My father had not been well after the war; a bomb had exploded in the tank he was in, killing his officer, wounding two of his fellow tank crew and piercing his eardrum with shrapnel. Towards the end of the war, battles became more intense with all the horrors that go with such madness.

He'd been kept busy doing MOD work after the war, cleaning up and dismantling concentration camps among other tasks. From this came the offer of a job working in the Black Forest in Germany, but because my mother's younger brother had been killed in the war she had no stomach for liaising with what had so recently been the enemy. So, feeling a wee bit deflated, he did what he could to provide for us in Scotland. With a cousin he worked cutting trees for firewood and selling bag-loads around the area.

Weem is the name of an underground tunnel built by the Picts to store food and supplies. There are several of these Weems in Perthshire, though only a few have been discovered of the many that previously existed. Experts believe that, over time, they have simply caved in.

Now, before we start on another tale, let me share this wee snippet with you.

I was once storytelling in mid-Ireland when a young man approached and said he liked my books. I was humbled by his praise and thanked him kindly. Apparently he had looked me up on the net and saw I was born in Aberfeldy. I chuckled when he informed me, 'There's another storyteller who lives there, but I think she's a lot more famous than you, Jess.'

Of course I knew he was talking about Harry Potter's creator, so respectfully enlightened him, 'Aye, lad, but she wisnae born there among the urisks, hobgoblins, fairies and broonies.' I added, 'but I can see where she gets her inspiration and ideas from!'

Many Tinker folks frequented the area, as I have said. Alder and hazel trees provided plenty of strong shoots for tent ribcages and to make washing pegs. In the village of Fortingall an ancient yew tree spreads her tired limbs supported by pillars of stone and gazes on the thousands of tourists who for one reason or another visit the place. As a lad my father made arrows from the branches of this tree. Pontius Pilate, the Roman who had Jesus crucified, was supposedly born there, and a beautiful Lairdess, young and lovely Mariota Stewart, wife of Niall the doomed, lies buried beneath its spreading canopy. Buried around the yew are more bodies than tree roots, according to fanciful myth makers.

However one looks at it the area has a mysterious atmosphere. Old Tinkers used to say the place had a smell of death about it. As an illustration of this I'm minded to share this dark and terrible story . . .

Three miles from the village of Weem, in a small strip of wood-land opposite Fortingall, near the Pictish plague circle of standing stones, little Charlie, his sisters and his parents were camped. It was 1919, and men had begun to trickle home from the war. Wullie, his father, had been discharged from the army the year before.

It was while they were cutting reeds and grasses at the water's edge and rolling them into bundles that wee Charlie and his sisters, Jessie and Anna, heard the snorting of a horse up at the campsite. The inquisitive threesome lifted their small heads above the level of the grass to see a stocky gentleman step down from a small buggy and harness his black horse to a tree. 'Hello there, folks,' they heard the visitor call. Margaret, Charlie's mother, was alone. Wul-lie, whose area of expertise was wood-cutting, was working on a nearby estate and was nowhere in the vicinity. The three children, like small chickens, stopped what they were doing and rushed to their mother's side, each grabbing an inch of her apron. 'There's nae folks here, sir, only me and the weans,' she told the stranger, adding, 'but my man will be here shortly and you'll not miss him, for he's over six feet, he is.' She thought that this description of her man's physique would put any ideas of harm from the stranger's mind. Although he was only seven, Charlie regarded himself as the man of the camp, and so gingerly released his grip of his mother's apron to step forward and give the man a once-over. He looked the man up and down carefully, and when satisfied with what he had seen returned to Margaret's side.

The visitor winked and smiled at Charlie, then pointed at the kettle hissing softly on a large stone at the fire. Margaret read his thoughts. 'We dinna hae sugar but there's a drap milk.' Usually she'd have lifted a stone, and brandished in her hand as a warning. She seldom entertained strangers, especially with her man not there, but perhaps, she thought, he was there to see her man; to offer him a job maybe. There was a gentleman-like air to the stranger, and as she detected no menace in his manner, she remained standing while he sat. They shared a crack over a strong cup of stewed tea while the children played, staying out of reach just in case he presented a threat.

One thing that upset Margaret was alcohol; she loathed it, and for good reason. So when the man took a flask from his pocket and poured some into his tea she flinched and stepped back. Again her brood flocked close, peeking from within the folds of her skirt, like baby rabbits, ever-watchful, missing not a single movement made by the visitor.

Margaret was a Christian woman and strong liquor never passed her lips. Wullie only drank on special occasions like Hogmanay, but once he was full of the stuff there was no reasoning in the man. That's why, from the hour of midnight and for two weeks after, Margaret took the children and hid away. The entire family stayed clear of him until the doldrums had passed and normality had been restored inside his brain.

Charlie well remembered a time when his mild-mannered father, with a half bottle of rum inside him, had become a first-class demon. One dark night, after waiting for his father as he shared a bottle with a shepherd mate, he was walking home with him when he became enraged. Charlie was terror-struck and shinned up a tree to escape from his flying fists. Wullie had got into a furious argument with a whispering yew branch. Only the good God knew what the conversation was about, but his son was so terrified he continued to cling to a branch until Wullie head-butted the tree and knocked himself out. Charlie had to act fast to stem the blood spouting from a deep gash to his father's forehead. Although he never used it, the boy thereafter kept a small penknife in his pocket just in case his drunken father needed a wee poke with it.

Back to the tale: there he stood, half hidden by long grasses, one eye on his sisters, the other on the stranger's movements, and warily watching his mother whom he adored. Small in stature, gigantic in motherhood, her children were her life, her son more than daughters. As a child he had been plagued by bronchial problems, which had give her another reason to fuss and fret over her boy. She was constantly treating him to words of wisdom followed by hugs.

Although the visitor at her fire seemed harmless enough she was more than relieved when she finally saw her husband sauntering up the road, a massive axe across his broad shoulders, and the sharp blade glinting in the evening sun. For a moment she'd taken her eye off the flask, but knowing the state its contents would have left her man in, hissed at the stranger to get rid of it. In a flash it was stuffed in a jacket pocket and a hand raised to greet Wullie. Wullie, on seeing the stranger, swung the axe like a feather above his head before burying the head into a log very close to the man's stretched-out legs. He jumped instantly to his feet, taking off his tweed deerstalker and revealing a headful of thick, greying hair. He continued to offer his hand in greeting. Wullie ignored him, and called out to his son, 'Charlie, I met wi' Andra Ness and guess whae's coming awhiley?'

Charlie dashed to his father's side and said excitedly, 'Ma wee pal Jeemy, ma best mate, wee wire legs! When, Da?'

'He'll be here tomorrow. Now, who's this?' Wullie stood a whole head and shoulders over the stranger, impatiently waiting for his wife to explain his presence at their campsite.

Margaret, Jessie, Anna and Charlie stood in a tight group, waiting for their protector to chase off the stranger, who they felt had stayed too long by their campfire. Margaret whispered in her man's ear that she thought he was a gentleman come there to see him. Wullie shook his head furiously.

'Well, if you're not here to speak with my man, then why are you here?' she asked the stranger, unceremoniously grabbing her cup from his fat fingers.

'Friends, calm down. I can understand why you folk are wary of strangers, but you've nothing to worry about with me. I'm a doctor, and I've come among you to see if there are any health problems I can offer you some sound advice about. I'm not asking a penny.'

This didn't sound right to Wullie and his wife. Doctors didn't go visiting Tinkers' camps at random, and they would be taking a risk if they did so. Wullie saw the man's horse tied to the tree. He brought it a bucket of feed and put it under its chin. At first the animal refused to eat, so he called to Charlie, 'Get a drink for the black mare, she's a dry lip.'

He then turned to the man at his fire and sat down, took off his bonnet and said, 'We keep sorrow and cold from our fireside by healing ourselves.' He looked at Margaret and added, 'Give me some soup, wife, and fill this yin's cup afresh.' He was curious, and wanted to know who this so-called man of medicine was and what his reasons were for such a friendly approach. Tinker people's strength lies in each other, the herbs and poultices they use and watching the seasons. His son's winter chest ailments were healed by a mother renowned for her herbal cures. He sat in silence for a while then asked his visitor, 'You have a name?'

'My name is Dr Smith. I come from the capital city, Edinburgh. I hired this horse and decided to keep to the drove roads and bridle paths. As I said, I want to help.'

'Na, lad, no man comes among us unless he wants something. Now, are you law or cruelty?'

The stranger seemed genuine, however. Though Wullie had already decided there was no malice in him, it was best to be extra sure, so he said, 'Open the bag and let's see what you have in there.' Without hesitation the doctor opened the bag and produced an array of small vials, bottles of pills and bandages. Satisfied that the visitor meant no harm, Wullie said, 'Aye, well, that's fine, doctor. Have a plate of soup and be on your way. As you can see there's nothing wrong with any of us.'

Margaret handed him a plate of soup which he ate gratefully. No one waved him goodbye as he trotted off. Margaret had the second sight She couldn't foresee anything distinctly, but there was something about him that she couldn't at that moment pin point.

Charles' pal Jeemy was the only son of Andra Ness's sister, Nancy, and her husband Joe. Joe had been killed in the first years of the war, and Nancy died shortly afterwards of a broken heart. Their son James, Jeemy for short, came to live with his Uncle Andra. The poor lad had no memory of his father, but he knew that he'd died for his country, and that meant that he was a hero.

In Inverness, where they had a decent house for wintering, there were plenty of dead heroes, but as far as Jeemy was concerned, his father was a greater hero than them all, because he fell while marching at the head of his column, playing the pipes. Jeemy told the story every chance he got. 'Not just one bullet, but five,' he'd say, as puffed up with pride as a peacock.

Andra, who had no family of his own, was very protective of his charge. 'Don't talk with strangers,' he would tell him. 'If a dog shows the white of its eyes, don't clap it. Listen to the river's flow, flash floods have washed many an old man to meet his maker. When lightning fills the clouds, don't go under trees.'

Wullie, on the other hand, thought this was over-cautious and said it was living in a house that had softened Andra and turned him into a sissy. Margaret said he needed a good woman. She believed men were useless without guidance and that only women knew the minds of men. Wullie always growled like a dog when she spouted her Amazonian wisdom.

Each spring, Andra and Jeemy were a regular sight setting off on the road south, mixing with other Tinker folk, enjoying the crack. Charlie, for one, was overjoyed to meet and share the countryside with his mate, Jeemy, who was a year younger than him. They had toddled out of nappies together and into short breeches. Both boys, when together, were inseparable, always the best of pals.

After the stranger had left, calm returned to the camp site.

'When will they be here, Da?' Charlie asked excitedly, straining to see if they had already reached the turn in the road that led to the campsite.

'Tomorrow sometime,' came the disappointing answer.

Seven-year-olds cannot master the art of patience, and Charlie was no exception. But he'd have to wait. As he did so his thoughts turned to the river raft the pair had worked on last year. They kept it in a strip of woodland at a quiet spot on the Tay over a makeshift bridge. What a fun they'd had building it! Margaret had promised him that when he reached seven she'd let him play further afield, and now that he was seven, they'd be able to explore the more distant parts of the river bank.

Their hideaway among the river grasses was a great place to romp, it was a play den for him and Jeemy. As he ran off to this place where his pesky sisters couldn't annoy him, he forgot everything, even the strange doctor man. Soon him and and Jeemy would be displaying their engineering skills. The river was flowing fast and furious in places, and his little heart beat fast thinking of the next day when they'd become riders of the river rapids. He had often been warned not to make boats from logs and jute bags because of the dangerous rapids on the river, but they were still going to do it. Rules were made to be broken, and that was another reason why he could hardly wait for Jeemy's arrival.

As he was surveying their private playground, there was a sound among the grasses. Peering through the reeds he saw a mother swan searching for a nest site, so he tiptoed away back to the camp site to leave her in peace.

His father was chopping a bundle of firewood for the cooking fire and immediately started to set tasks for his boy to do. 'Stack those cut logs, and when that's done, fill the watering cans, laddie.'

Charlie began to stack the firewood neatly next to the tent. Margaret was inside brushing her daughters' hair. Jessie had thick black locks where Anna's light brown curls were fine and flimsy. As they grew up, Anna would take on a fine and delicate appearance, whereas Jessie was a stronger, sturdier type. Both were beautiful children, and as the brush glided effortlessly through their hair their mother said proudly, 'You'll make perfect wives for lucky men, one day.'

That night Charlie lay for ages unable to sleep; his pal Jeemy was coming, with his wee wiry legs and his patched trousers, his poems and songs and all that made a real braw friend.

No prizes for guessing who rose first. The fire was hearted with kindling twigs and lit, the filled·kettle was plonked upon heated stones. Charlie even filled the porridge pot; on any other day he'd not have handled that boiling black cauldron or hung it on the chittie chain, but today there it was, bubbling away with a sweet aroma of hot oats, appealing to nostrils for miles around. He stood stridey-legged like a wee warrior, with his sleeves rolled up over pointy elbows; he was the replica of his father.

Margaret and the girls went off to make their ablutions by the river while Wullie scraped the stubble from his chin with a razor. When breakfast was over, the girls set about washing the dishes. Charlie finished his chores before sauntering the road to welcome their forthcoming visitors. It wasn't long before, from Fearnam way, came the sound he'd been waiting for so long – echoing voices mingled with the clippity-clop of iron on stone. It was Andra and Jeemy, sitting up on a high-wheeled buggy pulled by a fat-flanked palomino with sparks flying from its hooves. Andra wrenched back on the reins. 'Wait up, you bloody mad fire-horse,' he called. 'Whew, now, boy, good lad.' Charlie caught the flying leather straps, tied them to a roadside oak and called breathlessly, 'Come on now, Jeemy boy, let's get the raft built.'

His friend leapt from the cart and tumbled at his feet. It was hard to say who was more pleased, but as they ran off towards the campsite, Andra, who'd been completely ignored, grinned and shouted after them, 'Your Ma had best have the tea stewing!'

And of course she did. Margaret filled the biggest mug she had for him. The campsite resounded to children's laughter and sweet singing, while spirals of log fire reek danced up and over the silvery Tay. In no time Charlie and his best mate had completed the raft, and they had acquired a length of thick rope to tie it with from a local farmer in return for filling his shed with logs that Wullie had sold him.

The camp was a serene place that night. The boys had already made their plans for the next day. After a trot along the banks of the Tay on each other's horses, they'd go river rafting, not on the wild waters of the main river but on a small tributary flowing next to the campsite. That night the shenanigans of the excitable pair kept everyone awake as they howled and hooted like cowboys from each tent, until Margaret sternly told them to shush their nonsense. All went quiet at last.

Next morning it was Wullie who rose early. Late in the night he'd heard noises, but put it down to the boys' over-excitement. 'Come on, Charlie, let's be having you,' he called, adding that the midges were cannibalising the horses. Margaret suffered from the attack of Scotland's ravenous predators, but as protection for her face she had a supply of cotton masks with peep-holes for eyes.

Charlie was up like a linty and off over to the burn, soap in hand, and sang loudly as he rubbed his face. His toothbrush was his index finger covered in soot from the ashes of the fire. A rub over with this cleaned his teeth and got rid of mouth odour. 'Dirt to clean dirt,' he'd say.

Andra pushed a sleepy head from the tent mouth and stretched, scattering a million dust particles into the sunlight. 'Get out of yer kip, wee Jeemy. Charlie is up, washed and fed.'

Charlie slipped his empty porridge plate into the washing basin and seconded Andra's request. 'It's a braw day for river-rafting and horse-riding. Shift yerself, Jeemy.'

Andra and Wullie began to saunter off to get washed themselves when Charlie, who had looked in his pal's tent and couldn't see Jeemy called out, 'He's no here, the bugger's up and away! I'll kill him if he goes off without me.'

Andra came over and threw back the door flap exposing the entire tent. 'Jeemy must be down at the river, Charlie. You away and tell him to get back here or his lugs'll sting when I get him.'

Charlie ran off to look for Jeemy, but after checking every clump of long grasses, along the river bank, and even looking at the horses to see if he'd been for an early ride, he rushed back with the news that his friend was nowhere to be seen. It was too early for panic at first, but after everyone had been calling and searching for an hour, it was not hard to tell from the sombre pale faces and anxious looks that it was serious – Jeemy was missing.

Fear now gripped everyone. Normally the boy stuck to the campsite like a limpet, never leaving it unless his over-protective uncle knew exactly where he was!

Margaret took the girls and set off round the houses of Fortingall, while Wullie and Andra mounted the horses and galloped up and over the braes, leaving Charlie to search the riverbank again. He left no corner unchecked, calling all the time, 'Jeemy, lad, where are you?'

He was sobbing inwardly, a gnawing pit of grief replacing his usual calm optimism. Something was wrong. It would do no good and just alarm others if he started to scream, but that's what he felt like doing. Instead he continued to call on his friend.

Wullie had his own feelings but didn't let them appear; Andra was in a terrible state.

Exhausted with the search, everybody arrived back at the camp at the same time. Charlie's sister Jessie, two years older than him, and Anna, two years younger, were sobbing as Margaret kept herself busy in silence. If it had been another more spunky laddie she'd not feel so chilled to the bone, but Jeemy was such a timid little mite.

Wullie watched Andra with grave compassion as he went down to the river again, yet tried to reassure him. 'Dinna you be fretting, lad, yon wee man has seen a rare bird and followed it further downstream.'

'No, Wullie, I have a gut feeling that is tormenting me; my wee Jeemy is in trouble some place.'

Any other members of society would be banging on the local

policeman's door and asking for help, but as far as Tinkers were concerned this was a futile option.

Charlie thought they should widen the search and head on into Weem and Aberfeldy. 'Maybe Jeemy crept out during darkness to go to the toilet, fell and banged his head and has wondered off. I'm going to check the road, he might be lying unconscious in the ditch somewhere.'

This made Andra perk up. 'Aye, lad. I'll head along one side, you take the other.'

It was worth clutching at any straw. Wullie said he'd scour the fields and the wood. As he set off, a sudden thought flashed into his mind. Was the sound that wakened him during the night something to do with wee Jeemy? As he clambered up the wet, mossy braeside, a gaggle of wild geese screamed high above him and distracted him from his fearful thoughts about the lost child. The climb was steep, and on reaching the top he stopped briefly to catch his breath. Any other time he would have looked with pleasure and admiration at the view of Weem and Wade's Bridge, but not today. A rocky outcrop offered a welcome seat and as he made a track towards it through heather clumps and knotted tree roots he prayed that somewhere down on the road wee Jeemy would be found sitting nursing a bruise or two, none the worse of a bang on the head. Maybe he was already heading back to the camp, holding Charlie tightly by the hand.

As he reached the tumble of rocks he caught sight of something out of the corner of his eye; a patch of dark green, not the colour of leaves or grasses but perhaps an article of clothing. Rushing closer, he suddenly stopped dead in his tracks. He could see a small leg protruding from the rocks. Now all hope of finding the wee laddie unharmed failed. He was curled into a lifeless ball.

Wullie fell to the ground, panting for breath at the horror before him. This little child hadn't found his way here by chance; he had been brought here, and then he had been strangled. My God, he thought, the sounds he'd heard in the night were those of some demon pulling the boy from his bed. It was an easy task in the dark, to reach under the canvas and steal a sleeping child. It wasn't the first time it had happened and it wouldn't be the last.

Jeemy hadn't just been strangled. A crimson pool of dried blood beneath his body and his pale naked limbs were proof that whoever did this stripped and abused the innocent boy before killing him. His woolly jumper, shoes and trousers were missing. Wullie took off his jacket and wrapped the child in it. Andra and Charlie were already on their way back to the camp. Margaret, who saw her husband coming down the brae, limp body in his arms, quickly told her girls to get inside the tent. I can only leave the next scene to the imagination.

Tinker folk are different from other people faced with death; they go into a silent ritual of mourning. Andra and Margaret washed Jeemy's body and wrapped it for burial. It would take several days to reach Inverness where they would lay him to rest, so he'd need a double covering. She had plenty of muslin cloth and set about her gruesome task. Wullie took his mesmerised son down to the river and tried to explain.

'Can we no get the polis, Daddy?' asked Charlie. 'They'll catch the devil-man.'

'The police will not help us son. Come on now and let's burn the river raft.'

They stood side by side as the crudely constructed raft on which Charlie and Jeemy had planned, in their imaginations, to sail the seven seas as Blackbeard and his pirates, twisted and crackled in red and orange flames. As the raft disappeared, blazing up to the morning sky and covering the river reeds in thick grey smoke, so did his plans to grow up with Jeemy as his lifelong mate. Even for a boy as young as seven it was easy to see that life as a Tinker child was cheap.

For the rest of the day, after Andra and the others had said their farewells, if a pin had dropped on the stony ground the sound would have echoed and vibrated for miles. Death demands silence, and on that day that was certainly what it got. Then a clip-clopping of horse's hooves broke into their grief. Doctor Smith pulled on his horse's reins and jumped nimbly down from his buggy. 'Hello to you all,' he said, 'and how are you doing this fine day?'

Wullie nodded but said nothing. It was not the custom of his people to discuss anything like this with strangers. He walked away and began to cut up some logs, while Margaret told the girls to get back inside their tent.

'Can I have some tea please?' asked the doctor. His request was greeted with silence, but eventually Margaret brought him a mug. For a while the doctor chatted on about nothing in particular, sipping his tea. Charlie came back from the riverside and went over to his father to say a big swan had laid ten eggs in a massive nest among the reeds. A stream of tears rolled down his cheeks as he wondered what Jeemy would have made of the swan. His father patted him gently on the head, then asked him to go into the village shop to get him some tobacco. He took the money and walked off, still feeling desperately lost and confused about his friend's death.

On his way to the road he had to squeeze past the doctor's buggy. As he did so he caught a glimpse of a tiny piece of cloth sticking out from under the bench seat. There was something familiar about it. Gently he tugged at it and pulled it out. It was Jeemy's patched trousers! Stuffing them under his jacket he ran off for his father's tobacco.

Just as he arrived back the doctor was already on his buggy and ready to leave. Waiting until he was out of sight, he blurted out what he had found and showed them the trousers. Wullie ordered him not to say another word about them, but there was no need. Margaret and the girls had already recognised Jeemy's breeks.

A fierce wind was whirling around the plague circle of standing stones nearby as Wullie lifted his big axe and put it over his shoulder. He walked his horse slowly onto the road before straddling its back. He didn't have much faith in saddles and considered that a woven blanket was enough of a separation between rider and animal. In a few minutes he'd disappeared from sight. Margaret and Jessie knew why he'd gone; Charlie and Anna were too young to realise. Somewhere in the distance on the darkening horizon a dog fox lifted its sharp head from a patch of bracken and howled.

No one went to bed until the sound of footsteps crackling over dead twigs was heard once more. Wullie stood silent over the fire, stirred the embers into life with a stick, smiled at the little innocent head peeping at him from the tent, dropped a pile of bloodied clothes onto the flames and said, 'He'll not harm another bairn, Charlie.'

The Tinker child instinctively understood, crawled back under his bedclothes and said, 'Good!'

—

I'm aware that, if you are non-Travellers, this dark and evil tale will have you raising an eyebrow, and you are probably of the view that the laws of the land which are enforced in courtrooms don't permit vigilante tactics. But if you can put yourself in the shoes of my people, who seldom had any kind of justice in their favour from the authorities, then you will understand why Wullie would have taken matters into his own hands. It could also have been his devotion to his children's welfare as a father and his desire to safeguard innocent babes that moved him to act in the way he did – whatever that was! If there was no witness to Jeemy's horrific death, and a Tinker tried to have an officer of the law arrest a doctor dressed in a fine Harris tweed suit, the owner of a handsome buggy and sturdy thorough-bred horse, then which of the two men would the officer believe? I'm with the unwritten law on this one. The end result was that no other child would be violated or worse; there was one less demon crawling the land; that is my view.

I was a teenager when I first heard that tale. As a lassie of the road I'd been told innumerable horror stories. Many were invented to keep Tinker children alert and aware of ever-present dangers.

While recently I was researching standing stone circles and their relevance to my culture, I met a woman whose family, like mine, had travelled these parts in the old days. I was searching for the hound stone of Fionn on the roadside between Fortingall and Fearnam when we met by sheer chance. She offered to share a story with me, and being a lover of tales I happily sat upon a dry-stone dyke to listen. I'll tell it in her words.

'Roon-a-boot the war, the first yin [*during the First World War*], a shan gadji prowled aroon deekin amang te nawkens fur wee chavis [*a weird man prowled around Traveller campsites eyeing little boys*]. He'd pit te fear o deeth intae a the hantle, mithers couldnae gan hawkin or dukkerin fir te terror the gadji hud them in [*He'd put the fear of death into all the Travellers, and mothers couldn't go hawking and fortune-telling for fear the evil man should steal their boys*].

Yin nicht he pult a tottie wee chavi oot frae unner te tent and damaged it tae deeth [*One night after he had pulled a youngster from a tent and murdered him*]. A big Pavee fund the shan gadji intil a bush and paggert him within a inch o his life. The Pavee shifted yin o the gadji's fams, and blunt him in the yin ee [*An Irishman Tinker discovered him hiding, beat him, cut off a hand and blinded him in one eye*]. Efter yon carry on naebody wis feart nae mair [*After that the fear disappeared*]. The shan gadji, am telt, wis paggert tae deeth yin day by a Caithness faither seekin revenge [*One broken-hearted father from Caithness put an end to the man; he killed him*]. Travellers sort oot their ain trouble, an yon gadji hud whit wis comin tae him [*This was sweet revenge, it seems*].

Whether or not my father knew the people in this story, I cannot say, but he always held a fear of doctors (if indeed the murderer was one), and when stood by the fire always kept his back to the flames and his face to the vastness of shadows around the camp as if he was afraid of some terror catching him off guard.

21

THE URISKS AND THE BROWNIE

Wade's Bridge, which spans the river Tay, has a beauty of structure unequalled anywhere else in Perthshire. My folks used to share tales of the infamous supernatural beings, the Urisks, which haunted the river Tay in this area. I challenge anyone to sit near the bridge as a storm is brewing and not to be moved and unnerved by the swirl of water and sway of grasses as they come to life. It's all about imagination, no doubt, but the folk who live along the river will tell you there are more powerful forces at work here than rushing water. I'm led to believe that these arise from underground, linked to hell's black spirals of ley lines.

Here's another snip of folklore for you.

The Urisks never kept any company, preferring to travel alone, haunting at night and whispering to bairns who slept fitfully in their beds. They were nasty male spirits, clever, and far too fond of churned butter and thick cream. They would creep away from their homes in lonely moorland and deep ravines to intrude into the work of busy milkmaids and never-resting farmers' wives. Unlike the Brownie, a gentle spirit who was helpful around the house and farmyard, the Urisk was lazy and uncouth.

One night a dreadful Urisk called Black Breeks (*Triubhas Dubh*) sneaked out from his cavern behind a waterfall, disguised himself as a wee Brownie and set off to plunder the cream and scones left on the barnyard dyke by the mistress of Moness Farm for a Brownie who was her wee supernatural helper. It was a common practice by farmers' wives to seek out help from the Brownies with many chores which the farmworkers refused to do, like clearing out a chicken coop that had got full of muck, sweeping up scattered hay on a windy night and scrubbing down the pigs before taking them to market. When Black Breeks saw the bucket, brush and shovel that were always left for the helper to do his chores, he smiled mischievously and ignored them. He was only interested in the goodies left by the farmer's wife.

As the slee tod lawrie (fox) crept around the farmyard, sniffing around the chicken coop and putting fear into the hens, as the wise old owls eyed the glistening river under a shifting moon, and while the fairy folk danced in little rings around toadstools, Black Breeks gorged himself on cream and scones until full. As soon as he heard the earliest cock crow he slithered off.

When the mistress of the house saw that her night helper had come, ignored his chores and eaten his payment she was livid! Putting on her coat and hat, she set off up the brae to complain at the Brownies' Knoll. This good wife, who had always kept a seat by the fire in the family home for the good-natured Brownies, had second sight and many dealings with the spirit creatures; in fact she never took an important decision until after having a secret meeting with them. Making certain that no one was following her or was in the area, she sat down and tapped at the bottom of the grassy hump.

After a while she tapped again, and then a third time. This told those within that whoever was waiting outside was a friend. A door opened and in went the farmer's wife. When the Brownies heard her tale of the chaos that had been left for her, they knew what had happened. They gave her instructions about what to do. In the dark hours she should do as she had done before and leave cream and buttered scones for the helper. This time, however, she should put a dollop of treacle on the scones as well.

That is exactly what she did before going to bed. Once more Black Breeks sneaked down in his disguise as a Brownie and gorged himself on the tasty treats meant for his fellow supernatural being.

The next night, down he went again, but when he got there he was met with a sight that was not so pleasant as before but instead sent him into a fury. Two powerful Urisks, Peallaidh of the Upper Falls of Moness and Brunaidh of the Lower Falls of Moness, stood on either side of the entrance to the farm. One handed Black Breeks a bucket, the other a brush. 'You have to make all this farm spick and span, the hens' coops have to be cleaned and the pigs washed.'

'Why?' protested Black Breeks, 'what have I done?'

'You are a thief and have stolen from another spirit that which is not yours.'

Black Breeks lied and said he'd no idea what they were talking about; he was an innocent Urisk. Peallaidh stepped forward, took hold of Black Breeks and lowered his head into the farm well so that he could see his reflection. 'What is that around your mouth?'

With the tell-tale circle of black treacle around his mouth, the game was up.

In the presence of such powerful spirits he'd no choice but to work as he'd never done before, and only when the barn, hen coop and farm courtyard, along with the grimy porkers, were spotlessly clean, was he allowed to rest. Once he had finished his punishment, Black Breeks left the area and was never seen again.

22

Weem, Home of the Black Watch

My father used to say that if the authorities wanted to count the Tinkers they should sit down with pen and paper at the crossroads at Weem and after one summer they would have had thousands of names. Why was he so certain of this?

Well, one connection with Tinkers is that Weem was a Pictish settlement, but more relevant than this was the fact that the Tinkers' regiment, the Black Watch, was formed there.

There were campfire gatherings all around the Weem and Aberfeldy area in my father's younger days. As they sat around the flames, the Tinker folk would share stories as many as the petals of hawthorn blossom blowing into the night air. The storytellers would raise glasses to water kelpies, urisks, broonies, elves and fairy folk, but the most popular stories of all were about soldiers and the forming of the Black Watch, known to them as 'the Tinkers' Regiment'.

My relatives who came from around this area were quite clear about the Tinkers' role in the history of their regiment, but though I've tried hard to trace the original source of this tradition, the regimental histories have no record of this very important link. Most military historians agree that the Black Watch, the most famous of all Highland regiments, was formed at Weem in 1740 by the commander-in-chief of the British Army, Marshal Wade, although some say it could have been as early as 1725. He made his headquarters in the village inn, and proceeded with his ambitious plan to subdue the unruly Highlanders by building good roads on which an army could march without the hindrance of rough heather, moor and rock. His forward-thinking plan was well funded with money from the government. Like the Romans, and for the same reasons, in a very short time he had created a network of military roads and bridges where there had only been footpaths before. The roads included one through Weem and Coshieville, and over the hills to Rannoch. His finest work was the bridge spanning the Tay between Weem and Aberfeldy.

Wade despised the unruly Highlanders and relished the task of taming them. The crown had not forgiven the Jacobites for the 1715 uprising. It was a time when every Highlander was still suffering the degradation of being forbidden to bear arms. To keep order in the Highlands he formed six Independent Companies. This is where my Tinkers come into the story.

I really can only guess as to why the Tinker people no longer lived side by side with the settled clans. Long ago they had lost their links with them. The church was able to control many clansmen, but not the ancient Tinker bands who were constantly on the move, and who had a set of religious beliefs which in some aspects were older than even Christianity itself. They were living peacefully and were following their wandering lifestyle as their ancestors had done. It was these hardy men whom Wade and his generals press-ganged, armed and ordered to submit to the rules of the English army.

A few gentlemen were given the command of this regiment with a solemn promise that they and their men would never have to serve outside the Highlands. Their sole purpose was to keep law and order there. The historians describe this military police force as being a fine mixture of gentleman farmers or the sons of landowners, with ghillies or servants to carry their baggage and attend them when they were in camp. My research, however, indicates that most of the men had no such pedigree and whenever they moved across the Highland area their wives and children went with them. I have seen paintings of their officers as grand figures sporting the feather of a gentleman in their caps. It is assumed by many that they were landed gentry, but realistically, which noblemen in the Highlands would have sat upon a white charger and taken the King's shilling? To do so would have been suicide. The clans would have burned their homes to the ground and killed every living family member. In fact, it can be shown that many of the early Black Watch members did not live inside houses, not even in the low-roofed barracks of the time.

They wore a tartan which was mostly black, green and blue, and a plaid was sufficient uniform for them. Not for the Black Watch the red coats of His Majesty's army proper. On the banks of the Tay, in the heart of Menzies country, they were mustered and embodied as the 43rd Regiment. In 1887 a handsome memorial to mark the event was erected on the Aberfeldy side of Wade's Bridge. The monument was supposed to stand at the muster point in a field at Boltachan on the Weem side, but because of flooding it was not possible to put it there. It's said that the regiment was based at Weem for 14 years. If this is the case then Tinkers from the Menzies family would have been likely to join up in large numbers.

The leaders of the army had been promised rich rewards in land and wealth if they could recruit new troops of such high standards as would please the King. He was more than impressed by the new regiment, as was another of royal blood, the Duke of Cumberland. The Duke, of course, would later bring the Highlanders' dreams of ruling their own country and uniting the clans to an abrupt and bloody end. He was later nicknamed the Butcher and his story has been detailed by every Scottish historian who has ever touched on the campaign which was brutally suppressed on Culloden Moor.

Wade's new Highland regiment was the talk of military circles in London. The King wanted to see the cream of his northern soldiery, and three lads were invited to London to show off their prowess in swordplay. Among them was a Tinker lad called Alexander Macdonald, who was the best swordsman of the three and a great representative of the new troops. However, it seems that the other two men, who had no Tinker blood, decided to end his life prematurely. History does not say how this was done, but on many a summer night the fate of the Tinker lad had become a matter for serious discussion in that district and further afield. It would be the subject of debate under starry skies around camp fires and in cottar houses too. I myself listened to two uncles re-enacting the conversation between the other two swordsmen.

'How can this vagabond set foot inside a king's palace?'

'Aye, man, the heilans will buckle unner the shame.'

'Will we put a stop to him, then?'

'Aye. At the next turn you take him awa frae the body o troops and mak certain the cut gans well intae the ribs.'

'Will he expect it?'

'Tinkers sleep wi yin ee open. Nae doubt he'll be watching for dirty work.'

'Well, man, is he deed?'

'As a Fiann warrior following his faithful hound ower a cliff!'

Anyway, the upshot was that the two bonny lads went to entertain King George and received a guinea for their display of the military arts, which included the wielding of the axe that had belonged to Alexander Macdonald. Tinker blacksmiths called that style of axe the Lochaber axe, and it was a typical example of their work. I remember playing at hide and seek in and around cup stones, barrows and old gravestones on the outskirts of Pitlochry. One flat stone with an eighteenth-century date on it had an engraving of a large axe, and in Moulin graveyard there are grave slabs displaying swords running the full length of the stone in memory of the old craft.

It seems that a curse was laid on whoever used Macdonald's Lochaber axe after his death, but that's another story. There is also the tale about the guinea handed by the two bonny lads themselves to the porter at the gates of St James Palace in London as a tip. Now why would they give away such a large sum of money? Did it hold the mark of blood?

———

In March 1743 the new regiment was assembled at Perth and ordered to march into England. This they were told, was so that they could be shown to the King. On 14 May, after reaching London, they were reviewed by the top brass and then the rumours began to fly. The Highlanders, who had been told they would never have to leave their home district, realised they had been brought south by trickery. They heard that the government suspected them of being Jacobite rebels and planned to ship them off to the American Plantations. Only death could be worse than that!

Three days after the review, two hundred of them decided that they had seen enough of England. At a quick Highland pace, keeping away from main roads and using the cover of woods wherever possible, they set off on a return journey, and for two days and nights there was no trace of them. An advertisement was published urging people to look out for them and by the evening of the second day they were traced to Northamptonshire. Surrounded by cavalry they laid down their arms. A few weeks later they were lined up to watch three of their number being shot as deserters. The sentence caused a wave of indignation and disgust throughout Scotland.

This causes me to ask why Wade, with the King's blessing, formed a regiment that was proving its worth and then lured them south in order to break them up as a fighting force? If they were Highland gentlemen as is claimed this would not have been possible, but Tinkers, which I think they were, could easily be disposed of. The traditional account just doesn't ring true with me.

After news of the very public shooting, any sons of the soil back in Scotland who might have been tempted to join the government forces disappeared overnight into the mists of moorland and mountain. The disruption of their ancient clan ways added to the number of homeless wanderers who were to become Tinkers in later centuries. Two years after the mutiny of the Black Watch the King sent his own son, the Duke of Cumberland, to invade the Highlands and end the clan system on Culloden Moor. It seems to me that the plan to destroy the clans was long in the making and lay behind the way the Black Watch were treated. Wade may have built many good roads in Scotland, but here he was guilty of an act of treachery. He would no doubt say he was simply following orders.

It seems that many of the men who took part in the flight from London were indeed transported to the Americas. MacDonalds, Macgregors, Stewarts, McClellans, Mackenzies and Campbells among many others were forced to leave their native soil. I've drawn a blank on what happened to them, although in the US their names pop up throughout the country showing their strength of spirit, which enabled them to survive and carry their stream into new lands.

One of the three deserters who were shot was named Private Farquhar Shaw (not a name from the Weem district but at one time common in Glen Sheil). His statue stands on the monument in Aberfeldy commemorating the founding of the Black Watch. A fine young fellow he was. But rather than honour him as a simple Scottish soldier, and I'm guessing he was just that, the monument shows him with a single feather in his bonnet, which signified that he was a gentleman.

The government presumably thought that the condemnation and execution for desertion of a gentleman, rather than a poor man, would have more effect back home in the Highlands and encourage the clans to toe the line under British rule, and so might have invented his aristocratic status. Of course, as history shows, this brutal act paved the way for rebellion and war instead. What I'd have done to be a fly on the wall of the tent of Wade and his generals when all this twisting and turning of policy was being devised.

23

TALES OF THE TINKER SOLDIERS

Whatever the truth about Farquhar Shaw, he was a powerful giant of a man and has traditionally been seen as a brave and heroic figure in the Highlands. Let's listen to a tale now about him, and Bran, his faithful long-haired hound.

In those days no man worth his salt was without his bloodhound when traversing the wild and lonely mountains of Coe and Rannoch Moor. There was a fierce lightning storm on the night when Farquhar and Bran set off to hunt down a group of cateran cattle thieves. As the storm grew wild, lashing them with a nightmarish ferocity, he and Bran sought shelter in an old brokendown house.

In no time the soldier had built a fire and soon a welcome warmth filled the draughty abode. A piece of venison he had brought in his pack was cooking gently. Exhausted, while waiting for it to cook, he rolled his plaidy around both himself and his hound, and within minutes had nodded off.

He began to dream a strange dream in which he and two others were held captive, with their arms bound, in front of a gigantic castle with many turrets. On their backs they carried black coffins, and he and and the two others, whose faces were covered, began walking.

He wakened from this dream of death to see an old dwarf-like woman sitting warming herself at his fire. Bran was growling from the pit of his stomach.

'Shut yer hound or pit him oot intae the storm. He needs the temper knocked oot o' him – a blast or twa o' whirly win' up his erse would take the sting oot frae him.' Without another word, the hag reached into the fire, grabbed the searing hot venison and swallowed it whole.

Farquhar, taken aback at the sight of such a creature shouted, 'What manner of woman eats burning hot meat and is wandering about the moor on such a night?'

'Yer dream, Farquhar, I have come tae tell ye whit it means.'

'Who are you, woman?'

She stood up and changed from a tiny wee woman into a great lanky demon, with blazing red eyes and fanged teeth. The creature leaned over and stared down at Farquhar, while Bran continued to growl and bare his teeth.

'Yer dream was o' the great and mighty castle o' the south. There shall be mony Dhu men there, and I see for all but three a sea voyage from which they shall not return. I see wailing o' the weapon makers, Atholl's bairns shall burn under the sun of distant lands, and mony waste to death like the kinshin o' the mist. The saying is, "Early rising on a Monday gives a sound sleep on a Tuesday".'

With that, half the wall of the ruined house crashed down as the demon flew into the storm, screeching and screaming. Bran leapt after her. In the pitch dark, Farquhar was powerless to help as his faithful friend fought the demon. Suddenly everything went quiet as the wind dropped and a ghostly mist whirled around his feet. Then, with a bloodcurdling scream, out of the mist came his poor dog, torn, battered and disembowelled. Falling at his feet, with its last breath it licked his hand.

Now, as I've already pointed out, Farquhar Shaw was indeed murdered by the English, along with the brothers Macpherson. Eyewitness reports state that the three men were forced to carry their coffins, which had been painted black, along the streets of London until they were standing outside the Tower of London with its many turrets. As already described, they were shot as deserters there at first light the next morning, while the rest of the Black Watch mutineers were shipped off to work on the American plantations.

The Black Watch, regardless of the turmoil of its early years and the allegations of betrayal, raised its standard for many years to come, right up to the recent lowering of the colours and disbanding of the regiment at the dawn of the new millennium. The 'Tinkers Regiment' founded all those years ago in Weem, has its proud badge on many a cross and stone in graveyards where countless thousands of Scottish soldiers lie sleeping, having given the final sacrifice in battle. My father was in the Black Watch, and hundreds of Tinker lads like him fought and many died for their country. To them it was their regiment, and contained the best pipers and soldiers auld Scotia ever produced.

He would have been so proud of the landslide of TV, radio and media coverage of the disbanding of the Red Hackle and his beloved Black Watch; not so pleased with the faceless bureaucrats who decided on the streamlining of our fighting forces.

The tales of the regiment that Tinker folk have shared with me in the past about their ancestors who served with it would fill many books – and maybe one day . . . One thing that is clear is that no prouder soldiers ever died for their country than those without recognised roots, and what I cannot understand is, why were they never given credit and due gratitude for being part of the true story of Scotland?

> Your roots entwine the yew,
> Soft voices of the few;
> Scotia's hidden shame,
> Heaven's gentle rain;
> Soldier, will we see your face again?

A footnote to this is that I have in my possession several pages of the parish of Weem's baptismal records. Listed among hundreds of births there are a large number of Tinkers, hawkers, and pipers. Of these, the commonest names are Macgregor, Stewart, Macphee, Robertson, Campbell, Cameron and Mackenzie. If you happen to visit the Black Watch museum at Balhousie Castle, Perth, you will find that these names feature more than any others. I have been researching into Tinker folk for over 20 years and seldom does a military historian use his pen to acknowledge their contribution.

Before we move on here's a true story of Tinker sacrifice in war along the lines of the Hollywood film, *Saving Private Ryan*, starring Tom Hanks. This highly popular, award-winning film, was based on the case of a mother who, during the Second World War, had three sons enlisted in action at the same time. After two of her boys were killed, the US army went searching for the third son, intent on withdrawing him from action because for the mother to lose another child would be too much for her to take; a sacrifice beyond the call of duty of any parent. What I share with you now is a story of the British army during the First World War, when the military had no such tender sentiments.

The widowed Mrs Newlands of Orkney had three proud sons when the First World War broke out: John, Andrew and Isaac. For many years they worked in a small quarry near Moan at Harray, breaking stones for the roads. (Isaac, while working as a roadman at a quarry in Stenness, found a prehistoric burial site which is described on the Kirkwall British Legion website.) The brothers enlisted together at Fort George, Inverness-shire, and were initially recruited into the Royal Scots Fusiliers. Isaac had the regimental number 29766, John was 29767, and Andrew was 29768. It would appear that they were later transferred to the 6th Btn. (Morayshire) Seaforth Highlanders 51st (Highland) Division. Isaac became S/17856 in the 3rd Battalion, John became S/17857 in the 1st/6th Battalion and Andrew became S/17858 in the 6th Battalion.

Isaac was killed in action on 21 March 1918, aged 26 years, and is buried in the Bancourt British Cemetery, plot 1, Row G, Grave 4. This cemetery is in the Pas-de-Calais, two miles east of Bapaume. Andrew was also reported to have died of wounds on 21 March 1918, aged 32 years. His body has not been located and he is commemorated on the Arras Memorial, Bay 8. John was seriously injured on the same day, but survived and went on to die in action on 21 July 1918 and is buried in La Neuville-aux-Larris Military Cemetery, in the Marne region, Row A, Grave 29. The MOD Army Medal Office records that each brother was awarded the British War Medal and the Victory Medal.

It was common practice at that time to keep members of the same family together on the battlefields. It was considered that you would be less likely to desert or retreat if it meant leaving your own kin behind. The brothers were together in a machine-gun party and it would appear that, together with other similar units, they had been placed in front of the main front line to absorb the initial impact of the German attack. There were no officers with the units and they were given no instructions about when or if to retreat.

There was no saving Privates John, Andrew and Isaac Newlands; their mother's tears were not considered worth noticing by the Generals who were in charge of the slaughter.

Back home on Orkney, she and her family were not forgotten as waves of sympathy surrounded them, and on 31 October 1920, her brave soldier laddies' names were included on a newly erected war memorial designed in the form of an obelisk, which stands in Harray Churchyard.

While we're on the subject of war, in Dumbarton at the riverside church, where I was speaking on the travelling culture, an elderly lady of 90-plus years shared a piece of her family history with me. Her name was Annie.

'My dad worked in education and one of his duties was to visit with the Tinker folk who lived around Dumbarton. The war broke out, ye see, and every man was needed to fight for his country. When he was away visiting the Tinkers, he telt them that their menfolk should enlist in the municipal hall at a certain date and time. "Aye lad," said old Mr MacPhee, who had a fair few sons, "ah'll mak sure the boys will be there, dinna you worry about onything on that score."

'Well, Jess,' said Annie, continuing, 'the officers at the hall laughed and telt him that thon bloody Tinkers wid be pullin foxes oot o' their dens and bidin there until the war's ower. But my father, well, he believed in the Tinkers and defended them by saying, "Och no, man, I ken them folk, and when they say they'll be here, then you'd dae weel tae believe it." Now it was nearin time and there wasn't a sign o' the Tinkers. My Dad kept saying, "Just wait an' see, they'll be here." But as the hour approached, everybody said, "Thon tinks will no be seen until the end o' the war." Da stood on the steps for ages staring up the street, when suddenly his heart leapt. "Come here, you lot, and see this." There, coming doon the main street, pipers blawing their herts oot came marching – no just auld MacPhee and his boys, but every single tinker for miles around. My father counted over seventy! I don't know who survived or didn't, but I do know that one of those brave lads was awarded the Victoria Cross.'

I am so grateful to the Annies of Scotland, and I can assure you, reader, there are hundreds of them.

I'm away to refill my kettle, friends. It's a long road ahead, so why don't you do the same . . .

24

THE BATTLE OF KILLIECRANKIE

Here I would like to acknowledge John H. Dixon's valuable book, *Pitlochry Past and Present* (1925) in which I was able to find this description of the battle, almost identical to the ones I heard as a child.

The battle of Killiecrankie was fought on a hillside above Urrard, four miles from Pitlochry. The date was 27 July, 1689. It was a major battle between Viscount Dundee, better known as Claverhouse, commanding the army of the exiled King James II of England and VII of Scotland, and General MacKay, leading the forces of William and Mary, who had been invited to occupy the English throne.

The Marquis of Atholl and his eldest son had given their allegiance to William and Mary, but Patrick Stuart of Ballechin had seized Blair Castle, seat of the Marquis, on behalf of King James's army. Claverhouse, hearing of MacKay's advance and fearing to lose Blair Castle, made a hurried march from Lochaber before all the forces he expected to join him had arrived. When he reached the Castle, he had only two thousand infantry, about forty horse and three hundred Irish soldiers. General MacKay reached Perth on 25 July. The next day he marched to Dunkeld and bivouacked there. He sent forward two hundred hand-picked fusiliers to reinforce Athol's men who were guarding the pass. Next morning he left Dunkeld and reached Moulin before mid-day. He halted his army for two hours on the old road which is now the highest part of the Pitlochry golf course. Having ascertained that the pass was still open, he marched his forces with their baggage through the pass.

By the side of the path in the pass about a furlong above Garry Bridge is a well, called to this day 'The Trooper's Well'. Here the first blood was drawn. Ian Ban Beag Mac-rath (little fair John Macrae), a famous Atholl hunter, had kept pace alongside General MacKay's advancing army, but on the south side of the Garry, till they came to the Narrow Pass where he was within easy shot-distance of the enemy. He had only one bullet, so he took careful aim at a cavalry officer who fell dead by the well.

Mackay marched forward to the low ground beyond Killiecrankie station and below Urrard House. There he saw Claverhouse and his Highlanders coming over the hill to the north east of Urrard and only a quarter of a mile off, so he marched his forces forward and formed a line of battle with his right wing on the farm of Ochilmore above Urrard and his left wing on the knolls above Aldclune. His forces consisted of about four thousand, three hundred infantry and a hundred cavalry, and they had three small leather cannons. Claverhouse had halted a little above MacKay's army. The three leather cannon were used against Claverhouse, but with little effect, though some chroniclers say that several Highlanders were killed. The afternoon sun was in their eyes and Claverhouse restrained his little army until half an hour before sunset. The Highlanders then threw away their plaids and charged down the hill. They were met with a heavy fire as they came near the Government forces, but nothing could stop them. They kept back their own fire till they were close to their enemies, when they emptied their guns and pistols before discarding them and rushing on with their swords.

The upper wing of MacKay's army was almost annihilated and the centre was so badly cut up that the men turned and fled to lower ground. The left wing, being beyond the limit of Claverhouse's main attack, suffered the least, so General MacKay, with what little was left of his forces marched down to the Garry, forded it and fled during the night by Glenfincastle and Strathtummel to Weem.

Claverhouse, while riding into battle, was fatally wounded in the left side and fell off his horse into the arms of the Highlanders. Later he was buried in Old Blair church. Mackay lost two thousand, five hundred men and Claverhouse between seven and eight hundred. Many of the leading officers who fell along with their men were buried on the field of battle. Unaware of the turn of events, a lowland sentry stationed at the Pass of Killiecrankie was shaken to the core on hearing a battle-cry of a party of Highlanders racing towards him. With no visible escape route the terrified lad ran like a hare into

A Tinker mother and child – a newspaper photograph from the 1950s, but a timeless image.

The gravestone of the famous Gypsy chief Billy Marshall of Galloway, whose exploits were handed down in legend.

'The Tinker Widow'. Left alone in the world without a husband to support her and her children, she faces a dark fate, but holds her head high.

One of the many rich traditions of Travellers and Gypsies—the coronation of the Gypsy King, Charles Faa Blythe, down in Yetholm in the Borders.
Robert Dawson

Coronation of the Queen of the Gypsies at Yetholm.

Tinkers at Pitlochry in 1899, painted from the life by Edith Drummond Hay.

A vardo, or horsedrawn caravan, more typical of English Gypsies, is hauled through thick snow.

The Good Samaritan, by W. Small. A doctor examines a sick child in a Tinkers' camp as the family look on anxiously. *Leicester Museums*

LINDSAY'S CAVE, COVESEA, ELGINSHIRE.

Tinkers camped in a cave in Elgin.

Building a Tinker camp: this sequence of pictures shows the process.

My father's Aunt Jenny, a hard-working Gypsy mother hawking her handcrafted wares to farmhouses and rural cottages.

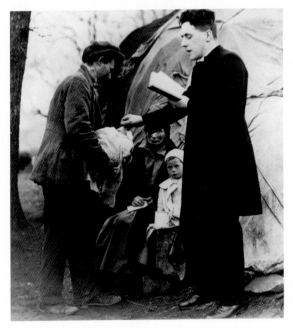

A minister, the Reverend Dr Hunter, baptising a Tinker baby.

Travellers moving camp, carrying the tent's ribs and covering with them.
Robert Dawson

A typical camp of Highland Travellers at Pitlochry. *Robert Dawson*

One of the Mars Training Ships by the Tay Bridge, where many young Tinkers were sent after being taken from their families.

Balnaguard on the banks of the Tay, where generations of Travellers camped. The area was surrounded by prehistoric remains, like this Pictish barrow.

Every year these nineteenth-century Travellers would head for Blairgowrie and the berry-picking, just as my family did. *Maurice Fleming*

Travelling show people with their performing dogs and monkey. This photograph was gifted to me by John Blackwood of Doune. He has no information about who these Travellers were.

Granny and Hughie at the roadside. This picture was gifted to me by a Comrie resident. Notice the bagpipes on the cart.

A travelling knife-grinder, his cart brightly painted.

* A GIPSY MULTIPLICATION TABLE.

Births of Children.	Mar- riages.	Births of Grand-chil- dren.	1												
1822, Oct. 1.	1842	1843, Jul.	1	2											
1824, Jan. 1.	1844	1844, Oct.	1	1	3										
1825, Apl. 1.	1845	1846, Jan.	1	1	1	4									
1826, Jul. 1.	1846	1847, Ap.	1	1	1	1	5								
1827, Oct. 1.	1847	1848, Jul.	1	1	1	1	1	6							
1829, Jan. 1.	1849	1849, Oct.	1	1	1	1	1	1	7						
1830, Apl. 1.	1850	1851, Jan.	1	1	1	1	1	1	1	8					
1831, Jul. 1.	1851	1852, Ap.	1	1	1	1	1	1	1	1	9				
1832, Oct. 1.	1852	1853, Jul.	1	1	1	1	1	1	1	1	1	10			
1834, Jan. 1.	1854	1854, Oct.	1	1	1	1	1	1	1	1	1	1	11		
1835, Apl. 1.	1855	1856, Jan.	1	1	1	1	1	1	1	1	1	1	1	12	
1836, Jul. 1.	1856		..	..	..	..	..	..	..	..	..	..	..	..	Total.
12			11	10	9	8	7	6	5	4	3	2	1	0	78

The ugly face of racism. A nineteenth-century report includes a table to show that the hated tribe of Gypsies, if left to breed, will inevitably grow in numbers, until there are too many to control!

Source: FHL Film 0203559 GRO Ref Volume 525-2 EnumDist 2 Page 28

Ref no: 352694 | Census Place: Lismore & Appin, Argyll, Scotland | Hi

ROAD, STREET, ADDRESS &c.	GIVEN NAME	SURNAME	RELATION to Head	CONDITION as to Marriage	AGE	SEX	OCCUPATION	BIRTHPL
Dwelling: Portnacroish Camp	Alexander	MC ARTHUR	Head	Married	36	M	Tinsmith	Appin, Argyll Scotland
Dwelling: Portnacroish Camp	Archibald	MC ARTHUR	Son	N/A	5	M	Tinsmiths Son	Ballachulish, Argyll Scotland
Dwelling: Portnacroish Camp	Bridget	MC ARTHUR	Daughter	N/A	12	F	Tinsmiths Daur	Strathfillan, Perth Scotlar
Dwelling: Portnacroish Camp	Margaret	MC ARTHUR	Wife	Married	33	F		Morven, Argyll Scotland
Dwelling: Portnacroish Camp	Mary	MC ARTHUR	Daughter	N/A	8	F	Tinsmiths Daur	Tobermory, Argyll Scotlar
Dwelling: Portnacroish Camp	Peter	MC ARTHUR	Son	N/A	10	M	Tinsmiths Son	Appin, Argyll Scotland
Dwelling: Portnacroish Camp	Susan	MC ARTHUR	Daughter	N/A	3	F	Tinsmiths Daur	Oban, Argyll,

GRT GRAND PARENTS

1881 CENSUS

Later in the nineteenth century, my own great-grandparents are counted in the 1881 census.

A visit to the Tinkers' Heart in Argyllshire, a poignant and spiritual memorial for all of Scotland's Travelling people. Our campaign to have it listed as an ancient monument succeeded in 2015.

Tinkers' Children

THE Church is often blamed for lack of enterprise, for running always in the old ruts and being slow to experiment. The somewhat prosaic illustration which accompanies this little article represents an experiment. The building is a small school recently erected by the Home Board on the outskirts of Pitlochry, and is for tinkers' children. The cost of the building (£800) was provided by the Girls' Association, and the President, Miss Eva Robertson, performed the opening ceremony. Dr. John White, who presided at the meeting, formally handed over the use and management to the Perthshire Educational Committee.

The wandering gipsy folk are a strange and picturesque survival from the early nomadic days of civilisation. One would be sorry to see these dwellers in tents and lovers of the open road pass from our countryside. But the training of their children presents a problem that is not

ALDOUR SCHOOL, PITLOCHRY, FOR TINKERS' CHILDREN

easily solved. It has been found that as a rule they make better progress when taught by themselves and not alongside of children from a different environment. So this school has been provided for tinkers' children only. It is by nature of an experiment, and its progress will be followed with keen interest.

Article in a church magazine about the new school for Tinker children at Aldour.

SCHOOL FOR BAIRNS OF WANDERING FOLK

IN the Spring of the year Scotland's wandering folk take the road, with their jingling carts. You see the sun-tanned children round nomad fires near the main roads.

Where do these youngsters go in the Winter time? These pictures supply the answers.

The first school for the education of these young wanderers has been opened near Pitlochry. The pupils come from their Winter camps, pitched in sheltered places around Pitlochry, and struggle with the three " R.'s."

You see them at lessons in the newly-opened Aldour Special School, where, between 1st October and 31st March, they must register at least half the number of attendances required from children who go to school all year round.

According to their teacher, they are smart pupils—" quick in the uptak'." They are particularly interested in nature study and art, subjects which require the observant eye developed in their mode of life.

Note the ear-rings of the girl on the right.

Part of another newspaper piece from October 1938 about the 'Tinker School'.

R. S. BRYDON, M.A., Ph.D.,
Rector.

5th November, 1940

Telephone No. 72.

-6.NOV.1940

R. Martin Bates, Esq.,
Clerk to Education Committee,
County Offices,
PERTH.

Dear Mr. Bates,

Aldour School.

This morning another Mrs.
Riley came here to enrol her child. She
is living with her mother Mrs. Power in
a hut. As you decided yesterday that Mrs.
Power's child should attend Adlour School
I told Mrs. Riley to send her child there.
She refused, saying that she was looking
for a house, and that if she did not succeed
she would live with her father-in-law, a
householder whose children attend this
school. From what she said I began to
think that one reason for this Tinker
revolt may be the absence of any Air Raid
protection at Aldour. Adhesive fabric
on the windows might help.

Yours faithfully,

Letter from the Head of Pitlochry High School describing my mother's refusal to accept second-class education for her child at Aldour.

My father Charles Riley, the inspiration for this book.

their midst. Muskets fired indiscriminately, and he took a volley to his shoulder. His only hope of escape was to jump the deep narrow gorge of the River Garry or prepare to meet his maker. Well, as history reports, the youngster closed his eyes and leapt! Somehow he made it to the other side. 'The soldier's leap' has become a very famous tourist attraction, but I have no knowledge of anyone else attempting such a feat from that day to this.

The wounded soldier was found and nursed back to health by Janet and Eliza Macgregor, daughters of a Tinker widower, Alan Macgregor. They took the man into their cramped black lum house in the forest, where he lived for two years. Many years after this he met Alan Macgregor and informed him that he'd got a job with Marshal Wade working on the construction of roads.

I have included this account of the Battle of Killiekrankie, because on many a damp summer's evening, sitting round in a circle of eager listeners, I heard the complete story of the battle being told over and over again. And like fishermen's tales of the biggest salmon, with each re-telling the story was added to and embellished. Why was this? Because to Tinkers, every part of their history is important – it is their identity; and additions or modifications to a tale gave it life. Through story, song and verse, many a truth has been handed on. Usually those that are telling the stories have a direct connection with the events they describe.

I have many vivid memories of laddies who, after a wee dram or two, went on at great length about this famous conflict. One lad named Mackenzie swore blind his ancestor was a weaponer, who melted and formed the lead musket balls that whizzed through the air on that fateful day. The other lad was also a Mackenzie, which indicates to me that they were related, although they denied this. He, with hand on heart, swore his ancestor forged and sharpened the broadswords used by the soldiers. Whenever they got to the part about the Highlanders ripping off their plaids, both lads stood up and acted as though they were about to attack each other; when they got to discussing the actual slaughter, their anger turned to tears. The amount of turbulent emotion they were going through convinces me that their ancestors really were there, but didn't live to tell the tale. That would have been left to their grieving relatives. What this shows is the importance of the oral tradition and Scotland's sean-nachies or bards in capturing the spirit of earlier times. As Hamish

Henderson said of us, 'There are many musical branches to a tree, but the travelling people [Tinkers] are the roots.'

25
WAR MEMORIES

One night as we sat around our expertly constructed camp fire I listened with pride to my father talking briefly of his days as a soldier in the Second World War. As mentioned earlier, after he came home he had a problem with shrapnel wounds. This was more than a nuisance, because not only did he suffer bouts of excruciating pain, but a piece had penetrated his eardrum and left him deaf in his left ear. To be honest he didn't talk a lot about the actual conflict, apart from telling us about an officer who he didn't get on with. When they were advancing into Germany, this officer was killed by the enemy. He said it would have been good to meet the officer in civilian life and get to know him. He thought the theatre of war made some men act in abnormal ways, and the officer might have come across differently when they met as equals. Talking about his role as a soldier, he used to say, 'A fighting man is a weapon, an extension of his gun. Once he is injured he is no longer of any use to the army.' He felt this matter of fact attitude had always prevailed in the British Army.

He was one of the many British soldiers who saw the real horrors of war when, as part of a group entering Belsen concentration camp, he was accosted by what he described as a skeleton with a covering of flesh. This human being rummaged through his pack, took out a tin of bully beef and tried to open it with his teeth. He said the poor soul's face was almost sawed in half as he desperately tried to feed himself. I know that for years after that he had nightmares about the Hitler extermination camps. It's recorded that over 6 million people were annihilated by the Germans during the Holocaust, mainly Jews, and their suffering is well chronicled. Many museums, books and films describe the dreadful atrocity against the Jews, but by comparison, there is little recorded about the death of hundreds of thousands of Gypsies in the camps. This is seldom highlighted and the balance should be redressed, especially when children are taught about the Holocaust in schools. Part of the reason for the neglect is because though the names and addresses of the Jews in the camps was recorded by the Nazis, there was no such account taken of the Gypsies. European Gypsies call this time Porraimos, a Romany word meaning the Devouring.

Sitting in a small circle around the fire watching a bright late spring moon spread its glistening beams over an unusually quiet Tay water, our parents shared a memory from 1947, the year of the snow. An enemy as bitter as any foe attacked so devastatingly that year it closed down the entire British Isles. Mother Nature, with a Siberian breath, buried the land in so much snow that everywhere was paralysed, and gripped every person who ventured out with an icy hand. Old folks who had survived German bombings were discovered frozen solid in their beds. It seemed that Mother Nature had forgotten to close the gates of winter. When the snow at last stopped, the land remained frozen through seven weeks of chaos and disruption. Trains and buses were buried under 30-foot drifts. Cities, towns and villages were cut off from supplies of food and other essentials. Ships remained out at sea unable to enter ports; harbours were closed.

Rationing was reintroduced and even the humble potato, which had escaped wartime rationing, got the same treatment as every other item of food. The blizzards caused power cuts; five hours every day had to be survived without light, warmth and cooking. Newspapers, for once unable to carry out their mission of getting the news to the people, were silenced as the print-workers failed to reach the presses. An entire country shivered and prayed for an end to the freeze.

My sister Shirley remembered it well; she was seven years old and had to walk with my older sisters a full three miles from our Weem chalet to Breadalbane School. Tree branches hung over a narrow path between walls of drifted snow, blocking the daylight. She laughs at the memory of racing from the road end to the twin towers of Wade's Bridge. Even Farquhar Shaw, the stone soldier, was more like a giant snowman than a monument.

When at last the return of the sun brought forth a thaw, faces frowned and folks living along the banks of the Tay held their breath.

Those hardy folk of the area feared that the melt would bring a flood that would shake the holy resolve of Noah. And indeed it did! But eventually the waters subsided. One season turned into another, and as I came into the world the country all around was praying that the snow queen would not return.

26

BALNAGUARD

Balnaguard on the banks of the Tay was a winter camping green for generations of Tinkers. At that time it was a small hamlet close to where the Tay meets the Tummel and was only reachable by ferry or by rolling up your trouser legs and crossing the river at the village of Grandtully. This is not a problem today, because there's a fine road to almost every house and farm in the district. Nevertheless, during heavy rainfall, the village can find itself cut off until the water subsides. In the old days, where everyone had an old rowing boat, I'm told they now have 4x4 vehicles.

The River Tummel's meandering is cut short at Grandtully as it loses its regal independence and gargles angrily into the mighty Tay. Many of my relatives were born in this area. My father had a habit of shouting to us as we passed the meeting point of the rivers, 'Are you a Tay or a Tummel bairn?' And we'd all call back, 'Nae way are we the Tay weans; we hae Tummel in oor veins.' In other words our hearts lay with our forebears who chose to settle on greens among Pitlochry's standing stones by the quiet River Tummel. Scattered in secret places along its banks and wooded places lie many relatives who were not accepted for burial in a sanctified ground until recent years. When the church at last opened its heart and allowed burials, the designated place in the graveyard was a narrow strip called the 'Paupers' line'. This was usually located out of sight of graveyard visitors down next to the end of the wall, as this was all that church officials would spare for such use.

I'm told that the wee bowdie legged queen, Victoria, preferred the Tummel to the Tay. Beyond Pitlochry there's a very famous beauty spot known as 'The Queen's View' (not named after Victoria but Queen Mary), before which unfolds a panorama which, once seen, can never be forgotten.

Even so, it has to be admitted that the Tay is Scotland's longest and most powerful body of water, and all the other rivers, including the Tummel, Earn, Almond and Garry, are really tributaries of the great river. She winds her way through Perth and on to the town which is named after her, Dundee (Fort of Tatha), before making her grand entrance on the east into the North Sea.

One day, as the bus engine ticked over quietly, we were waiting outside a bonny wee house, in the village of Balnaguard, to see the farmer to ask his permission to camp in his ground for a few days. We had been sitting for ages, and my father, who was obviously becoming impatient, thought he'd share a wee tale with his brood before we got restless. He turned in his driver's seat to face us and explained why we were waiting to speak to the farmer before parking our bus. He told us that when he was a young lad he had witnessed the drowning of an entire family who were camped between Balnaguard and the neighbouring village of Dalguise. In a flash the water rose to such furious heights that they didn't stand a chance.

He'd often warn us not to go near the river during heavy rain. I can't remember ever being in our bus on that low marshland but it didn't seem a problem on the opposite bank, where the land rises higher and allows for a swift escape. Our green near Balnaguard was always behind the village and not in front of it.

Yet again, and you must be fed up hearing me repeat this description, the green was surrounded with standing stones, pictish barrows and even cross-stones, cup-stones and much more. My mother even tied her washing line between two of the highest trees on the Balnaguard Pictish barrow. On folding her laundry she'd stroke it gently and say, 'Ye can tell the auld yins breathed on my washing; it's as soft as butterfly wings.'

The Caird

My tinsmith from Lochgilphead who said, 'Don't call me a Tinker, I'm a Caird,' left me chasing an elusive butterfly – who was the Caird? I spent hours searching through documents and books without finding anything. I was beginning to think no such people existed, when I discovered in an old dictionary that a Caird was a Scottish Gypsy. Later this was confirmed by a section in an 1894 book, *The Scottish Gypsies under the Stewarts* by David MacRitchie, who writes: 'The genuine Gypsy, the swarthy, fortune-telling Romany of our fairs and race-courses is unmistakeable; but the term " Gypsy" has been and still is loosely applied to many people of fair complexion, who cannot speak a word of Romanes, and whose chief claim to be so designated is that they lead a wandering, unsettled life. These latter are also known by various other names; of which the most popular in Scotland are tinker or tinkler,—and, in earlier times, caird,—as also horner, mugger (i.e., potter), and faw,—these last terms being more specially limited to the Border districts.' I followed this useful information up on the internet, and was able to verify the tinsmith's statement as fact.

Now that I knew what a Caird was, could I find out their history? There just wasn't anything firm to go on, so I sent out feelers. Lo and behold, much to my astonishment, a parcel fell through my letterbox one morning. Courtesy of a Mr Jim Caird, it was like manna from heaven to me. It was two rare publications by Dr Alexander Caird called *Caird the Surname* and *Caird the Clan*. I'd been referred to Jim by a lady who was related to the Caird family – isn't life just simply wonderful when out of the blue comes gold?

I must thank both from the bottom of my heart, because this generous gift is a valuable resource and one that has helped me find the answers to many questions that I might never have found on my own. Scotland's Travellers owe you a lot.

Let's take a look inside this revealing book.

According to the author, Caird was a surname in Scotland long before Gypsies came to the country in the sixteenth century. It is a Gaelic name which is mentioned in numerous books, in which Cairds are erroneously described as strolling merchants and wandering friars, 'noisily entering village market squares by striking a kettle, demanding princely sums for cheap merchandise'.

Did the Cairds belong to a clan? In 1913, the author of the book put the question to several highly qualified historians. Among them was John MacNeill, B.A., a professor of early and mediaeval Irish history, and also the Duke of Argyll, whose archive of clan history and old census records is held in the private library at Inveraray Castle, and includes a substantial collection of interesting writings regarding Cairds.

The Duke responded:

'For a northern Scot to trace his name he can only go as far back as his clan. For the origin of the surname Caird, there is no evidence. Yet in every town and house there were skilled hands working their crafts in metals, either precious or not.

The Sinclairs (English) of the west of Scotland (Islay and Argyll) are called in Gaelic 'clann-na-Cearda; children of the craft, or craftsmen. Records and documents of the fifteenth and sixteenth century abound with the name M'Nacaird (Glenlochy, 1590), M'Necaird and M'Nokard (*Black Book of Taymouth* 1594, 1561), M'Nakard (1688–1733). In Islay and Argyll generally, it still exists as mac-na-Cearda, and is anglicised by the Norman name of Sinclair. It is to the Irish rather than the Scottish we must look for the first establishment of the growth of the clan, the patriarchal system, and the hereditary head. The very name Scots is Irish or Erse, and Ireland was Scotia or the land of the Scots – the Erinach.

Prior to this the clan system was in full force in Ireland. There must have been constant journeying between Erin and Caledonia before the movement of any multitude from across the narrow sea took place. At a very early period, the Scots (Celts) of the western shores of Britain went to Ireland. Before the commencement of the fifth century the Scots gave their name to the whole of Ireland. Igbernia, which we call Scotland, is surrounded on every side by the ocean – A.D. 850.'

Professor McNeill provides the following information:

'This is how the Irish records of families in Scotland stands: down to about A.D. 700 the Irish Annals contain fairly abundant particulars about affairs in Scotland, but only the affairs of Kings, the struggle among the Scots, Picts, Britons and Angles. After 700, they say little about Scotland. There must have been a large migration of Irishmen, gentles and commons to Scotland in the earlier times, and, but for the severance I have mentioned, we might expect that many noble pedigrees, besides those of the chief ruling family, would have been written in Ireland, as happened in the case of Irish pedigrees. Cerd means a skilled craft, and secondarily a craftsman. Mac-na-Cerda comes from it. The oldest Irish surnames in Mac and Ua (O) originate in the tenth century. There was, however, an older phase of surnames which became obsolete about A.D.700. The last dated instance is about 692. These were formed from the old tribe names. There was an ancient tribe in Ireland named CERD-RIGE. The ending -rige means kingdom or the folk governed by a king, and the element preceding -rige is normally the ancestral name of a tribe or place after some person or craft, trade. Cerd-rige would thus mean descendants of an ancestor named Cerd.

The origin of such names is in every known instance prehistoric. The Cerdraige folk were located in S.W. Ireland, and though the name Cerd is taken as their ancestral name, there is good evidence that they were really the Cerd folk, i.e. a race of hereditary craftsmen. In the *Yellow Book of Lecan* it is stated that the King of Munster who reigned in Castel was supplied with Cerda (blacksmiths) and umaige (bronze smiths) by the Cerdraige.

Amongst the ancient Irish a master craftsman ranked with nobility and a Cerd was a name of honour. In Rome the craftsmen were mostly slaves. In modern Gaelic (Irish and Scottish) Cerd has been largely replaced by the soar, a "craftsman". Bur soar (old Irish – soer) primarily means a noble, and is also used to mean a "freeman".'

My belief is that this ties in with the information from my Lochgilphead Tinker. In the Bible, goldsmiths and silversmiths are listed as being the earliest crafts: see for instance *Acts* 19, verses 24 and 38. In Gaelic 'ceard-airgid' is a silver craftsman or professional worker in silver. If those early craftsmen who were slaves of the Romans were deserted by their masters and enslaved by the Picts in turn, is it not likely that some of them were granted their freedom or bought it, went on to form a community and left the country? There is evidence that the Cerdraige appeared in Ireland around the fourth century. The Romans left Scotland around the mid-fourth century, which would be about the time the Cerdraige set forth for Ireland. Other historical accounts say the Cerdraige formed the kingdom of Tara and were great rulers of parts of the country for centuries.

At the nearest point there are a mere twelve miles of sea, give or take a mile, between Ireland and Scotland, and it was easy for people to move back and forth. The Caird of old could choose at a whim to be a trader in one country or the other. Some of our Cairds who were introduced to Britain as Roman slaves would rise in society and grow in status. Those who were not so fortunate would live as wanderers as their forefathers did, living as close to the land as possible. This would mean that there were Caird traders long before the clans were formed.

In later times, were those early century craft-slaves, who I believe bought their freedom from their masters, already marrying into different sects of old Scotia and forming their own clans? The to-ing and fro-ing between Ireland and Scotland over the years will have elevated some of them from being just dark-skinned workers in metal who once lived in tents in the desert to illustrious merchants; they evolved and progressed. It is known that the Cerdraige did in fact hire out craftsmen to work for others, acting as a kind of job centre of old. Freemen employed fee-d men.

Forbes of Culloden describes the clan system as follows: 'A highland clan is a set of men bearing the same surname. In each clan there are several subaltern tribes, who owed dependence to their own immediate chieftain, but all agree in owing allegiance to the supreme chief of the clan or kindred, and look upon it to be their duty to support him in all adventures.' Dr Skene adds: 'While the clan, viewed as a single community, consisted of the chief and kinsmen and depended on individuals of the same blood bearing the same name, septs of native men, but not claiming the same links to the chieftain's bloodline, were probably descended from the more ancient occupiers of the soil, or broken men from other clans and of a greater age.'

Just as my tinsmith related in our original conversation, I can see the exact same clan system among the nomadic tribes of today who roam the desert regions of North Africa and live in tents.

Some writers say that after the clan system in the Highlands was broken up, the tinker cairds were given sanctuary by what remained of the clans but according to Sheila Stewart, the eminent Scottish author, singer and folklorist, it was the other way round. The Highlanders, deprived of home and protection by the shattering of the clans were forced to take on the mantle of the tinker and live as they did. My belief, given the evidence of how closely linked the clans and the tinkers were, is that it's hard to imagine one without the other. Through historical circumstances, whether of upheaval through wars or intermarrying, the fates of clan-members and Tinkers would have been intertwined. Perhaps this was why, both before and after Culloden, the King and his authorities wielded such a heavy sword against the clan system and the Gaelic language. Nowhere else in Britain was the destruction of a way of life and a language carried out more thoroughly than in the Highlands of Scotland. The native tongues of the Irish, Welsh and those on the Isle of Man were allowed to continue unhindered and I have been unable to find out the reason for this.

A friend of the culture who has traced many lineages of Tinkers in the north says, 'No doubt at one period Cairds were makers of armour and ornaments to more than one clan in the West Highlands.' This is echoed by the *Glasgow Weekly Mail* in 1915: 'Travelling artificers, tinkers,' it says, 'probably are the first tradesmen found in the Highlands.'

28

CAIRDS, TINKERS AND SINCLAIRS

When in 1786 Robert Burns was invited by gentlemen in Edinburgh to write a poem in honour of the Highland Society, he was not amused. This was a group formed in London to hunt down 500 Highlanders who, wishing to escape their lives of virtual slavery on the estates of Lord Glengarry, were trying to escape to Canada and freedom and were hiding in the forests and caves of Glen Garry. Burns, whose lineage came from the Highlands, was so incensed by this attempted enslavement of innocent people, already hounded from their homes, that he wrote the poem in the voice of Beelzebub, in other words, the Devil, to Lord Glengarry. In his furious satire, Beelzebub thoroughly approves of the noble lord's vicious and degrading treatment of his tenants – it is truly devilish!

Here are the final verses:

> An' if the wives an' dirty brats
> Come thiggin at your doors an' yetts,
> Flaffin wi' duds, an' grey wi' beas',
> Frightin away your ducks an' geese;
> Get out a horsewhip or a jowler,
> The langest thong, the fiercest growler,
> An' gar the tatter'd gypsies pack
> Wi' a' their bastards on their back!
> Go on, my Lord! I lang to meet you,
> An' in my house at hame to greet you;
> Wi' common lords ye shanna mingle,
> The benmost neuk beside the ingle,

At my right han' assigned your seat,
'Tween Herod's hip an' Polycrate:
Or if you on your station tarrow,
Between Almagro and Pizarro,
A seat, I'm sure ye're well deservin't;
An' till ye come – your humble servant,
Beelzebub, Hell.

In his famous *Jolly Beggars*, featuring a fight between a fiddler and a Tinker over a beggar woman, the Bard describes his Tinker as a Caird. Here are a couple of verses:

My bonnie lass, I work in brass,
A tinkler is my station.
I've travelled round all Christian ground
In this my occupation.
I've ta'en the gold, I've been enrolled
In many a noble squadron
But vain they searched, when off I marched
To go and clout the caudron.

As it turns out, the Tinker gets the girl, not the fiddler.

The Caird prevailed – the unblushing fair
In his embraces sunk,
Partly wi' love o'ercome sae sair,
And partly she was drunk.

The Duke of Argyll noted how important the Gaelic chieftains' hereditary office bearers like the Seannachies, or bards, were to the clan.

'The Seannachie kept the records of the hereditary distinction of those at all levels of society, from the King to the lowest knave. Nothing must be lost to memory, and memory must continually be refreshed. At births, weddings, deaths and festivals, the descent of the King or the chief from famous ancestors must be "repeated over and over again." [Here we see the importance of 'balladeers', like those the great travelling families, the Stewarts of Blairgowrie, and the O'Rileys from Ireland, stem from.]

There is mention of Cairds in other old Scottish histories. Robertson of Atholl once said to his Tinker, after a fierce fight in which many were slain, "Well done, little Caird." Mrs. S. Robertson Matheson, a historian of Clan Robertson wrote: "Alistair M'Coll [a Robertson] slew nineteen foes at Inverlochy. Montrose referred to M'Coll as 'Little Tinker'. Montrose wished all Atholl men had that day been Tinkers." After this incident, Robertsons were sometimes called the Tinkers of Atholl.

The small clan of Caird apparently lived in relative security under the banner of the Argyll Campbells. In the records of the Parish Register of Inver and Glenaray, and Argyll Testaments and inventories (1653–1752) the name Kaird (with various spellings) appears just under 200 times. My source and other authentic records inform me that, along with Macalister, Macarthur, Macnab and Macnaughton, and others, the Cairds carried the Campbell banner onto battlefields and skirmishes with other clans.

The different spellings and pronunciations of names add to the confusion about clan relationships. To reach the Highlands before there were proper roads (before the Wade roads were constructed), communication from the south was geographically easier through Buchan and Moray to the east end of Glenmore. This was the route by which the language of the south reached the lonely western glens, and as is well documented the southerners did not bother to pronounce Gaelic names with any accuracy. What has now been kept is the English translation of names, and sadly we have lost forever the old and true pronunciations. For instance Malnroichs became Munroes, and Macnokairds was anglicised to Sinclair. In the Inveraray Parish Registers to about 1720, there are plenty of entries for Macnokairds, but no Sinclairs. After 1720, numerous Sinclairs appear while the name Macnokaird vanishes. Today the Sinclairs are a well recognised clan with their own crest and tartan.

After Agricola's campaign in Scotland, the Romans sent a fleet to sail round Britain and apparently conquered Orkney.

The late fourth-century writer Eutropius penned a piece claiming that this had happened which historians refused to believe. But lately the claim seems more credible because at the broch of Gurness, fragments of Roman jars have been discovered. Was this Roman invasion the time tinkers first arrived in the far north? These ancient craftsmen may have been the forefathers of the noble Earls of Orkney, the Sinclairs. It is more than a coincidence that the northern clans of Caithness, e.g. the Gunns, Wilsons and Mackays, to name a few, are also common names among Tinkers.

Curiously I find that, after the Reformation, the Sinclairs of Orkney went to great lengths to establish that they were not Tinkers but rather descendants of the Norsemen. "No Romans or their slaves ever came here," I was told by a staunch Orcadian who added, "yes, we had our Tinkers and proud people they were, but they are indigenous to the islands."

There is no mention in the histories that Cairds or those of that name were Egyptian in origin, and I feel that this may have been because of the dominance of Christianity in Scotland. Those from an alien culture would have wanted to conceal the fact.

In a few books I find indications that Tinkers spoke a language similar to Hebrew. In the *Domestic Annals* it is recorded that when James I and VI arrived at Holyrood Palace to celebrate his 51st birthday, at the gates a young lad called Andrew Kerr "did sing him a song in his ain Hebrew tongue."

There are some grounds for believing that the Hebrides on Scotland's west coast have a secret history which the ancestors of the present islanders concealed. Many inhabitants of the islands refused to observe the Sabbath on Sunday, clinging instead to the Saturday as the day of worship and rest. Why was this so important in those places? Some believe the name Hebrides is itself taken from the word Hebrew.

I have also read that the ancient Irish Cerds were faithful to a religion much older than Christianity. Their God was Jacob, and their two main teachings were that you should have nothing in excess and that you should know yourself!

Throughout the tumultuous history of the Scottish clan system I can recognise a struggle on the part of the Cairds and

Sinclairs to be recognised, not as craftsmen of slave origin, but as loyal Highlanders on the one hand and fair-haired Vikings on the other.

There is a story of a great battle in which many Sinclairs and Cairds stood side by side as one clan. This was the Battle of Muckairn, named after the hill where it took place. Muckairn means the place of the Phucks (fairies) – they were known as this in Shakespeare's time, which is why he named his character Puck. Many lives were lost in this battle and it is said only two men were left standing; both were called John.

One John was of Gaelic origin and referred to as the Erse. The other John was from Caithness and had his own language. At the end, as both Johns stood together in the dead of night, an evil fairy whispered in the ear of one of the Johns, "Cut the Erse from him," meaning to remove his tongue, "and I'll show you where a pot of gold is buried." A knife was slipped into his hand, and in a moment the deed was done! Immediately the Phuck jumped upon the shoulder of the other John, who was now dumb, and said, "Kill him and I'll show you where a pot of gold is buried."

But this lad recognised that the wee imp was playing evil tricks on them, so he grabbed him by the throat and strangled him. He then rolled the dead Phuck in his plaid and threw him into a fast-flowing river. The other John, thinking that he was going to lose the promised gold, jumped in after him and was drowned. The dumb John died of blood loss. From that day of battle there were no survivors.'

In Alexander Caird's book he takes great pains to write about the Cairds who rose to high positions in the professions and society. They achieved great things in whatever line of work they chose, whether it was medicine, law, education, engineering, bridge-building, church ministry etc. The list of Caird and Sinclair high-achievers is extremely long. Could this be because they are descended from the elite of Rome's smiths and craftsmen who were taken all over the Roman empire? I know of thousands of people from the modern day Travelling community who have risen to greatness from humble beginnings in the same way.

Finally, here is a footnote to the story of the Cairds which Travellers Donna Whyte and Hamish Jupp shared with me.

Around the early eleventh century, Caird craftsmen formed a group and bought a stretch of land which they called Kincardine, their 'new lands'. They had various surnames – Robertson, Stewart, Whyte, Marshall, MacPhee among others – and were collectively known as the clans of the Newlands. Sometime after they had settled on the land, fighting broke out between them. Many left and reverted back to their original clan names. Those left behind continued to feud. Some bought out of the 'Newlands' deal and were referred to in cant as the Cala agus magi, meaning dark and mysterious (in Gaelic, dorcha agus cunnartach), and also as the Red Landless Newlands, or Seventh Clan. Another group turned to the Church for protection and were called the White Newlands. They were given more land by the Church and built Lauriston Castle as their seat. Somewhere in the Northern Isles stands a gravestone with an inscription on it: James Newlands – Tinker – killed in a brawl. He may have been a member of the Seventh Clan, 'dark and mysterious'.

A complete history of the Landless Newlands and their journeys through Scotland would be fascinating, but apart from the oral tradition from my informants, it has vanished. At every turn my research into it has drawn blanks. Donna and Hamish proudly added that the clans of Kincardine played the bagpipes. Their shoulder-clasp was a silver thistle, the emblem of their land, since the Latin for thistle is Cardus.

29
GYPSIES

I know that historians state unequivocally that Gypsies originally came from India; linguistically this has been proven beyond doubt. I would not dream of going against such a distinguished group of scholars, but after sixty years living the culture, I feel that I must disagree with their conclusions to some point. It seems to me that a nearer place of origin for Tinkers and Gypsies is Egypt.

The Egyptian word for clan or family is *makhaut* which in Irish appears as Maccu and in Scotland as Macca. Mac, meaning family of, prefixed the name of the head of the clan; for example, as in MacDonald, MacGregor, MacIntosh etc.

Just as Rome brought her highly skilled craftsmen back as slaves from whichever country she had conquered, so had Alexander the Great before them. If tribes and nations are to be conquered then it makes sense for the conquerer to seize the best of their resources and their best workers must be enslaved. In those ancient times Egypt produced the elite of craftsmen. This is shown in the majestic masonry of the Pyramids, the ornate golden statues, in the carving of the Sphinx, in the wares of the merchants; all have stood the test of time. A visit to the ancient history department of Cairo Museum will confirm this. This was a great prize to fall into the hands of the country's conquerors.

The word Egypt itself conjures up the mysteries of a time without history. The Greeks called her 'Chemia' and thought of her as the source of wisdom, wherein lies the answers to all the mysteries of alchemy. It was believed that Egyptians knew the appearance of the Gods and that the Gods chose Egypt from all the countries of the earth to smelt precious metals and pour molten gold and silver into casts to make their images so that mortal men might look upon the infinite beauty of their heavenly rulers. Another gift given to Egypt was the secret of building castles and mighty burial mounds for the earth gods, where they could rest when they had reached the end of their mortal paths. The Sphinx, the resting lion with the head of a man, is supposed to represent the 'watcher of the horizon', Horus, the son of God. Egyptians believed Horus was the sun, and his name means both light of the world and he of the horizon. The Roman emperor Constantine is supposed to have taken the virgin birth story from Egypt when he had the New Testament transcribed, replacing Horus with Jesus and Isis with Mary and the twelve astronomical heavenly guides by the disciples. The Sphinx was believed to represent the binding together of all life forces, both human and animal. Gypsies from the south of England told me that the tribal enemies of Egypt feared the Sphinx, naming it the 'Father of Terror'. They thought that while the man's head slept during the night the lion's body hunted. During the daylight the spirit within opened its eyes to look upon the horizon, and sent desert storms and plagues to punish those which it didn't like. These ancient beliefs gave rise to the very popular gypsy names of Heron, Hawron and Horn.

Barry is a word used by Travellers, Gypsies and Romanies meaning good; I use it myself daily. I'm not alone in thinking it originates in Egypt from the word meaning a mode of transport. The first Gypsies were not only travelling merchants and nomadic tribes, they were also masters of the seas and rivers. Flat-bottomed boats from Egypt are called baris, and this becomes barge in English. And yes, there are bargee Gypsies throughout the canal systems of the British Isles. So when we say barry, I think we are referring to a solid hull without weakness; a barry thing.

One very strong superstition among Gypsies is fear of a bird with red and gold wings. The commonest bird with these colours is the Peacock. I've seen women refuse to set foot inside a caravan if there is the slightest sign of the bird and its colours, either on fabrics or upholstery or on dishes in a display cabinet. This relates to the Egyptian myth of the Binyat bird or the Phoenix. Every 500 years, the Binyat bird would fly out of Arabia, spreading its mighty wings of red and gold plumage on its way to bury its father in the Egyptian city of Helipolis. The Binyat bird's beloved father was so precious that his body was wrapped in an egg of myrrh, then placed in the temple of the sun. The flight of the Binyat bird comes after global terrors like wars, pestilence and famines, and coincides with a rare solar association. The father of the Binyat bird's rising from the ashes signifies a war in heaven between the god of the sun and the god of peacocks.

Welsh gypsies call a Pigeon an 'ompe', ancient Egyptians called it the Aly-n-pt, 'bird of Heaven'. These are all pointers to the origin of Gypsies in the Middle East and not India. I could go on and mention other things that connect Egypt to Gypsies – bull-fighting, belly-dancing, veil-dancing, Arabian horsemanship, gladiatorial skills (bare-knuckle boxing), wrestling, Moorish dancers, dog-racing and snake-charming, to name a few. And to what, if not Egypt, do we owe the word 'caravan' to? For centuries, trains of horses and camels laden with all manner of merchandise travelled over all the lands of North Africa taking metalwork of gold, tin, copper and brass, as well as silks and precious gems, to the waiting kings and queens and their peoples in far-off lands, all anxious to acquire the wares of the travelling merchant. When 30,000 Gypsies and Travellers converge on the tiny Cumbrian town of Appleby each year to immerse their horses in the waters of the River Eden, they are re-enacting the same custom of their ancient Egyptian forebears who would baptise their own ships of the desert in Mother Nile before embarking on a journey that might be beset with sandstorms, thieves and roving lions.

The ancient Egyptian word for 'man' is pi-rome, pi meaning the and rome meaning man, and the word also means nobleman. I wonder if the word has any connection to the name Roma?

My father's pedigree was derived from Ireland and Scotland, but he sometimes wondered if he was connected to Gypsies in earlier times. I remember how black his hair was and the sallow hue of his skin must have come from some place other than Scotland. Even in winter my father's colouring remained darkish.

As Andrew Sinclair notes in the following extract from his book, for a period in history protection was afforded by the authorities to travelling craftsmen. After this, however, when the Gypsy from the south ventured among the wild men of the north, seemingly he was not welcome. Why this was so may simply be down to clannish mistrust of strangers. Whatever the reason, writers varied between calling Tinkers Gypsies and vice-versa. This made my research into eighteenth and nineteenth century accounts very difficult as it has been difficult to distinguish between Scottish Tinkers and Gypsies from down south. One thing which early writers didn't mince their words about, and I'm sorry to say they seemed to relish it, was the ill-treatment of Gypsies – there were witch-burnings, hangings, they were punished for causing plagues, there was an endless list. They were scapegoats for society's ills.

If Tinkers had it bad, then their suffering was minor in comparison to the inhumane treatment meted out to the Gypsy. Never in the history of man's inhumanity to his fellow man was his bestiality more evident than when the Gypsy set foot on British soil. It was on a par with Hitler's slaughtering of over a million Gypsies without keeping any record of their names or identities. My father could go into the doldrums and not speak a word to a living soul for weeks after having an argument with some ignorant person on this subject.

If we could for a moment forget the propaganda of the establishment that has led to the prevailing derogatory attitude towards Tinkers, we should ask ourselves this question: 'How much does this land owe to those ancient metal workers and craftsmen?

This is the subject of a chapter devoted to Tinkers and Gypsy craftsmen in Andrew Sinclair's fascinating book, *Rosslyn: The Story of Rosslyn Chapel and the True Story behind the Da Vinci Code*. He relates everything to weaponry. At the forefront of the change when one culture has given way to another, there has been the development of weapons. The Greeks and the Romans recognised how they had won their empires. It was not just brought about by the fighters, but by those who had made their arms. That is the key question of the past, which is seldom asked and hardly ever answered. Who forged the warrior's sword? Just as the fighter pilots of the Battle of Britain could not fly without the ground crews and mechanics repairing their battered Spitfires and Hurricanes, so the Knights Templar, who were known as the men 'of the trowel and the sword', could not continue their interminable skirmishes and sieges without the support of their armourers and metalworkers. In Palestine, they were totally dependent for their weapons and castle building upon Semitic and Arabic craftsmen, and at the time, the Saracen sword was superior to the Frankish broadsword. After their expulsion from the Holy Land, the Templar would have taken their armourers with them, as the

Roman legions once had. These craftsmen would become known as Romanies or Egyptians or Gypsies. They were accustomed to a vagrant life with a cart and a forge, as camp followers at the back of an army. Without them, the military could not sustain a campaign.

The smiths and tinkers with these vital skills came to Scotland with the Knights Templar, and ended up under their protection. The path of those Templars who fled to Scotland was recorded in gravestones near Loch Awe in Argyll, which charted their progress from the Western Isles to Lothian. In Muckairn churchyard there was a tomb carved with a piece of the staff of a cross, on which a sword was incised. At Taynuilt, a gravestone was carved with a crusading sword, surrounded by leaping thistles and dogs and a hare, while another showed a battle-axe and a Lombard Sword, as on the monument to William of St Clair at Rosslyn.

Andrew Sinclair writes:

'The most telling evidence of the arrival of the Near Eastern armourers at Loch Awe lies in their clan name. They were known as the Mac Nocairds. In medieval times, Muslim ironworkers and doctors and dancers were called Moors or Saracens. An Arabic inscription on a Grail tombstone testifies to their presence at Corstorphine church. Excluded from Spain, a troupe in 1491 received from King James IV the sum of twenty unicorns for dancing the Moorish or Morris dance, later a staple of folklore. And before the arrival of the first recorded Egyptians in Scotland at Leith in 1504, along with the illustrious Faa family, vagabond metal craftsmen already travelled the land.'

These craftsmen were Irish tinklers with their Shelta language and the Highland Cairds with their vocabulary based on Gaelic – e.g. 'pan' for frying pan and 'pal' for friend.

In contrast to other historians, Mr Sinclair thinks there is another side to the highly documented treatment of the Gypsy as an undesirable creature who should be killed on sight.

'When King James V became the special patron of the wanderers, it was not out of a romantic interest in their nomadic lifestyle, even if the ballad of the Gaberlunzie Man is to be believed, in which he disguises himself as a blue-cloaked bard and beggar. During his reign he was re-arming Scotland against an English assault, and he needed to favour the makers of armour and weapons. The Lord High Treasurer referred to the migrants in 1505, "to the egyptianis be the Kingis command" while their leader Gaginus, Lord of Little Egypt, was given safe conduct to the King of Denmark. His successor Johnnie Faa was granted an even more remarkable position in 1540. Under the great seal, all the Sheriffs and Baillies were bidden to assist the Lord of little Egypt to govern his people and collect his dues. The reason why the kings of Scotland extended this extraordinary protection to the Scottish gypsies and tinkers was their important role in the armaments industry, under their protection by the Lords of Roslyn. From the time of Robert the Bruce, the St Clairs had been recognised as the protectors of the early smiths and masons. Yet at Rosslyn they were also the guardians of the royal family and its holy treasures in Edinburgh. They could not have fulfilled their role without an intense interest in weaponry and those who made the weapons. They were chief patrons of the metal-working travellers who tended to follow the armies.

Although their role is disputed by modern historians, it is proven by one of the few manuscripts to survive the sacking of Rosslyn library after the Reformation. Commissioned by the Earl William St Clair in 1488, the thousand pages written in longhand are the earliest surviving examples of Scottish prose. They contain Guild Laws and Forest Laws and "the Laws and Custumis of ye shippiss". The Earl was then dealing extensively with the craft masons working on Rosslyn chapel, also the carpenters and hammermen or iron-workers, who were constructing a Scots navy on the firth of Forth. He had to have authority over their disputes, if he was to protect the Crown by land and sea.

The patronage of the wandering Near Eastern iron workers helped the St Clairs to be the suppliers of arms for the defence of the realm. With the white monks of Newbattle, they had been working on the coal seams near Dalkieth since the latter part of the twelfth century, also establishing foundries nearby in Lothian and Fife. They held all the necessary resources to become makers of weapons. And through their control of the guilds, they could use the Romanies among the armourers of Scotland.

The leading metal workers were gypsy families, who took the name Smith – based on the mythical Wayland Smith, who had made the weapons of the gods of old.'

What I think is happening here is that in addition to the Cairds who remained attached to the clan system, many smiths and metal-workers spread out into the south and beyond.

I hope I have shared enough evidence gathered from the works of these professional historians to paint a picture of the movements through the early centuries of the ancient metalworkers and smiths leading onto the Gypsies and Tinkers. I saw that the thread which linked them all together was their craft skills. I'm also of the belief that the majority renounced their links with old Egypt, settled, formed guilds and became prestigious in whatever community they lived. Their guilds had a voice and established themselves in society. In this position they took on apprentices, so the skills were soon being handed along a line of workers who were not of the Tinker bloodlines. In time the workers from the east would pass on, leaving future generations with no knowledge of their forefathers. Those who chose to remain nomadic and carry their tools around with them would in time be seen as different to the craftsmen of settled society and become a form of pariah, as they have often been labelled.

In the 16th century it was the Church that held the reins of government and laws would not be made without Church approval. When damning laws against Gypsies were passed it was through the auspices of the Church, and it was through the Church that anti-Gypsy propaganda was spread.

In Tudor England 'vagrant craftsmen' were outlawed. This did not extend to Scotland until after the Protestant Reformation of the sixteenth century. The Catholic Church was in danger of an-nihilation, and she needed all the strength at her disposal to stop her churches being demolished and holy artefacts dating back centuries from being smashed to pieces by marauding soldiers and religious fanatics. Unable to protect herself, it is understandable that she couldn't offer protection to Gypsies or to any others under threat of the new enlightenment, by means of which a set of lies about the Gypsy people was being spread. Overnight they changed from being peaceful wanderers, working their crafts, to dark-cloaked night-creeping bogeymen, who stole children, practised witchcraft, were filthy vagrants and had no allegiance to Christian values. How could this propaganda be believed? I expect in those days, without telephones and news media, people could be led to believe almost anything. Ignorance and fear would make close-knit communities receptive to horror stories and hostile when strangers arrived in their midst. A typical example of this attitude is this so-called lullaby which used to be sung to children.

'Hush ye, hush ye, dinnae fret ye; the black tinkler winna get ye.'

I think there were theologians whose sole task was to sit at a desk and write the most awful inhumane lies about the Gypsy/Travelling people wherever they were to be found. The passage of time only seemed to make things worse. Nations throughout the western world held these same hateful attitudes to Gypsies, which makes one despair of human nature.

30

GYPSY SLAVERY

Following Cumberland's destruction of the Jacobite forces at Culloden in 1746, laws to eradicate the Highland clans once and for all were hastily forced through parliament. These laws saw the wearing of tartan forbidden, Gaelic banned and mass clan gatherings outlawed. Under the Saxon yoke, the proud men of Argyllshire, Macgregors' people of the mist, Macdonalds and Macphees, smiled no more. The next generation of Highlanders would not be able to rebuild their shattered homeland; it was left to the rich gentry and the shooting of the deer. Once more the conquering army created slaves. The Romans of old who came and stole the British Isles for their mighty Empire left in their wake a people who would one day follow in their footsteps. Britain would call itself 'great' and conquer lesser nations for its own empire.

The British empire-builders looked towards America, a place of magnitude beyond anything the Romans had taken over. There was gold, oil, land, perfect weather and plains on which to sow thousands of acres of wheat and to breed millions of cattle. It had its own natives, of course, native Americans, but once the colonisers were armed with the right propaganda they'd be dealt with in the same way as the old clansmen, along with the Cairds and Tinkers of Scotland. Those who had been oppressed in Britain now became the oppressors.

There are plenty of books in libraries telling of the ships laden with spices, tea, coffee and human cargo which sailed between Europe, Africa, the Caribbean and America. The horror stories of enslaved Africans sent in shackles in crowded ships to work on plantations for greedy British merchants until they dropped are well known.

What has been up to now a hidden history is that before one single black man set foot on American shores, Gypsies were already dying in their hundreds working on the plantations. The government of the day didn't see Gypsies as individuals with rights or feelings, and when labour was needed, they, along with thousands of prisoners, were sent abroad in chains. Gypsy men who were enslaved left behind women and children whose fate I cannot write about because it is unknown. John Bunyan, author of *The Pilgrim's Progress*, which in its day was referred to as the second Bible, was the son of a Tinker. While in prison for his beliefs, Bunyan referred to his ancestors as the 'cursed and chained ones'.

I expect that the widespread and forcible removal of gypsies from the shores of Britain to the West Indies and America was covered up. My friend Robert Dawson is what we call 'a wee burro mole'. In other words, he is like a mole smelling a worm – if he gets on the trail of something he'll keep on tunnelling until he has found what he is looking for. Hunting for a few scanty documents from county to county, was sometimes soul-destroying, and he met one brick wall after another. But as I say, a burro mole never gives in. So he transferred his search across the Atlantic, and there had more luck.

Among the Creoles of Afro-Caribbean descent he found that many words were Anglo-Romani (English-Gypsy dialect) and cant. This demonstrated that Gypsies and African slaves were kept in close proximity. Also several of the Eastern seaboard Native Americans used the Anglo-Romani language along with their own. They told tales of Gypsies who joined their tribes and lived their ways. Sheila Stewart tells a similar story of meeting a Native American chief who could speak cant in her autobiography *A Traveller's Life*. There is also a claim that the Mandan Indians spoke a form of Welsh. Carolina Indians used a strange form of Irish Gaelic in their speech.

In Andrew McCormick's 1907 book *Tinkler Gypsies*, he describes links between North American Indians and Scottish Gypsies (Tinklers). One Christmas he was invited to listen to three Gypsy girls singing beautiful songs called *Navaho* and *Idaho*. McCormick goes on to say, 'There are lot of striking similarities between Indians, Red Indians in America and the Gypsy.' For example, Billy Marshall, the famous eighteenth century King of the Gypsies, was said to wear around his wrist the skins of lamprey eels, which is commonly done in India and also by Native Americans.

Let's now look at some of Robert's findings, in quotes from his book *Empty Lands*.

'The official books on slavery make no mention of all the slavery of British Gypsies. It was, presumably, either too little known or not significant set against the wholesale slavery of peoples from Africa. In much the same way, the holocaust has tended to be seen as a Jewish event because of the vast numbers murdered, whilst the number of Gypsies killed was probably no more than 20% and perhaps fewer, and therefore seems to be numerically not very significant when set against the Jewish disaster. Only in very recent years has this balance begun to be redressed.

Slavery of British Gypsies is therefore even more problematic, as the number of these peoples taken as slaves to the Americas probably never exceeded a few hundred over 150 years. Many more non-gypsies were taken and even they have been forgotten. The difference – as with the horrors of Gypsy extermination in the holocaust – is that while numbers were relatively small, the percentage of Gypsies thus affected was, in both cases, high.

Indeed at best the official slave histories make only passing references to Gypsies and then, so far as I can discover, only in the context that Gypsies "were occasionally slave traders" especially in Brazil, where they were in competition with Jews! (No evidence given and a nice bit of anti-Semitism from one of the official chroniclers here, combined with a bit of anti-gypsyism too.) The mass slavery of Gypsies in other countries is never mentioned, except in very special literature, yet vast numbers of Gypsies from Spain and Portugal were shipped in irons to their American colonies and even to Africa. So there is no hope in non-specialist texts that Britain's part with Gypsies is reported, and I would therefore like this to redress some of the balance.

In the seventeenth century slave trading was big business. Up to that point it was a privilege of European profiteers trading with the West Indies but after that British slave ships were sailing at full capacity. Black slaves were much more desired because they worked harder and were considered more resilient. British white slaves were mainly derived from poverty so were undernourished and weak. The truth was that death aboard ship was prevalent and costly.

The African was a triangular trade, in which British ships brought their human cargo from Africa, took them to the West Indies where they were sold, bought tobacco, cotton, sugar and rum with the blood money. These goods sold well in Britain and then back to Africa. The white slave trade was two-way, and in the first quarter of the eighteenth century very profitable. Merchants were paid to take prisoners to the Americas where they were exchanged for tobacco for sale in Britain. By now of course Gypsies were well established in Europe and had already entered into official slavery in several countries, especially Rumania, Spain, Portugal, Russia and Hungary. In England, slavery had not yet occurred, as in any case the existence of the Egyptians act provided a more permanent solution by hanging them. But an implied slavery certainly existed, in which children of the executed were taken as indentured apprentices by merchants and tradesmen, to be used as semi-official slaves. Clearly the triangular trade was efficient, but there was a cheaper way to get slaves and trade, and solve a growing crime problem due to poverty. Convicts could be sent direct from Britain to slave markets in the Americas. Criminal or political, off they went! Gypsies could be sent under any pretence because it was a crime simply to be one.

Legislation in England and Scotland designed to rid the country of Gypsies held its own warrant. What a cheap cargo. Another reason was that so many hangings were a drain on the public purse.

More women than men filled the slave ships. This had a sinister reason. The women were used for breeding with the black slave, especially in the Caribbean; to breed out the black skin and create a more acceptable slave. My belief is that this is how the Gypsy forebears of current day Afro-Caribbeans must mainly have occurred. In Barbados particularly, "young and full-breasted women" were preferred to any other. In Virginia, North and South Carolina, best prices were always paid for "breeding women" and "uncommonly good breeders". Overall, however, men outnumbered women 4 to 1 in convict transportations. Certainly, convict slaves were seen as no better than black or native Indians. A 1748 Virginian Statute banned these from testifying in court because "convicts as well as negroes, mulattos and Indians are commonly of such base and corrupt principles".'

Robert also describes the Acts of Parliament that were used against Gypsies:

'For slavery of Gypsies to occur during the time of Henry VIII (known among Tinkers as "shan Harry wha scourt the morts", in English, the evil king who destroyed females; a royal control freak with total power over women). Henry VIII's "An Act concerning Gypsies" (1530–31) ordered Gypsies to leave the realm within 16 days on pain of imprisonment (where few survived) and seizure of goods. The second such act was "For the punishment of vagabonds" (1547) which, whilst not mentioning Egyptians by name, states that previous acts had been unsuccessful. The act orders masters to take up any such vagabonds and bring them before the justices who would immediately arrange for the person to be branded with a "V" and they would be given to the master to hold the said slave for two years. The slave was fed on bread and water and put to work "however vile" and punished with chains and beatings. Escapees would additionally be branded with a letter "S". Escape a second time resulted in death. Children could be kept in slavery until the age of 24 (men) and women until aged 20. If parents or other relatives tried to rescue the children, they would be enslaved for the rest of their lives. Cities and towns had the power to seize vagabonds and sell them as slaves to masters, and this included any foreigners or people who falsely stated their place of birth.

Even although one Act followed on another's heels to hunt and kill the Gypsy, at long last slavery to all within the British Isles was officially abolished in 1772, and transportation to the Americas in 1775 as a result of the Revolution, but it continued to be legal for Britons to take slaves from Africa and transport them to the Caribbean/Americas. This was only four years before the Act of being a Gypsy punishable by death was itself repealed. Slavery was finally abolished in 1833, thanks to William Wilberforce and others.

When one door of evil closes another opens. Australian colonies awaited and little did the indigenous natives realise the fate that had been planned for them.'

———

Blues, soul, reggae and many other rhythmic forms of music have come down to us through the sufferings of African slaves brought by force into America and the Caribbean, but there is another, more modern style of music, that came from the descendants of the Gypsy slaves in America – rock and roll.

According to some experts, the term rock and roll comes from words used by sailors; rock is the fore and aft movement of the ship on the ocean, roll is the port and starboard motion. But surely it is stretching belief to think that a seafaring phrase should come into the homes of American youth 1950s and be transformed into a term meaning dance music and lyrics.

I have been given another explanation, though it has to be said it is one not accepted by Americans generally or by music historians. Rokker is Gypsy cant for talking, and roll is the word used when the caravans are on the move. The rokker songs of the Gypsies who lived in America during the fifties were very popular amongst the young. In cafés it was not uncommon to see teenagers from both the settled and the Gypsy cultures enjoying each other's company and 'rokking' together. This wasn't acceptable to the parents of the settled population, so they banned their kids from fraternising with the 'trailer trash'. It was always a relief to these parents to see the Gypsy 'rolling' his wheels and taking to the road in summertime as they usually did. It wasn't such a pleasure when they came back. It seemed to the Christian middle-class parents that their youngsters were being brainwashed by the rokker rollers, according to the scare stories.

But the tide could not be turned, especially when rock and roll began to take off and the mega-bucks began to mount up. From the birth of this music came a new voice which swept across America and out into a waiting world. Now, at the time everyone knew what the phrase rock and roll was referring to, but heaven forbid that the trailer trash be given the credit, so the story of rock and roll coming from a sailors' expression was invented and the truth was forgotten.

Traditional music among American Gypsies came originally from England, so folklorists came from the States to seek out the roots of the music and when they did so found that there was also a wealth of traditions from Scotland too. Alan Lomax was one such collector who spent years among the travelling Tinker folk of Britain, and like Hamish Henderson and Ewan McColl gathered a considerable amount of our root music and song.

The African-Americans who suffered under the yoke of slavery have had a public apology and have successfully progressed in society. Today America has a black president, a sign of true equality. In Britain there has been no such apology to Gypsies or any other wandering group. My father cursed successive governments for not addressing this. He said, many times, 'Those bastards have no soul.' He was, of course, referring to the entire establishment rather than particular politicians.

31

Next Stop on the Road

Back on the road now, where our next stop was Logerait, and it was there I had the pleasure of making a true Gypsy friend. Her name was Middie Lee and I loved her to bits. Never in all my days of travelling in our old bus had I enjoyed the company of such an intelligent friend. She was self-taught and had the keenest eye for nature, history, geography and anything else that took her fancy. With her fresh approach to people she would have made a brilliant teacher; and to tell the truth she could have done whatever her creative mind set itself to do. She was one of those unique people who seemed to shine on a dull day. I had never been so keen to wolf down my porridge and head on out as when I shared my days with Middie Lee.

We played all over the area, paddling in the Tay and then sitting on the hotel wall watching our toes turn from red to blue with the cold, before rubbing life into them and running off in bare feet. With her unusually long thick black plaited hair and yellow gold loop earrings, my dark-skinned friend was quite an eyeful. For that brief time we were simply two teenage lassies with the world at our feet.

Middie's people were horse folk who went annually to all the horse fairs in England. Her parents had not been that far north before, and after that summer we never saw them in Scotland again.

An only child, my friend had strange pets, two pigeons which she carried around in a cage. Every day she'd let them out, only to see them return within hours. She told me her ancestors had kept pigeons for hundreds of years. I've since learned from research that the Romans used the birds all the time as did most armies before more modern methods of communication.

Middie had a strange way about her when she'd open the cage and watch the birds stretch their wings ready to fly. She always kissed their wings and said, 'Safely back'. Then she would look at me and add, 'When I die, I'm coming back as one.'

I shared a tale with her about a Highlander who was assigned the duties of looking after the carrier pigeons during the Great War. Along with his friend, a tinker lad, he got into a bit of bother. One night, when the supply lorry hadn't managed to catch up with the troops, the Highlander wrung two of the birds' necks and then they cooked and ate them. Middie astonished me when she said, 'The buggers should have been shot.' However, when I told her the birds were already injured then she forgave the men.

An officer who came on them when they were eating the birds was not so forgiving. This officer was 'tipping the heights as a radgi gadji', in other words he had let the war get to him and was on the verge of going mad. He insisted that the pair be court-martialled come the morning, and sentenced them to be shot for killing His Majesty's birds. Another officer intervened at the last minute, or the two fellows would have been executed.

Our friendship ended abruptly when her mother took ill and the family had to go home to England.

Now, readers, you must be wondering why I have included this lovely lassie in a book about the Scottish travelling culture? Well, word reached me a couple of years later that she had been accidentally shot by a gamekeeper in Cumbria while waiting for her birds to return from a short flight. For obvious reasons this awful news affected me deeply.

So many gifted Gypsies never get to realise their dreams or get the chance to shine and make a contribution to the world in which they live. It was this thought that plunged me into a spiral of depression. My dreams of one day becoming a great writer or achieving anything in any form evaporated. I went deep into a black hole of depression. I began to feel a morbid fear of the settled people and their attitudes towards my kind. I felt utterly worthless.

To help me out, my sister Shirley wrote this beautiful song and sang it to me. It has been this song that has kept me going, reaching, sometimes blindly, for the realisation that every day is for living.

Don't Lose the Dream

Don't lose the dream,
Don't let it die,
Now that you've come this far,
Reach up and touch the sky.
For there are no answers
When hope has all gone,
Your dream hasn't vanished,
You've got to be strong.
Don't lose the dream,
Don't turn around,
Now that you've come this far,
You must tread upon new ground.
Your destiny beckons,
It's calling your name,
Endure to the finish,
Your quest's still the same.

Charlotte Munro (Shirley)

There's a graveyard at the top of the Logerait hill road where many Tinkers are buried. I think it's because there was a poorhouse in that vicinity which was their last port of call. I haven't got exact information as to why many of my relatives are buried there, I just know they are. If you visit, look out for their names – Johnstone, Riley and Stewart. There are many more and I just wish I knew their history. If my research into paupers' graves in small enclosures has any bearing, then it suggests that in Logerait, whereas locals were interred in the church graveyard, the hillside cemetery may have been set aside for the poor.

32
DESCRIPTIONS OF GYPSIES FROM THE PAST

In contrast to Andrew Sinclair's book in which metal-workers are given great status and respect, I'm now going to quote from other writers who go to the opposite extreme, and who go out of their way to describe the elusive and secretive Gypsy in negative and derogatory terms. It is almost as though they want to change history and leave their distorted version of it in book form as truth for ever more.

I have many books on Gypsies of this kind, from a wide range of authors and dates. Here are a few samples from my collection, beginning with William Chambers' 1821 book *Exploits and Anecdotes of the Scottish Gypsies*.

'Grellman, author of an 'inquiry concerning Gypsies' indicates Gypsies came originally from Hindustan. His reason for this, however, is a dubious one, and points to a similarity of language. He compares the Gypsies with the Pariahs, the lowest class of the Indians. He thought the cause of their emigration in 1408 and 1409 was the war of Timor Beg in India. All who made resistance to this evil conqueror were destroyed or were made slaves; of these slaves 100,000 were put to death. Universal panic spread across the region and a scattering of terrified Gypsies fled from India. This is not proven however. Salmon, the English geographer, endeavoured to prove Gypsies came from Egypt; although there is no historical documentation.

It is in the 15th century when they are first recorded in Britain under the assumed titles of Kings, Dukes, Counts and

Lords of Lesser Egypt. They entered Bohemia and Hungary from the east, travelling in numerous hordes, calling themselves Christian Pilgrims, who had been expelled from that country by the Saracens for their adherence to the true religion. They had the audacity to address some of the principal sovereigns of Europe, and even the Pope himself, for real pilgrims; and obtained, under the seals of these potentates, various privileges and passports, empowering them to travel through all Christian countries under their patronage for seven years. Having once gained this footing the Egyptian pilgrims took no time in establishing their territory and setting tribal footings across the land. They seem to have been legally protected by most of the European governments for the greater part of a century, and why this is the case I cannot say.

But with their different customs and living in a land where the enemy was never far off they were soon despised and loosely tolerated. Rumours ran wild of them being thieves, non religious and mostly undesirable. Severe measures were adopted by different states to expel them from their territories. Decrees of expulsion were issued against them by Spain in 1492, by the German empire in 1500, by France in 1561, with England taking harsher methods of expulsion. From this came a human fox-like existence and around this air of fear came stories of demons hiding in deep forests; ghostly spectres that haunted the unsuspecting innocent traveller who just happened to have the misfortune to cross paths while they danced with the devil himself.

Referred to across Europe as the Cingari, Zigeuners, Tziganys, Bohemiens, Gitanos or Gypsies, no matter where they are dispersed, they refused to change and remained a dark, deceitful, disorderly race, just as they were when their wandering hordes first emigrated from Egypt or from India. Warlockry, fortune telling, pilferers who could at the drop of a twig be up and gone in the wildest night.

As far as the pilfering Gypsy who first set foot on Scottish soil is concerned around the beginning of the sixteenth century we read of them being fairly treated by James V, who wrote a Privy Seal (1540) in favour of a Johnnie Faw, Lord and Earl of Little Egypt, in the execution of justice upon his company and folks, *conforming to the laws of Egypt,* and in punishing those who rebelled against him.

I don't know whether it was their cunningness to survive, or their skill of hands, but through time they mixed with many different sets of Scottish peoples, which in time led their Middle Eastern characteristics to diminish in favour of the fairer complexions of northern highlanders and their habits. They travelled in different bands, and had rules among themselves, by which each tribe was confined to its own district. The slightest invasion of the precincts which had been assigned to another tribe produced desperate skirmishes, in which there was often much blood shed.

Some rude handicrafts were entirely resigned to these itinerants, particularly the art of trencher-making, of manufacturing horn spoons, and the whole mystery of the Tinker. To these they added a petty trade in coarser sorts of earth ware. Such were their ostensible means of livelihood. Each tribe had usually some fixed place of rendezvous, which they occasionally occupied and considered as their standing camp, and in the vicinity of which they generally abstained from depredation. These tribes were, in short, the Pariahs of Scotland, living like wild Indians among European settlers, and like them, judged of rather by their own customs, habits, and opinions, than as if they had been members of the civilised part of the community. Some hordes of them yet remain, chiefly in such situations as afford a ready escape either into a waste country, or into another jurisdiction. Nor are the features of their character much softened. Their numbers, however, are so greatly diminished, that instead of one hundred thousands, as was calculated by Fletcher (about a hundred years ago) it would now be impossible to collect upwards of five hundred throughout all Scotland.'

After reading the above my heart almost stopped – 100,000 individuals reduced to 500 in the space of a century. Where did they go? Europe had decreed they were not welcome there, and their family groups were too close-knit for them to desert each other and join the settled community.

Was this genocide? Were they hunted down like foxes? Whenever they were seen, they were apprehended and hung or worse. Blamed for crimes they were innocent of, they were put to death without mercy. In the Great Britain of our forefathers it was an unquestioned belief that the Gypsies were below the sewer rats, unworthy of breath. Every unforeseen problem whether of plague or war, was thought to have been brought about by the Gypsy's curse and his evil eye.

In his introduction to the subject, Chambers affords very little in defence of the Gypsy. He had already decided that they were undesirable, subhuman. He had made no attempt to communicate with them. There is no mention of Gypsy babies, children, elderly or infirm. He doesn't touch on their home life or speak of their beliefs.

As I delve into the history of religious fervour in those days, I'm strongly led to the conclusion that the Gypsy was not discriminated against because of his criminality or his skin colour but because of his religion, which was different from that of the rest of society. The black-clothed gentry of the pulpit regarded Gypsies as being guilty of heathenism.

I feel this wasn't just a matter of them having no religion but rather relates to where they originally came from. Egypt was the land of the Pharaohs. The book of Exodus in the bible is one of the most important ones because it introduces the sacred laws known as the Ten Commandments. It also records a fantastic struggle between man and the elements, the establishing of the Jewish faith and the war between God and the Devil. In the end the chosen people come out of the fire refined and cleansed. It ends with God's people finding a country, Palestine, the land of milk and honey, replacing its previous inhabitants and settling there. It took a long time, 40 years to be exact, for the Jews to escape the captors who had enslaved them. According to the Bible, the Egyptians were the vilest people on earth. To save his chosen ones, God turned the Nile red with blood, the Angel of Death killed all first-born Egyptians, plagues of frogs and sores were rained down from heaven on the whole country – none were spared.

The persecuted Gypsies' fate was sealed – it was written in the Bible, so it was what God decreed. If he could kill the Egyptians and inflict a multitude of plagues on them, part the Red Sea to help his chosen people to escape and then close it to drown the Egyptians who were following them, then it was perfectly acceptable to kill those pestilent Gypsies, their descendents who shared their evil nature. What perfect anti-Gypsy propaganda!

In H. N. Hutchinson's 1856 book, *The Living Races of Mankind*, the same theory about the origins of Gypsies is found. This states, in reference to the Gaelic tongue:

'Gaelic descended from the lost tribe of Manasses, the Jewish tribe who refused to go into Canaan. Members of this tribe wandered into western Europe, eventually settling in Britain, Wales, Ireland and Scotland. Within the Bible we find yet another branch of this tree in Isaiah which states that God will cast the Egyptians into the hands of other nations and peoples, where they will suffer to be homeless and wander.'

The persecution of Gypsies had begun in earnest when an act was passed by the Privy Council in 1573 as follows:

'The commonweal of this realm was greatly damned and harmed through certain vagabond, idle, and counterfeit people of diver nations, Egyptians living on stealth and other unlawful means. These people were commanded to settle to fixed habitations and honest industry; otherwise it should be competent to seize and throw them into the nearest prison, when, if they could not give caution for a due obedience to this edict, were to be scoured throughout the town or parish, and so to be imprisoned and scoured from parish to parish, till they be utterly rendered forth from this realm.'

Little more than three years later (27 August 1576) it was declared that this act had failed to be executed – 'a very common misfortune to acts of council in those days' – and it was found that 'the said idle vagabonds has continued in their wicked and mischievous manner of living, committing murders, theft, and abusing the simple and ignorant people with sorcery and divination.' Men in authority were now warned to deal more strictly with these wanderers, or else be held as their accomplices.

Then came another law by which more Gypsies could be killed off. This was the statute under which all subsequent witch trials took place. On 4 June 1563 it was enacted that:

'No person must take upon hand to use any manner of witch-crafts, sorcery, or necromancy, nor give themselves forth to have any such craft or knowledge thereof, there through abusing the people; also, that no person seek any help, response, or consultation of any such users or abusers of witchcrafts . . . under the pain of death.'

The great protestant reformer, John Knox, was also busy sending Gypsies to their death. It is recorded that after hearing that Queen Mary had attended Mass in a chapel in the Highlands, he sent soldiers to capture as many of her unfortunate followers as they could and put them to death. They found many Gypsies – 'Egyptians' – there instead and killed them all.

It strikes me that John Knox was a most superstitious churchman; strange that a man of such faith should be so steeped in fear. Retribution for his harshness towards Gypsies waited for him, though, when at the age of 50 he married his second wife, Lord Ochiltree's daughter, Margaret Stewart, who was only 17 at the time. A Gypsy fortune-teller professed that she was present at the ceremony and spread a rumour that she had seen a black-cloaked apparition at the couple's side on the altar. This dark figure was the Devil, who had put into the lassie's head an image of her husband as a young and handsome man rather than the auld, decrepit creature he'd become. People had spoken in whispers of how strange it was that Knox's bride was besotted by him. His Papist enemies who, it is said, paid the Gypsy handsomely to spread this tale around, were soon telling everyone that the 'guid man o' God' was all the time in league with the de'il – his true master.

The Gypsy woman's sons were at the time awaiting hanging for petty crimes, but with the money she made from spreading the rumours about Knox she is supposed to have bribed the jailers to let them go free. Her family left the Peebles area to make a new life in England.

33
MORE STORIES FROM CHAMBERS

Before I finish with Chambers' historical outpourings there are a few snippets that are worth noting.

Sir Walter Scott's novel *Guy Mannering* contains one of the most well-known Gypsy characters in literature, Meg Merrilies. Though Scott did not divulge her identity, Chambers is adamant that Meg's character is based on that of the real-life Gypsy, Jean Gordon, and most readers at the time believed this. His description of Jean contains the following information.

Jean was born in 1670, somewhere in Roxburghshire, probably Kirk Yetholm. She was married to a Patrick Faa or Faw, a Gypsy chief of high degree. They had twelve children.

In May 1714, Patrick and eleven others found themselves facing an anti-gypsy judge at Jedburgh. He took no time in finding them guilty of wilful fire-raising, of being thieves, vagabonds, sorners, masterful beggars and whatever else he could name without taking a breath. Greenhead House in Roxburgh had been burnt down and only the Gypsies could have lit the flame.

The principal fire-raiser was named as Janet Stewart, who was sentenced to be scourged through the town, and afterwards to stand a quarter of an hour at the crossroads with her left ear nailed to a post. Patrick, and another six of his companions, were sentenced to be transported to the Queen's American plantations for life. Before Scotland parted with poor Paddy the locals enjoyed the spectacle of him being frog-marched through town, then horsewhipped and left to stand in agony for half an hour with his left ear nailed to a post. And for a further treat the onlookers could relish hearing his screams as his two ears were hacked off. Another Gypsy was banished, and three were acquitted.

In the same year, one of Jean's sons, named Alexander Faa, was murdered by another Gypsy named Robert Johnston. He escaped justice for nearly ten years until captured and brought before the court.

'In the evidence we find the following curious account of their savage transaction:

"John Henderson, feuar in Huntley wood, depones, that time and place libelled, Robert Johnston, and his father, came to Huntley wood and possessed themselves of a cot house belonging to the deponent, and that a little after, Alexander Faa, the defunct, came to the door of the said house, and desired they open the door: that the door was standing ajar, and the deponent saw Robert Johnston in the inside of the door with a fork (graip) in his hand. He pushed open the door and struck Alexander in the breast with the fork. Alexander staggered outside to a midden. The distance between the said midden and the house is about a penny stone cast. Before he died he called out, 'Run for your lives, for I have got my death.' The witness saw Robert Johnston come out of the cot house with fork in hand and say, he had sticked the dog, and he would stick the whelps too! He ran after the defunct's son with fork in hand into the house of George Carter. In a little while after he saw him running down a balk and a meadow; two hours later saw him on horseback riding away without his stockings or shoes, coat or cape.

Another witness swears that she heard Johnston say, 'Where are the whelps that I may kill them too?'

Johnston went into Carter's house searching for Alexander's son and found him beneath the bed, but before he could stick the bairn, the cries of those finding the defunct's dead body scared him off. Johnston was captured and sentenced to be hanged on 13th June 1727, but he escaped. Jean had her own plans for him. She followed him to Holland and from there to Ireland where she had him seized and brought back to Jedburgh. Revenge for Jean was sweet when she saw him hanged on the Gallow-hill."

Her cup, sad to say, was filled with heartache, for just as their father's killer had been hanged, her sons also suffered the same fate. They were not hanged for murder but at the whim of a half-wit judge who tried them for theft.

Jean was heard to scream out at the verdict, "Lord help the innocent in a day like this!"

Her own death was accompanied with circumstances of brutal outrage, and of which the poor lady was undeserving. Now Jean, among merits and demerits, was a staunch Jacobite. One day while attending Carlisle Market, soon after the Jacobite defeat at Culloden in 1746, she gave vent to her political partiality, to the great offence of the rabble of that city. A cry of condemnation rose and filled the air, and Jean was grabbed and ducked in the Eden. It took some time to drown the stout lady because she was a strong and tall woman. But before she succumbed to her murderers she managed to get her head above water and shout, "Charlie yet! Charlie yet!"

Jean possessed the same virtue of fidelity of Meg Merrilies, spoke the same language and in appearance there was little difference. However some believed that it was not her but her grand-daughter Madge on whom Sir Walter Scott modelled his heroine in *Guy Mannering*.'

Here are some more anecdotes from Mr Chambers.

'Selkirk-shire was at one time greatly celebrated for the Gypsies it contained. The Faas and Baileys were the two principal gangs which infested it. They used to traverse the country in bodies of from twenty to thirty in number, with their horses and ruddies, among whom were many stout, handsome and athletic men. They generally cleared the waters and burns of fish, the farmer's out-houses of eggs, and the lums of all superfluous and moveable stuff, such as hams, etc., that hung there for the purpose of resting. It was likewise well known that they never scrupled to kill a sheep occasionally, but they always managed matters so dexterously, that no one could ascertain from whom they were taken. These Gypsies were otherwise civil, full of humour and merriment, and the country people did not dislike them. They fought amongst themselves, but were seldom the aggressors in any dispute or quarrel with others. The following instance of their depravity may be depended on as authentic.

About a hundred years ago (1721) in the month of May, a gang of Gypsies came up Ettrick; one party lodged at a farm house called Scobcleugh, and the rest went forward to Cossarhill, another farm about a mile further on. Among the latter was one who played pipes and violin, delighting all that heard him; and the gang, principally on his account, were civilly treated. Next day the two parties again joined and proceeded westward in a body. There were about thirty souls in all, and they had about five horses. On a sloping grassy spot on the farm of Brokhoprig they halted to rest. Here the hapless musician quarrelled with another of the tribe about a girl, who was sister of the latter. Weapons were instantly drawn, and the piper losing courage or knowing that he was no match for his antagonist fled, the other pursuing close at his heels. For a full mile and a half they continued to strain most violently, the one running for life, the other thirsting for blood, until they came again to Cossarhill, the place they had left. The family were all gone out, either to the sheep or the peats, save one servant girl who was baking bread at a kitchen table when the piper rushed breathless into the house. She screamed and enquired, what was the matter?

He answered, "Nae skaith tae you – for God in heaven's sake hide me!" With that he essayed to hide himself behind a salt-barrel that stood in the corner. His ruthless pursuer instantly entering, his panting betrayed him; the ruffian pulled him out by the hair, dragged him into the middle of the floor, and ran him through the body with his dirk. The piper never asked for mercy but cursed the other as long as he had breath. The girl was struck motionless with horror, but the murderer told her never to heed or regard it, for no ill should happen to her. By the time the breath was well out of the body of the unfortunate musician, some more of the gang arrived, bringing with them a horse on which they carried back the body and buried it on the spot where they first quarrelled. His grave is marked by a stone at the head, and another at the foot which the gypsies placed themselves. The grave is looked upon by rustics as an eerie place to be on a stormy or misty night. Some say while passing the place even to this day they feel a sudden chill at hearing a lone piper play a melancholy lament. No one is seen, but it's a certainty there is the presence of something supernatural.

Another short tale in a similar vein relates to a murder committed at Lowriesden on Soutra hill by one Gypsy or another. It happened before many witnesses. They fought for a considerable time most furiously with their fists till one overpowered the other and drew his knife, then assisted by his wife despatched his opponent by repeatedly stabbing him in the chest. When he pulled out the weapon the blood sprung to the ceiling, where it remained as long as that house stood.

The story goes that the assassin fled but was pursued by Walter Scott, who at the time was a very young man, along with Mr Fairbairn, the Blackshiels Innkeeper. They were passing at the time of the murder, and shocked by the indifference of the bystanders, along with a blacksmith chased and apprehended the murderer, who was later tried and hanged.'

Another similar tale was one about the infamous William Faa I listened to many a summer night around a camp-fire.

Old Wull, round about the year of 1830, along with others of his clan, was deeply involved in the smuggling trade on the coast of Northumberland. They were engaged in this on a night as dark as the Earl o' Hell's waistcoat when suddenly a bloodcurdling scream rent the shadows; a company of dragoons on horseback were on every side, swords in the air. One cavalry lad was looking for Gypsy trophies and waving his weapon like a madman. William saw him bearing down on him and lifted up his only defence – a stick! With his wooden cudgel in his dexterous hand he set about the dragoon. But a weapon of wood was no match for solid metal. The horseman galloped round in circles, swinging and cutting at the stick, trying to put an end to Wull's defiant dancing and louping. Chunks of the stick went skywards until all that was left was a short stump. Wull was on foot and might have been split in two; the dragoon eventually cut his hand almost off. As William was taken prisoner, the bystanders heard him shout to the dragoon, 'You've spoiled a good fiddler!'

Wull Faa, the lineal descendant of John Faa, Lord and Earl of Little Egypt, who'd fought three battles with Young, between Dunse and Coldstream, died on 20 October 1847. The *Scotsman* newspaper paid a fitting tribute to the great man and here it is – a lament for Will Faa.

The Deceased King of Little Egypt

The daisy has faded, the yellow leaf drops;
The cold sky looks grey o'er the shrivelled tree tops;
And many around us, since summer's glad birth,
Have dropped like the old leaves, into the cold earth.
And one worth remembering hath gone to the home
Where the king and the Kaiser must both at last come,
The King of the Gypsies – the last of his name
Which in Scotland's old story is run on by fame.
The cold clod ne'er pressed down on a manlier breast
Than that of the old man now gone to his rest.
It is meet we remember him; never again
Will such foot as old Will's kick a ball ower the plain,
Or such hand as his, warm with the warmth of the soul,
Bid us welcome to Yetholm, to bicker and bowl.
Oh, the voice that could make the air tremble and ring
With the great-hearted gladness becoming a king,
Is silent, is silent; oh wail for the day
When Death took the Border King, brave Wullie away.
No dark Jeddart prison ever closed upon him
The last Lord of Egypt ne'er wore gyve on limb.
Though his grey locks were crownless, the light of his eye
Was kingly – his bearing majestic on high.
Though his hand held no sceptre, the stranger can tell
That the full bowl of welcome became it as well;
The fisher or rambler, by river or brae,
Ne'er from old Willie's hallan went empty away.
In the old house of Yetholm we've sat at the board,
The guest highly honoured, of Egypt's old Lord,
And marked his eyes glisten as often he'd told
Of his feats on the Border, his prowess of old.
It is meet when that dark eye in death has grown dim,
That we sing a last strain in remembrance of him.

The fame of the Gypsy has faded away
With the breath from the brave heart of gallant Will Faa.

I must say the *Scotsman* newspaper did the Gypsies proud with that poignant tribute. Gypsies and Tinkers all across the country had cuttings of the poem faithfully preserved in family albums and Bibles along with other precious keepsakes like wedding and birthday photos.

Here's another extract from Chambers.

'It was around 1780, when the title of Gypsy changed to Tinkler, that there lived old Will o' Phaup, a well-known character at the head of Ettrick who was known to give shelter to Tinkler friends. They asked nothing but house-room and grass for their horses, and though they sometimes remained for several days he could have left every chest and press open with the certainty that nothing would be missing, for he said, "he aye kent fu' weel that the fox wad keep his ain hole clean!" But sad to say, times altered with honest Will. The Tinklers were lodged at a place called Potburn, and the farmer having bad grass made them turn their horses over the water to Phaup ground.

One morning about daybreak Will found a stout man, Ellick Kennedy, feeding six horses on the Coombdean, the best piece of grass on the farm, which he was carefully haining for winter fodder. A desperate combat ensued, but there was no man a match for Will – he thrashed Ellick and hunted him and his horses out of the country. Five years of warfare ensued with the Tinklers, which nearly ruined Will. One day he decided he'd had enough, so they buried the hatchet and settled their differences. He never told them, but a neighbour's wife said of the affair, "I think Will was scared that they'd put a curse on him, his farm or his cattle."'

Before I leave the eighteenth century, I really have to write something of the greatest Gypsy of all time –and that, as you may know, is none other than King of the Galloway Gypsies, Billy Marshall. Born in 1666 in Galloway, Billy was in his youth a soldier in the army of King William, and fought at the Battle of the Boyne.

He also served as a private in some regiments under the Duke of Marlborough in Germany in 1705.

I love the following story about him.

'After Billy was proclaimed King over all Gypsies, he decided to visit and punish those among the rival Gypsy clans who were planning invasions of his empire. It was on a Sunday morning in the month of April, 1707, that he, along with part of his clan, came to a solitary farm house on the borders of Dumfries and Roxburghshire, in a quest of a gang of Teviotdale gypsies, who had quartered there the night before. The family were all at church except one female left to look after the house. No sooner had Billy and his men arrived than their antagonists turned out and instantly gave them battle. The poor woman shut the door and remained in the house terrified until the door was suddenly forced open and one combatant rushed into the apartment. She stood fixed to the spot in utter horror, seeing the man's left hand had been severed. Without saying a word he thrust the bloody stump against the glowing bars of the grate. Having staunched the flow of blood by cauterising, he seized a sheep-gutting knife from the table and rushed outside to continue the fight.

When they'd carried off their dead and wounded they left a shocked maid to explain the pool of blood outside the house. Her experience left her momentarily struck dumb, and all she could do was point at the severed hand lying on the kitchen table.'

Incidentally, as well as being King of the Gypsies, Billy Marshall was also leader of the dyke levellers of the Border counties. As such he was considered a hero by all poor people. Landlords were erecting dykes and stone walls to divide up the fields and keep the poor out of what used to be common land. Billy Marshall and his gang would wait until the dyker was well on with his building, then they'd loosen the weight-bearing stones and push the dyke over. This was a constant thorn in the side of the land dividers but a godsend to the poor who were being forced from their homes and land because of greedy seizing of land by landowners. A great rebellion followed, with small farmers, crofters, labourers and Gypsies fighting against the proprietors over this annexing of fields, moors and community land.

Joseph Train describes Billy Marshall in his memoirs as 'King of the Randies, who encouraged the insubordination of the peasantry of Galloway in their last ebullition of discontent. This happened in 1724, and their attack was principally directed against the King's fences. In this they were led by Marshall, who despising all rule and authority, was a proper person to direct the movements of the rebellious peasantry.'

Many are the exploits of Billy Marshall, who passed away in Dumfriesshire in 1790 aged 124 years. He is buried in Kirkcudbright.

Entertaining as these stories are, I have to say at this point that I'm seeing a pattern here. Every book about Gypsies that I have studied mentions the people described above, give or take a few other hardy stalwarts, but no one else. Writers stay in their comfort zone; when writing about a subject that they know little about, they keep to familiar ground. The reason for this, as I've mentioned before, is that few writers ventured into the caves, dark forests and far out-of-the-way places where the bulk of the Gypsies and Travellers existed. Instead of exploring the lives of these individuals they chose a few famous characters from the herd and ignored the rest. What a different story I could tell if more attention had been paid to the Gypsies of old as a community where strong baskets were woven, horn spoons carved from sturdy rams' horns that would last a lifetime, earthenware, thick and watertight, was fired, ropes twisted that were strong enough to circle hay bales, brooms made to sweep a fine skelp of farmyard, and pot-scourers that could scrub a pot clean and would last for ages, with washing pegs able to prevent the wildest winds from roaring off with the weekly wash. Gypsies made horse tack second to none, because they respected the horse and understood its soft palate, and therefore designed a bit to suit the animal and not the master. These beautiful objects could only be produced by the most expert and painstaking of individuals. I'm convinced that, if given half a chance, those nimble-fingered people could have been a major asset to this land. Things could have been so different, so positive, but an ignorant, racist establishment passed from generation to generation its fear and hatred of those who didn't fit within society's norms.

Richard McKay, otherwise known as the Bard of Armagh, was one of the many Irish famine survivors from Tinker stock. He was married to my great-great-great-grandmother Sally Malloy, widow of Charles MacManus.

Mary McKay is a gifted poet and author from the same seed. She was raised in Dundee and thanks to the marvel of genealogical research we have been brought together. Here's her gift to this book.

A Life Long Gone

I've never walked the lang, lang road
Nor cooried in a tent
My back sair bent wae heavy load
For me was never meant.

Not for me the berryfields
The lee lang simmer day,
When corncrakes crawed their bonny song
Amangst golden parks of hay.

The heather hills were not my home,
Nor the midnight's sky my ceiling,
Voices roon an open fire
Bairnies listen, laughing, squealing.

The wandering life was not my own,
No basket weaver I.
No hawker, peddler, chimney-sweep,
I cannot tell a lie.

I'll never mend a fairmer's riddle
Nor mak' a milking churn,
Nor thin the neeps, nor sow the corn,
Mak' tea aside the burn.

Nor have I felt the Hornie's boot,
As he shouted to 'Move on!
Dirty tink get oot, get oot,
And dinna be here the morn!

That time has gone this lang time syne,
When their ancient crafts were needed;
Progress, machinery and hate,
Have alas the tink succeeded.

But in my veins rins thick rich blood,
Of these much maligned God's craturs,
And pride swells bravely in my breast
With love for my forefaithers.

I'll wave your banners proudly high,
Shout your praises to the skies,
With gusty voice I'll mak' them hear,
Renting heaven with my cries.

You've had your day, I'll not deny,
Your need is over now.
But the fight goes on and will not die,
For we'll win through somehow.

Mary McKay, 2009

34
SIMSON'S HISTORY

Simson's *History of the Gypsies* (1878) contains a range of attitudes to the wanderers, but generally is much more positive and realistic when describing them. See what you think.

'In 1848 bands of Irish Gypsies made their appearance in Scotland. Many severe conflicts they had with our Scottish tribes, before they obtained a footing in the country. But there is a new swarm of Irish Gypsies at present scattered, in bands, over Scotland, all acquainted with the Gypsy language. They are a set of the most wretched creatures on the face of the earth. A horde of them, consisting of several families, encamped at one time at Port Edgar, on the banks of the Forth, near South Queensferry. They had three small tents, two horses and four asses, and trafficked in an inferior sort of earthenware. On the outside of one of the tents, in the open air, with nothing but the canopy of heaven above her, and the greensward beneath her, one of the females, like the deer in the forest, brought forth a child, without either the infant or mother receiving the slightest injury. [In days gone by, a hole was usually dug in the ground near where a woman was giving birth, filled with water, and after the baby was born it was shown to the tribe, washed in the hole and handed back to mother for feeding. Usually, within an hour, the babe was on its mother's back and off both went.]

The woman, however, was attended by a midwife from Queesferry, who said that these Irish Gypsies/Tinkers were so completely covered in filth and vermin that she durst not enter one of their tents, to assist the female in labour. Several individuals were attracted to the spot, by the novelty of such an occurrence in so unusual a place as the open fields. Immediately after the child was born, it was handed about to every one of the band that they might look at the "young donkey", as they called it. In about two days after the accouchement, the horde proceeded on their journey, as if nothing had happened. Gypsies are generally noted for a remarkable attachment to their children.

But there are Irish Gypsies much superior to the above in Scotland. In 1836, a very respectable and wealthy master-tradesman informed me that the whole of the individuals employed in his manufactory, in Edinburgh, were Irish Gypsies. Several authors have brought a general charge of cowardice against the Gypsies, in some countries of Europe; but I never heard or saw any grounds for such a charge against Scottish Gypsies. On the contrary, I always considered our Tinklers the very reverse of cowards. Heron in his journey through parts of Scotland, before the year 1793, when speaking of the Gypsies in general says: 'They make excellent soldiers, whenever the habit of military discipline can be sufficiently impressed upon them.' Several of our Scottish Gypsies have even enjoyed commissions. But the military is not a life to their taste. There is even danger in employing them in our regiments in the seat of war; as I am convinced that, if there are any Gypsies in the ranks of the enemy, an improper intercourse will exist between them in both armies. During the last rebellion in Ireland, the Gypsy soldiers in our regiments kept up an intimate and friendly correspondence with their brethren among the Irish rebels.★

★Two gypsies in battle between the French and Spaniards, in the Peninsula, in Bonaparte's time, met under the direst circumstances. Confusion and desperation all around them, sword to sword, bayonet to bayonet the French soldier singled out his enemy. After a severe personal contest, he got his knee on his breast, and was about to run him through when his intended victim whose cap fell off, caught his eye and called out, "Zincali, Zincali!" The Frenchman shuddered, relaxed his gasp and wept. He produced a flask, poured wine into his brother's mouth; and as they both sat down on a knoll said, "Let the dogs fight, and tear each other's throats till they are all destroyed: what matters it to us? They are not of our blood, and we shall not shed it for them!"

The Scottish Gypsies have ever been distinguished for their gratitude to those who treated them with civility and kindness, during their progress through the country. The particulars of the following instance of such gratitude are derived from a respectable farmer, to whom one of the tribe offered assistance in his pecuniary distress. [Simson adds that he knew both of them.] The occurrence, which took place around 1868, will show that gratitude is still a prominent feature in the character of the Scottish Gypsy.

The farmer became embarrassed in his circumstances, in the spring of the year, when an ill-natured creditor, for a small sum, put him in jail, with a design to extort payment of the debt from his relatives. The farmer had always allowed a Gypsy chief, with his family, to take up quarters on his premises, whenever the horde came to the neighbourhood. The Gypsy's horse received the same provender as the farmer's horses, and himself and the family the same victuals as the farmer's servants. So sure was the Gypsy of his lodgings that he seldom needed to ask permission to stay all night on the farm, when he arrived. On learning that the farmer was in jail, he immediately went to see him. When he called, the jailer laughed at him and refused to let the farmer know of his visitor. With tears in his eyes, the Gypsy said one way or other he'd get in to see his friend. At last an hour was fixed when he would be allowed to enter the prison.

He appeared with liquor for his friend, but the jailor laughed again and refused the visit. He spoke to the jailor, "Weel man," said he to the turnkey, "is this yer hour now?" The jailor once more refused and said, "You surely must be joking." [No doubt a Gypsy visiting a farmer was unheard of.]

"Joking, man?" exclaimed the Gypsy, with tears glistening in his dark eyes, "I am not joking, for into this prison I shall be; and if not by the door, I'll find another way." Seeing his determination the jailor at last allowed him entry. When he saw the farmer he took hold of both his hands and threw his arms around him, burst into tears and was overcome with grief. Recovering himself, he asked if it was the laird that had put him in prison, but on being told it was a writer, one of his creditors, the Gypsy exclaimed, "They are a damned crew, thae writers! Aye, and the lairds are little better." He then said, "Your father was an honest man, aye good tae my horse, and your mother, poor body, was kind to me when I came to the farm. I was aye treated like one of their own, and I can never forget their kindness. Many a night's quarters I received, when others would not suffer me at their doors." The grateful Gypsy offered the farmer fifty pounds to release him from prison adding, "We are not as poor as some folk might think." He put his hand in his pocket then added, "here is part of the money which you will accept; and if fifty pounds won't do, I will sell all that I have in the world, horses and all, to get you out of this place. Oh my bonny man," continued the Gypsy, "had I you in my camp, at the back o the dyke, I would be a happy man. You would be far better there, than in this hell hole." The farmer thanked him for his kind offer but declined to accept it. "We are," resumed the Gypsy, "looked upon as savages, but we have our feelings, like other people, and never forget our friends and benefactors. Kind indeed, have your relatives been to me, and all I have in this world is at your service." When the Gypsy found that his offer was not accepted, he insisted that the farmer would allow him to supply him, from time to time, with pocket money during his confinement for the necessities of life. Before leaving the prison the farmer asked the Gypsy to share a meal with him; but at first the Gypsy modestly refused, then changed his mind saying, "I am a black, thief-looking devil, to eat in your company; but I will, this day, for your sake, since you ask me." The Gypsy's wife and family also insisted in visiting the farmer in prison.

This interview took place in the presence of several persons, who were surprised at the gratitude and manner of the determined Gypsy. He is about fifty years of age, six feet tall, small black eyes, normal weight, and a swarthy complexion. He is styled King of the Gypsies and his by-name is "Terrible.'"

Simson doesn't say what happened to the farmer, but I expect in time he paid his dues and went back to his farm.

From a case of kidnap in the seventeenth century came one of the most famous Gypsy traditional songs of all time. 'Awa' wi' the Gypsy Laddies' is a powerful song in its own right, but the true story lying behind the song is seldom mentioned when it is sung. However, there is a version in Simson's *History of the Gypsies*, backed up with the facts of the case, which gives Johnny Faa, the Gypsy laddie, back his dignity and proves his innocence.

Johnny Faa, the Gypsy Laddie

The gypsies came to my Lord Cassilis' yett,
And Oh but they sang bonnie;
They sang sae sweet, and sae complete,
That down came our fair lady.

She came tripping down the stair
And all her maids before her;
As soon as they sawn her weel-far'd face
They coost their glamourie ower her.

She gave to them the good wheat bread,
And they gave to her the ginger;
But she gave them a far better thing,
The gold ring off her finger.

'Will ye go wi' me, my hinny and my heart,
Will ye go wi' me, ma dearie;
And I will swear by the staff of my spear,
That my lord shall nae mair come near thee.'

'Gar take from me my silk mantel,
And bring to me a plaidie;
For I will travel the world ower,
Along with the gypsy laddie.

I could sail the seas wi' my Jockie Faa,
I would sail the seas wi' my dearie;
I could sail the seas wi' my Jockie Faa,
And with pleasure could drown wi' my dearie.'

They wandered high, they wandered low,
They wandered late and early;

Until they came to an auld tenant's barn,
And by this time she was weary.

'Last night I lay in a well made bed,
And my noble Lord beside me;
And now I must lie in an auld tenant's barn,
And the black crew glowering ower me.'

'Oh hold yer tongue my hinny and my heart,
Oh hold yer tongue my dearie;
For I will swear by the moon and the stars
That thy lord shall nae mair come near thee.'

They wandered high, they wandered low,
They wandered late and early;
Until they came to that wan water,
And by this time she was weary.

'Often I have rode that wan water,
And my Lord Cassilis beside me;
And now I must set in my white feet an' wade,
And carry the Gypsy laddie.'

By and by came home this noble lord
And asking for his lady;
This one did cry, the other did reply,
'She's gone with the gypsy laddie.'

'Go saddle me the black,' he says,
'The brown rides never so speedie;
And I will neither eat nor drink,
Till I bring home my lady.'

He wandered high, he wandered low,
He wandered late and early;
Until he came to that wan water,
And there he spied his lady.

'Oh will thou go home, my hinny and my heart,
Oh will thou go home, my dearie;
And I will close thee tae your room,
Where no man shall come near thee.'

'I will not go home, my hinny and my heart,
I will not come home, my dearie;
I have brewn good beer; I will drink of the same,
And my lord shall nae mair come near me.

But I will swear by the moon and the stars,
And the sun that shines sae clearly;
That I am as free as the gypsy gang
As the hour my mother did bare me.'

There were fifteen valiant men,
Black but very bonny;
And they lost all their lives for one,
The Earl of Cassilis' lady.

After the Earl brought his wife back to his home, Johnnie Faa and all his Gypsy companions were executed by hanging.

The truth behind the story was later to be unearthed, but not until both Lord and Lady Cassilis were dead. The lady, before she met her husband, had had a long and tempestuous relationship with a merchant called Sir John Fall. During one of his many voyages across the Atlantic buying and selling in the spice trade, the lonely and bored young lass was courted by wealthy Lord Cassilis. This led swiftly to marriage.

One day her ex-lover came back, thinking all he had to do was sweep up his beloved and she would be his alone. Now that she was a married lady this was impossible; but when she saw him again it was easy to see where her heart lay, and it was not with Lord Cassilis. They planned an elopement; they would escape across the sea and live in peace and harmony on one of his plantations.

Ah, 'the best laid plans', as Burns wrote, don't always succeed. The couple made their escape, but when they got to the port, they found their ship had set sail an hour earlier. There's no explanation for why this had happened, but with nowhere to escape and the spurned husband on their heels, they rode off with him in hot pursuit. When

Lord Cassilis, who was an expert swordsman, caught them up, Sir John galloped off and left his lover to her fate.

. Lord Cassilis had never met Sir John, so when he asked who she had gone off with, she lied, threw herself into her husband's arms and said she'd been kidnapped by the wicked Gypsy, Jonnie Faa. Fifteen Gypsies died on the scaffold for Lady Cassilis' lie. Yet again we see Gypsy as scapegoat, blamed and hung for another's act.

Whoever penned the song knew how to upset the blue-blooded aristocracy; forever more it was thought that Lady Cassilis had given up her life of luxury to go a-wandering with the despised Gypsies.

. In another interesting section of his book, Simson writes:

'Every author who has written on the subject of Gypsies has, I believe, represented them as having remarkable dark hair, black eyes and swarthy complexions. The Gypsies in Scotland of the last century were of all complexions, varying from light flaxen hair and blue eyes and corresponding complexions, to hair of raven black, dark eyes and swarthy countenances. Many of them had deep red and light yellow hair, with fair complexions. I am convinced that one half of the Gypsies in Scotland, at the present day [1878], have blue eyes, instead of black ones. According to the statistical accounts of the parish of Borthwick, Mid-Lothian, (1839) the Baillies, Wilsons and Taits at Middleton, the descendants of the old Tweed-dale Gypsies, are described as, "a colour rather cadaverous, or of a darkish pale; their cheek bones high; eyes small, light-coloured wiry hair of a dingy white or red colour, and their skin drier and of a tougher texture than that of people of the country." This question of colour has been illustrated in my enquiry into the history of the Gypsy language; for the language is the only satisfactory thing by which to test a Gypsy, let his colour be what it may.'

Simson's account of the marriage and divorce ceremonies of the early Gypsies is also very informative.

'Scottish Gypsies married at an early age. I do not recollect ever having seen or heard of them, male or female, unmarried after twenty years old. There are few instances of bastard children among them; indeed they declare that their children are all born in wedlock. I know, however, of one instance to the contrary; and of the Gypsy being dreadfully punished for seducing a young girl of his own tribe.

The brother of the female, who was pregnant, took upon himself the task of chastising the offender. With a knife in his hand and at the dead hour of night, he went to the house of the seducer. The first thing he did was sharpen his knife upon the stone posts of the door of the man's house; and then, in a gentle manner, tap at the door to bring out his victim. The unsuspecting man came to the door in his shirt, to see what was wanted; but the salutation he received was the knife thrust into his body, and the stabs repeated several times. The avenger of his sister's wrongs fled for a short while; the wounded Tinker recovered, and to repair the injury he had done, made the girl his wife. This took place in the mid-nineteenth century in Midlothian. The girl's name was Baillie, and her husband, Tait.

I have not been able to discover any peculiarities in the manner of courtships, except that I was informed by an elderly male that it was the universal custom, among the tribe, not to give away in marriage the younger daughter before the elder. In order to have this information confirmed, I enquired of a young woman, one of eleven sisters, if this was the custom. Evidently from fear, she didn't venture much information, but in time she told me that it had been the custom, but caused many unhappy marriages. She said she'd often heard the old people speaking of the customs which were not truly apprehended by force in the present day. In the Book of Genesis, where Laban excuses himself to Jacob for having substituted Leah for Rachel, saying, 'It must not be done in our country, to give the younger before the first-born.'

The nuptial ceremony of the Gypsies is undoubtedly of the highest antiquity, and would probably be one of the first marriage ceremonies observed by mankind, in the very first stages of human society. When we consider the extraordinary length of time Gypsies have preserved their speech, as a secret amongst themselves, in the midst of civilised society, all over Europe, while their persons were proscribed and hunted down in every country, like beasts of the chase, we are not at all surprised at their retaining some of their ancient customs; for these, as distinguished from their language, are of easy preservation, under any circumstances in which they have been placed. Marriage laws were to be daily observed and as important to them as are their choice of wives, and love of their offspring – the most important and interesting transactions of their lives; their very existence depended on this.

The nuptial rites of the Scottish Gypsies are, perhaps unequalled in the history of marriages. At least I have never heard of any marriage that has the slightest resemblance to it, except the extraordinary benediction which our countryman, Mungo Park, received from the bride at the Moorish wedding in Ali's camp, at Benown; and that of a certain custom practised by the Mandingoes, at Kamalia in Africa, also mentioned by Park. "I was soon tired," says Park, "and had retired into my tent. When I was sitting, almost asleep, an old woman entered with a wooden bowl in her hand, and signified that she had brought me a present from the bride. Before I could recover from the surprise which this message created, the woman discharged the contents of the bowl in my face. Finding that it was the same sort of holy water with which, among the Hottentots, a priest is said to sprinkle a new-married couple, I began to suspect that the lady was actuated by mischief or malice; but she gave me seriously to understand that it was a nuptial benediction from the bride's own person; and which on such occasions, is always received by the young unmarried Moors, as a mark of distinguished favour. This being the case, I wiped my face, and sent my acknowledgements to the lady." Park's *Travels*, pages 205, 206.

This custom with the Mandingoes and the Gypsies is nearly the same as that observed by the ancient Hebrews, in the days of Moses, mentioned in the Book of Deuteronomy. When we have the manners and customs of every savage tribe discovered, including the Hottentots and Abyssinians, described, in grave publications, by adventurous travellers, I can see no reason why there should not be preserved, and exhibited for the inspection of the public, the manners and customs of a barbarous race that have lived at our own doors for centuries – one more interesting, in some respects, than any yet discovered; and more particularly as marriage is a very important institution among the inhabitants of any country, whether civilised or in a state of barbarism. How much would our antiquarians now value authenticated specimens of the language, manners and customs of the ancient Pictish nation that once inhabited Scotland?

In describing the marriage ceremony of the Scottish Gypsies, it is possible to clothe the curious facts in language fit to be understood by every reader. But I must adopt the sentiment of Sir Walter Scott; "not be squeamish about delicacies, where knowledge is to be sifted out and acquired."

A marriage cup, or bowl, made out of solid wood, and of a capacity to contain about two Scots pints, or about one gallon, is made use of at the ceremony. After the wedding party is assembled, and everything prepared for the occasion, the priest takes the bowl and gives it to the bride, who passes urine into it; it is then handed for a similar purpose to the bridegroom. After this the priest takes a quantity of earth from the ground, and throws it into the bowl, adding sometimes a quantity of brandy to the mixture. He then stirs the whole together with a spoon made of a ram's horn, which he wears suspended from his neck by a string. He then presents the bowl first to the bride and then to the bridegroom; calling at the same time upon each to separate the mixture in the bowl, if they can. The young couple are then ordered to join hands over the bowl containing the earth, urine and spirits; when the priest in an audible voice, and in the Gypsy language, pronounces the parties to be husband and wife; and as none can separate the mixture in the bowl, so they in their persons cannot be separated till death dissolves their union.

As soon as that part of the ceremony is performed the couple undress and repair to their nuptial bed, where they remain for a while to allow some of the most confidential relatives of the couple as witness to the virginity of the bride. If all the parties concerned are satisfied, the bride receives a handsome present as a mark of respect for her remaining chaste till the hour of her marriage. Those matters settled the couple, dressed in their finest attire, join their guests and dance away the night; in some cases, several days.

The nuptial mixture is delicately bottled and the bottle marked with a Roman character – M. It is then buried in the earth or kept in their houses or tents, and carefully preserved as evidence of the marriage. When it is buried in the field, the husband and wife frequently visit the spot and look at it in remembrance of their vows. Small quantities are also given to individuals of the tribe, to be used for certain purposes, such as, perhaps, as pieces of the bride's cake are used for "dreaming bread."

What is meant by employing earth, water, spirits, and of course air, cannot be conjectured; unless these ingredients may have some reference to the four elements of nature. I would like to inform you of the use of a ram's horn, but as not a single Gypsy would part with this sacred information I am at a loss.'

One last piece from Mr Simson, who has given us so much I shall be forever in his debt, before we leave him. Here he discusses the divorce ceremony. This was a widespread practice throughout Europe and very old.

'In whatever country the Gypsy appears, the first thing that makes him noticeable is his respect for horses. In the first place, it was and still is a general tradition over all Scotland, that when the Tinkers parted from their wives, the act of separation took place over the carcass of a dead horse. My informant Mr Alexander Ramsey, a retired officer of the excise, who died in 1819 at the age of 74 years, stated that he saw a MacDonald Tinker and his wife separated over the body of a dead horse, on a moor, at Shieldhill, near Falkirk, in the year 1760. The horse was lying stretched out on the heath. The parties took hold of each other by the hand, and, starting at the head of the dead animal walked – husband on one side, wife on the other – till they came to the tail, when, without a word to each other, they parted, in opposite directions, as if beginning a new journey. Mr Ramsey said he never could forget the violent swing which MacDonald gave his wife on parting. It was daybreak when this happened. My informant, at the time, was going with others to Shieldhill for coals and happened to be passing over a piece of rising ground when they came upon the gypsies, in a hollow, quite unexpectedly to both parties.'

In the memory of my family's older members the customary wedding ceremony included both bride and groom urinating in a pail, mixing it together and pouring it over a flaming fire; the higher the flames rose and the more they hissed indicated the length of their union.

Another custom had the married couple jumping over a broom-stick. This had nothing to do with witches or witchcraft. The broom-stick represented a brush or besom. When the couple held hands and jumped or stepped over the broomstick it meant that together they were sweeping away evil influences from their past history. Together they would sweep a clear path to walk on in their future life.

Having spoken at length to many Gypsies and Tinkers from Scotland I understand that they believe that the Christian ceremony favoured by settled people is not a binding one and that they are aiming for a deeper and more meaningful union than that symbolised by two gold rings. Rings were a sign of slavery to the Gypsies of ancient times and they considered that no one should have a master. Blind Pate (Peter Robertson from Lochgelly) was a nineteenth-century priest to the Gypsies who conducted hundreds of Gypsy and Tinker ceremonies.

35
THE COTTAR FOLK

I hope that I've covered enough of Gypsy history to give you an insight into what it was like to be on the road during times of religious upheaval when a superstitious and bigoted establishment was determined never to show mercy to the wandering nomads of this land. This may explain why, to this day, Gypsies keep their distance from settled people, and a long and painful period has had to be got through before either side has been able to show a degree of trust to the other. I know that in earlier times Gypsies and the settled community mingled and intermarried. During the Reformation and afterwards the Highlands went through a terrible time of rape, burnings and murder. Clans were broken up, and then in the following years people were forced from their homes to make way for sheep. Widespread famine and the clearances helped destroy what pride of place remained among Highlanders. Fleeing from instability and poverty, hundreds of country folk, those who didn't leave for foreign shores, were forced to join the wanderers on the road. In the search for food to feed the babies and some kind of home, a new breed of Gypsy/Tinker was born.

Many wanderers of the road intermarried with the hardy farm workers from rural parts of Scotland, who are often referred to as the cottar folk. These workers had no permanent home, but had to move from place to place in search of temporary work which would provide wages and lodging for as long as they were employed. I don't have as much information about them as I do about the Cairds, Sinclairs, Tinkers and Gypsies; suffice to say that their ancestors had originally lived for generations in the same area, and usually in the same house. When hard times came and there were clearances of the Highlands and Lowlands in the nineteenth century, many of the workers' houses went into the ownership of the local laird. He was charging extortionate rents, money that the poor farmworkers didn't have. Cast out onto the lanes and byways, for a time these people were indistinguishable from my raggle-taggle Tinkers of the road, joining a human snake wending its way from place to place, searching for sustenance. These skilled workers found jobs to do on farms up and down the land, and as long as they were employed were given a house to stay in. When the job came to an end, out they went and became 'Johnnies of the road' again.

This next piece is about the children of these migratory farmworkers. It is from an article in the *Scottish Educational Journal* of October 1929 by Joseph Duncan, which I came across in the National Archives of Scotland. It begins with a descriptive poem simply called 'The Cottar's Child'.

> I took up hoose at Duncrahill,
> That's fifty year this Whitsuntide;
> Next year I went to Humbie Mill,
> And then frae there tae Chaukie side;
>
> And syne I gae'd tae Nethertoon,
> For, O, I was a rowin stane,
> As shure as Whitsunday cam' roon,
> I was Johnnie on the road again.
>
> Whippilaw and Kippilaw,
> Outerston and Esperton,
> Falaha' and Sherriha',
> And Johnnie on the road again.
>
> At first I flitted for a wage,
> Like mony anither glaikit fule;
> Syne, when the bairnies were the age,
> I flitted tae be near the schule.
>
> Then the neebor's wife was ill tae bide,
> She widnae lea' ma wife alane,

I lookit roon the countryside,
And was Johnnie on the road again.

Tyningham and Whittingham,
Dowfiston and Elphinston,
Mungoswells and Lempockwells,
And Johnnie on the road again.

I've flitted for a better hoose,
And, when I got yin decent like,
I couldna stand the ill abuse –
The maister wis a girnin tyke.

And then for Bob, or Pate, or Neil,
Anither jaunt had tae be ta'en –
Frae Ferniehirst tae Brithershiel,
And Johnnie on the road again.

Mortonha' and Monktonha',
Comsliehill and Whitehouse Mill,
Hermiston and Clermiston,
And Johnnie on the road again.

The language used by the government inspectors about the wandering cottar folk in the following piece is insulting but not surprising. In those days, with people of low status it was taken for granted that the children wouldn't be very bright. The writer, Joseph Duncan, however, thinks that the reason for their poor performance in school lies in their migratory lifestyle, shifting from place to place and never staying anywhere long.

'Scotland and the northern counties of England have the unenviable distinction of being singular in having a migratory population of farm workers. My problem is not to discuss the causes or the many social problems created by a migratory farm population, but to direct attention to the educational problem involved.

An extract from His Majesty's inspectors focuses the problem.

"I fear that the migratory child who has almost all the disadvantages conceivable in home life and who seldom comes of a stock of much mental worth is a problem that cannot be solved by education alone. All we can do is to see that he gets the best education the circumstances will permit."

That phrase, "who seldom comes of a stock of much mental worth," raises a problem in heredity. How far is the backwardness of the migratory child due to disadvantages of home life and the passage from school to school, or how much can be set down to inherent defect? It is the old problem of assessing the respective effects of nature and nurture, and until we have proper research into the problem it would be wise to keep an open mind.

But the lowering of the mental activity is a serious drawback to the children in the formative years. It sets a tone which does not stimulate the children. The elders who are their immediate exemplars make little effort to make their destiny; they are indifferent and drift along. They have no stimulus of tradition due to migrations which leaves them without attachment to any place; they never get their roots down in any society. Because movement is second nature it is easier to pack their kit and seek a mode of living where life promises a reward of effort. The effects of migration are not confined to the disturbances in school work due to changing schools so often but it is sufficiently serious to investigate the extent to which children are retarded by this alone. Most parents seem to view it merely as a grievance because there is more cost; new books, uniform etc, but teachers have a better understanding of the loss to children. While I agree with the Inspector quoted above that the problem cannot be solved by education alone, I am as certain that the evidence of the waste of child life, and the fruitless expenditure of public money would do much to assist those who are making efforts to break down the migratory system if the evidence could be gathered and presented to the public and to those in authority. The rural community in Scotland is generally so limited in point of numbers that corporate or club activities (boy scouts, girl guides etc) would be difficult under any circumstances, but the annual upheaval makes such efforts pointless. With a settled population, even if the most active did flee the scene, it would be possible to make the school a centre which could create a sense of belonging to a place and community and they could be carried on from school into adolescent activities and even into adult life. I still hold the faith that it is from the school as a centre that we could recreate a social life in rural Scotland if we had a more settled community to "work" upon, and were rid of the curse of migration.

It may seem that I am pessimistic about the "Cottar's child". I can only plead that for the past eighteen years I have been handling the product of our rural schools. It is exceptional to find a cottar house child attend secondary education. My experience is that the proportion going from the homes of farm servants, who have left the farm to follow other occupations, where the wages are not so much better as to account for the difference, is quite as good as from any other classes of workers similarly situated. I cannot charge it to any defect in the rural schools, because amongst other rural workers whose standard of living is similar to farm workers, I find the children going to secondary schools in larger numbers. There may be something in the stock, but I'm inclined to put it down to the more obvious difference in the school: permanence of the home and the continuity of school life.

If it can be established that the cottar's child is not being given a reasonable chance in life because of the migration in which it suffers, I do not think we can salve our conscience by giving it the 'best education that circumstances permit.' We cannot ask the teachers and inspectors, to do more, but we can ask the agricultural industry to prove that it is necessary to deny the children to maintain the industry. We tend to forget that the human output is the most important product of any industry and there is evidence that the agricultural industry is failing in that respect, if the evidence of the schools is considered.'

My father's best mates came from the 'cottar folk'. I've had numerous conversations with elderly people who previously suffered from the 'cottar child syndrome', who tell harrowing tales of hunger, deprivation and bullying. The children of cottar families quickly deteriorated in health and became malnourished. I've heard of factors using dogs to rouse families in the dead of night when either the head worker was ill or the temporary work had ended. The end of the job meant they were unemployed and often without a house and job to move to.

I agree with Joseph Duncan when he speaks of the poor educational achievement of cottar children being down to the fact that their parents wanted to get farm work in different locations, but he does not offer a solution. The desperate parents simply do not have an option. I believe that those anxious parents would have given the world to stay put, give their children a proper education in a settled school and reap the rewards.

I have heard many Tinker folk reminisce about taking wandering cottar folk into their tents and feeding them until they were able to find work. For a generation, each needed the other, and this close contact led in many cases to marriages, which were referred to by tinkers as buck unions. Although some of these relationships were lifelong, others were not so. When Tinker men married country girls, the 'culture shock' for both could be dreadful. In summer such marriages seemed idyllic, but on winter campsites, the unwary lass, used to a roof and four walls, could find everything very different. In most cases the winter tent, if erected properly, could withstand the ferocity of the worst storms, but if a wayward husband hadn't respect for his scaldy wife and his half-caste children and housed them in a shabbily built canvas home, it could mean injury and even death. Often the lassie would leave and go home, wherever that might be, while the Tinker husband, lonely and rejected both by his kin and in-laws, might take to the highway and become a tramp. I remember a tramp known as Old Stewart who was believed to have wandered the roads until his death for this very reason.

36
The Report That Condemned the Tinkers

Tinker folk throughout the country have had for centuries their own little places that were no man's land where they could camp and overwinter. However, in recent years, inch by precious inch, the land has been commandeered; now acres of ground have been swallowed up by councils armed with a string of compulsory purchase orders. The old places, where the Picts slept in peace and which offered a form of freedom to the Tinkers who followed them, have gone, fenced, dyked, walled and gated. Nowhere in Scotland is there a free stretch of common that hasn't been parcelled up by councils, Trusts, landowners and anyone willing to offer money for it. The land is now worth more than gold: even the wild heather moorland has factors who drive around the hill roads and bridle tracks in 4x4s ordering walkers, or heaven forbid, campers to go home. No place is free. Most of it lies unused and empty, but that doesn't matter; as long as it is rented or caravan-clubbed there isn't a patch of soil where a man can rest for longer than a few hours. As the old poem tells us:

> The law locks up the man and woman
> Who steal the goose from off the common
> But lets the greater villain loose
> Who steals the common off the goose!

As a child my father suffered the hardships of settling down for winter in the era of the horse and cart, no easy task. His father was the first Tinker in Perthshire to buy a proper wagon, but sold it after finding that negotiating the steep hill roads pulling a wagon was cruel on any horse no matter how heavy it was. Grandad put his horse before his woman and would sleep by its side when it was sickly. He was a quiet man who, I was told, lived by the code of the 'Horseman's Word'. His father, William senior, was a woodcutter from Waterford in Ireland and another typical horseman.

My father remembered as a teenager easing his father's horse and wagon, fully loaded with the family's entire belongings, up an almost vertical Perthshire hill road. They nearly lost all their life's possessions as the horse began to lose control and began to be dragged backwards. My father jumped into a nearby field at the top of the brae and gathered stones, which he used to break the cart-wheels. His attempts at getting the horse uphill were helped by a young lass who was camped down in a wood nearby and ran to his assistance. He told me affectionately that the beautiful raven-haired lassie, who rushed to help him successfully control the cart and horse, was none other than my mother, Jeannie. Her family would be living near my father's on the usual campsite where they'd see the winter through. Their chance meeting on that day would lead to a relationship that would last for over fifty years.

His father's plan that his son should become a horseman like himself never came to pass: my father was a born mechanic, and warned his father that the road was being upgraded to take faster wheels and they weren't going to suit the wagons any longer. There were a lot of clashes between them on this point until the old man relented, and accepted that his son would never take hold of the reins of the old way of travelling.

My dear friend Robert Dawson from Derbyshire, who works tirelessly for the culture through buying out-of-print books and searching through documents, must be commended for bringing this next piece to light. While delving through mountains of archives, he stumbled across the government report of an enquiry which had been undertaken in 1895, under the chairmanship of Sir Charles Cameron, and entitled *Educating the Rural Poor and Dealing with Vagrants, Itinerants, Tramps and Tinkers*. Its 700 pages of small print would have been a nightmare for the keenest healthy eye, but Robert suffers from poor eyesight and various others forms of ill health. Yet he spent weeks sifting through the documentary evidence and vividly remembers thinking that if my father had been alive he would have chained himself to the railings at 10 Downing Street and told everybody what this country had done to his people. I am glad that he and Mammy have passed away; it would have been difficult showing them this official government publication.

I'll let you make up your mind as to what you think of its description of the wandering Scottish tinker who, as will be seen, was not consulted about the planned eradication of his way of life. As we study the questions and answers in this report it becomes crystal clear that the eventual aim of the authorities was to remove the Tinker children from their families and bring the Tinker himself to his knees.

To achieve this, not only was there an army of expert witnesses lined up to testify to the enquiry, but from the first minute of its sitting the press were involved. The report of the enquiry was being fed to the press on a daily basis. The authorities had realised that propaganda, if administered in the right way, could do tremendous damage and turn the general public against innocent people. The saying 'The pen is mightier than the sword' was never more true than in this denigration of the Tinkers of Scotland.

The Secretary of State for Scotland, Sir George Treveleyan, set up the committee 'to call attention to habitual offenders, vagrants, beggars and inebriates in Scotland . . . to enquire whether the numbers of such persons was increasing. To establish what were the causes of such increases and to suggest deterrents likely to bring about their reformation and to prevent increase in their numbers.' In other words, the committee were to seek out wandering tinkers, do a head count, and then decide how to proceed with the eradication of the entire lifestyle.

The committee met in Glasgow, Edinburgh, Aberdeen, and London to hear its evidence. The report gives the dates on which witnesses were heard and lists the members of the committee present, this varying in number but always with Sir Charles Cameron in the chair. The tone of the report was established at the very outset.

The persons grouped together as beggars and vagrants may be sub-divided into three classes – Tinkers or Gypsies, professional vagrants, and working men on the tramp. The Tinkers and Gypsies form a class apart. They live principally in tents, and marry among themselves according to their own rites; support themselves ostensibly by petty industries, such as Tinker work, umbrella-mending and occasional field labour, but really to a large extent by begging. The number of them reported by Chief Constables as having camped in their counties in 1893 was 977 adults and 725 children. As their movements extend through several counties, the same Gypsies must have been returned as passing through their districts by several Chief Constables, so that the number recorded should be considerably over the truth.

The Tinkers and Gypsies were represented by chief Constables, landowners and others as not given to stealing or poaching, but as inveterate beggars, levying contributions in the shape of food, money and sites for their encampments on the rural population, spending what money they obtain on drink, and when drunk fighting amongst themselves. In their domestic relations, they are depicted as faithful to their marriage ties and fond of their children. The charges against them, as far as the general community are concerned, is that they are troublesome beggars; that their unions not being recognised as marriages, their children increase the illegitimacy ratio in the counties in which they abound; and that, owing to their wandering habits and mode of life, their children are exposed to hardships amounting to cruelty, and grow up practically devoid of education, except in the border counties, where they seem to have settled down. Various drastic proposals were made to us, especially in Perthshire, for getting rid of a nuisance which was described as intolerable. These included the suggestion that living in tents should be made illegal, and that the children should where necessary be forcibly removed from their parents and sent to industrial schools.

Education of Gypsy Children

As to the education of gypsy children there is a twofold difficulty. The families being constantly on the move, it is practically impossible as the law now stands to enforce the compulsory school attendance of the children. In the second place, witness after witness informed us that if the children were to go to school they so abounded with vermin that the general population would not allow their children to sit in school alongside them. And Mr Stewart, schoolmaster, told us that were they to present themselves at his school he would refuse to receive them. Suggestions were made that the law should step in and forcibly separate Gypsy children from their parents by sending them to industrial schools, or that the parents, while their children were of school age, should be compelled to select a district of settlement and to send their children to school within it. Your committee see grave objections to any legislation that would render migration, which to other men is lawful, a crime in the case of one particular class or which would deprive parents belonging to that class of rights of guardianship of their children which other parents enjoy.

If, as a class, Gypsies and Tinkers are remarkable for the excessive percentage of their offences, as would seem evident from the number of their arrests, the law prescribes conditions under which lawbreakers of all classes may be deprived of the custody of their children. At the same time, we fully recognise the evil of permitting any class of children to remain outside the pale of the law which enforces compulsory education. We believe however that the enforcement of the law against begging, vagrancy, cruelty to children and drunkenness, on the one hand, and of existing powers as to committal to industrial schools on the other, might greatly mitigate the evil of the want of education among Tinker children, and we believe that one of the chief reasons why the law is not enforced is because to do so would entail expenditure on the parish enforcing it.

In illustration of this, we would refer to the evidence of the Chief Constable of Perthshire. He issued a circular to his police, explaining how the law stood. One of them acted on his circular and arrested a little girl for 'begging', but the Magistrate declined to proceed with the case because of 'the expense that would be incurred in sending the girl to an industrial school.'

A. In order to diminish costs falling on any particular parish, powers should be given to School Board Districts and parishes in a county to unite for the purpose of enforcing school attendenance of vagrant children. Where districts refrain from this, and where there is evidence that a class of vagrant children is growing up in their midst without education, it may even be advisable to enforce their duty on the school boards by withholding their share of the Imperial grant.

B. We recommend that powers should be given to school board districts and parishes in a county or adjoining counties to unite in enforcing the attendance at schools of the children of nomadic parents, and that such united districts and parishes should be empowered to frame bye-laws for the purpose of carrying on the education of such children, which bye-laws, if approved by the Secretary of State for Scotland, should have the force of law.

C. The effect of this recommendation would be (1) to enable the power of compulsory officers to extend over a very large area, and so to bring home to the parents the responsibility for the education of their children, and remove the obstacles which exist to their being brought within the scope of the ordinary law; (2) to enable to be borne by an extensive area the expense (a) of the contribution of the maintenance of children liable to be sent to Industrial Schools, under any of the provisions of the Industrial Schools Acts, but whom, to avoid expense, Local Authorities at present refuse to send there, and (b) of the erection of a Special Day Industrial School or schools with provision for lodging children when their parents were out of school range, or the setting up of any special educational machinery which might be deemed necessary in consequence of the aversion of the general population to receive Gypsy children into their public schools.

The eradication of the culture was in its final stages. From this heavily loaded report came the testimony of witness after witness; all prominent figures at that time, with the single aim of eradicating the Tinker's lifestyle. As I read page after page a blind man could easily see what was planned. Churchmen and police spouted one lie after the other, saying that Tinker parents were nothing more than drunkards who had no love for their children nor cared about a decent form of shelter. The pages were full of the same repetitive propaganda. The end result was that laws were passed to burn tents which were seen as unfit for habitable homes. Landowners had the laws for their employment of Tinkers changed, so that they were forbidden to employ them unless they lived in houses. The most devastating finale to this indecent report was a recommendation for the forced removal of the Tinkers' children, who were to be handed over to orphanages. In later years children were sent to the orphanage at Aberlour, to Barnardos and Quarriers Homes. Parents were left wandering around in a state of shock at the loss of their children. Once admitted to these institutions, hundreds of children were given false identities and sent to Australia and Canada. Some were given to childless couples, and others raised to work in service. Young boys were sent to Mars ships in Dundee and Hull to be trained for the army and navy. Others were handed over to work for farmers.

The report goes on to discuss adult Tinkers and Gypsies and propose measures for dealing with them.

One witness who states that he holidays in Perthshire says: 'They are all drunkards, both men and women, and the children are of all ages, and are as absolutely neglected as the cattle in the field around them. No man cares for them.'

This witness offers a remedy: 'Dwellings should be registered and brought under the control of the local authority for inspection, and if unsanitary and indecent as to be unfit for human habitation, they should be closed; and where no other provision existed for their housing the local authority or the parish council should provide refuges. I would not send them to the poorhouse. I think they should be told, "there is a shelter for you. You cannot remain here any longer," and in the comfortable refuge provided I think they might gradually be absorbed with the labouring population, their children looked after and sent to school, and the whole Tinker clan thus gradually brought into association with the other labourers with whom they were already, to a certain extent, in touch. They can find labour in fields at certain times of the year. The object of the committee, I think, might be to get these Tinkers absorbed in the labouring population by driving them into the villages and giving them refuges for a year or two.'

Another witness commented on the tent homes: 'They are open to all the winds that blow. Of course they are unsanitary. There is no bedding there, there is no furniture; it is almost like living in the open air with an umbrella, little more than that.'

Do they spread infectious disease?

'One particular case came under my notice when one went to a poorhouse suffering from typhus fever, and the Matron's daughter took it. And that is a disease almost stamped out! But further may I say that I do not think that these Gypsies are altogether idle. The Townies for example, make baskets, and work a good deal, but most of the others do a considerable amount of farm work at various times; and I think it requires to be considered that they afford cheap labour to farmers when labour is not to be had otherwise, and in these depressed times of agriculture that requires to be taken into consideration.'

Is there any powers to get rid of them if they encamp on any place without the consent of the tenant?

'Yes, under the Vagrancy Act.'

The questions about the education of children were the most loaded, and it was easy to detect the constant thread underlying their thinking was, 'If a child is separated from its parental environment, it will cease to follow the travellers' culture.' Yet I did find one single witness who doubted the effectiveness of this:

'Children cannot be found as under the Education Act because they move around so much or under the Industrial Schools Act because it is nobody's duty to send them to an industrial school; and further I do not think there are any funds provided under the Protection of Cruelty to Children Act and there is always a great objection to separating child from parent.'

Chairman Cameron seems to have a settled view as to what should be done with Gypsies and Tinkers when he bluntly asks a witness:

'Is there any way of ending the Gypsy race as such except by taking forcible possession of their children and sending them to Industrial Schools and training ships?'

The witness did not think this was a humane act.

Referring to Perthshire it was asked how many Gypsy families were there in the county.

'Forty-four families of which are 49 adult males and 47 adult females – a total of 96 adults; and of children less than 14 years of age there are 63 boys and 51 girls, a total of 114 children,' came the extremely precise and detailed reply.

Do they winter camp in Perthshire and make short excursions into the neighbouring counties during summer months?

'Yes.'

Describe their mode of living?

'They live principally by begging and live in small primitive tents.'

Do they move about?

'They probably stay a day or so in one place.'

A police inspector was questioned.

Do they annoy the inhabitants?

'Very seldom' came the answer.

Do they steal?

'No, they have seldom been known to steal.'

How do they fight?

'Just with their fists.'

In your experience have there been any serious results from quarrels?

'Two years ago we had a case of culpable homicide; but, generally speaking, they do not hurt each other much.'

You do not think anything can be done in reforming the adults?

'I think it is hopeless.'

What do you suggest?

'I think their condition would improve if the present system of camping was prohibited, and something in the way of parochial shelters provided instead.'

Would you propose to make it illegal for a proprietor or tenant to give the use of his land for such purposes?

'Yes, for these small tents.'

If a man had a Gypsy cart, would you allow the tenant to draw up his cart and live in it?

'I would, but as a rule Tinkers have no carts.'

What about the children?

'I think the only way of dealing with them is, after having them compulsorily educated, to send them away out of reach of their tribe. I am certain that, if allowed to join their friends, even after spending some years in an Industrial School, they will just relapse into their old habits.'

Do many of them find their way into industrial schools at present?

'Comparatively few.'

What are the principal names here in Perthshire?

'Reid, Townsley, Macgregor, Macallum, Stewart, White, Macdonald and Johnstone.'

Do you think the Gypsy is quite a different race from the vagrant?

'Yes, it is ingrained in him to wander; and it will take a couple of generations to tame down his roving spirit.'

Have you any complaints of their invading farms and smoking and that sort of thing?

'No, not the Tinkers.'

Have they any other livelihood than begging?

'The men do a little tinkering, and the wives go about selling the pots and pans.'

One witness in Edinburgh told us they are valuable at harvest time?

'They do some harvest work in the county and some potato lifting.'

And in that way they make themselves useful members of the community?

'To a certain extent.'

You say they have a moral code of their own?

'Yes, they stick to each other as man and wife, and among them illegitimacy is almost unknown. They are very kind to their children and to each other.'

Then you think that within their own code they are moral people?

'Yes.'

Does that code of morality extend to stealing?

'They very rarely steal.'

Is he more violent when drunk than the ordinary labouring man?

'No, I do not think so.'

Then, on the whole, the Gypsy is not such a formidable pest of society after all?

'Certainly not!'

The questions and answers sometimes favour the Tinkers and sometimes not, but Chairman Cameron every now and then throws in his own views, for what they are worth.

'It appears to me a great evil that there should be this miserable camping out of men, women and children all huddled together.'

One witness is asked, would you say the Gypsy's life is unhealthy?

'No, it is healthy. It is a question of the survival of the fittest. The weakest die early and those who survive are as strong as horses.'

At what age do Gypsies marry?

'They marry very young, the girls at 17 or 18 and the men about 20.'

What is the average size of the family?

'Some are large – perhaps seven or eight – and others three or four.

How then, do you account for the population not increasing?

'I think a number of the weakest children die from cold.'

Do they spread disease?

'Not that I know of but they must do it tramping about.'

Have you known of any boys being sent from this county to the Mars Training Ships?

'Yes.'

What was the result?

'I am not aware that many of them done well afterwards.'

The next witness was a member of the Church.

Do you propose to take the children from parents as the only solution?

'Yes, unless something were done in the way of getting them to settle down. I think the children ought to be educated compulsorily if necessary.'

Have you any suggestions to make as to bringing the Gypsies themselves into civilisation?

'I think it is rather hopeless, unless something was done in the way of village shelters.'

Do you know that, under the Industrial Schools Act, any parent who allows his children to beg can be fined and the children sent to an Industrial School?

'Yes, but Tinkers do not let their children beg.'

Have you any suggestions to make as to how these children should be dealt with?

'I think something should be done in the way of sending them to an Industrial School, and I do not think the parents would object if they were allowed permission to come and see their children.'

Colonel Williamson from Lawers Estate on the outskirts of Comrie was asked if the statement of one witness who said the Tinker was an honest man was accurate. His frank response was one of the very few positive voices in the Tinkers' favour.

'I have lived in this county for 60 years and I quite agree with that statement. I would go further and say that they are more easily managed than worthless strollers who call themselves working people.'

The Chief Constable also says that they do not poach – is that your experience?

'My gamekeepers would rather manage the Tinkers than any of the loafing communities of the village.'

The Chief Constable mentioned the case of a child of one of the Tinkers, who was brought up, and the Fiscal and Magistrates of Alyth refused to deal with the case, because of the expense that would be entailed on the town if the girl were sent to an Industrial School. In the view of the Chief Constable, does the law have power?

'It gives the power, but the power cannot be applied. I believe that you could take these children and educate them, but you cannot apply the law to "catch" them.'

Have you any remedies to suggest?

'Yes, I have. Our committee and myself think, first of all, that we aught to insist upon these families locating themselves in some particular parish, and if they won't do that, the sheriff should be called upon to give them a location. Secondly, we think that a certain number of homes should be provided for these Tinker families in different districts of the county. Thirdly, we ought to insist upon all their children being educated, either at the public schools or in some special school provided for them. And fourthly, that the expense incurred in providing these homes and educating the children should ether fall upon the county generally, or be borne by the Imperial Funds. Speaking for myself, as an individual, I think that the law ought to step in and declare that camping out or living in camps is an illegal form of life.'

I am told you have had some notable examples of the hereditary tendency on the Gypsy to remain a wanderer?

'Yes, I had a very striking example of that last night. Yesterday was an extremely cold day, and the frost was succeeded by pelting rain. It happened that two Gypsy families had returned to the district of which I am speaking, and I had to provide a shed for their shelter. I also gave them something to eat, and material for a fire, and hoped they would take advantage of the shed. They pretended to do so but they did not, and remained out in the pouring rain all night, simply because they love their life of independence and outside living. I had another story of a child not being allowed to be born in a house, but in a shed. I had a little christening money raised for her, and put in the Savings Bank, but after she had grown up and been to a situation, she returned to her former life.'

Do they do good work?

'They do very good work when at it. They work at our oak-peeling, at turnip-shawing and at harvest. When I was a boy the Gypsy would not eat "baker's" bread but now they all eat it, so that there is a great advance in their manner of living.'

The majority of us are of the opinion that the chief work is to get hold of the children and bring them under educational influences; it cannot be achieved unless someone is given the responsibility. As it stands if a school board was to try and get hold of them, they'd slip away to some other place and we would not have the locus standi for a prosecution. The magistrate won't enforce the Industrial Schools Act at present against these children, because they are with their parents. Through sympathy or sentiment they make the Act which is at present in force quite powerless. But you think that, if the parents were in a fixed home and within range of the Board schools, and you got that attendance order, the children would attend the school?

'It is very much what we desire because they are very fond of their children and that might serve to make them a resident population.'

Do you think if these people were educated in Board Schools up to 14 that they would become ordinary settled down members of the community?

'If they did not, I think their descendants would. It has taken a very long time to make us all good Christians and it will make some little time to make the Gypsies or Tinkers good members of the community.'

The Chief Constable of Roxburghshire told us he was quite able to deal with vagrants under the present powers of the Trespass Act?

'The Gypsy population that he has to deal with is quite different from the Tinker population we have floating about in Perthshire.'

In what way?

'They have their settlements in Yetholm and Morebattle, and are a distinct class, moving amongst themselves.'

Witness MacCallum now offers a solution to the Tinker/Gypsy problem.

'The class on which I wish to give evidence is that of the Tinkers, consisting of small bands of human beings, travelling over a definite area, and living all the year round in tents, with no ostensible means of livelihood. These bands consist, as a rule of one family of three generations. Their tent is rudely made of stakes, bent so as to meet in the centre, and over this is stretched a covering. Under this shelter the whole family sleep, without, as far as I know, any division. In case of sickness, straw or dried ferns form the mattress covered with an old blanket. The privilege of fixing this tent is accorded to the tenant farmer who, in return, gets help during harvest, potato and turnip lifting, and tree peeling. Of course, the Tinkers get paid, and this is the only useful work they do. The money thus earned is seldom spent in bettering their condition, but nearly always in drink. Amidst surroundings such as these, the children are trained from one generation to the next. They never attend school, and from birth, are ill-used and ill-cared for. I am scarcely in a position to speak of the morality or immorality of these people but one thing is clear, the same couple live year after year as man and wife. I don't think many are married according to any rites but their own, so I would hereby point out that their children are entered by the Registrar as illegitimate, and I consider it is this that swells the percentage of illegitimate children in our rural districts and not the immorality of the Scotch.

No effort is made to educate the children of these people, and herein lays the backbone of the whole case. Philanthropic efforts however well meant can never be of service as long as the mode of livelihood, training and surroundings remain as they are. ERADICATION, in my opinion, is the only CURE.

How this is brought about is a difficult problem. A great deal of nonsense (if you'll excuse me saying) has been talked about breaking ties. Family ties should be measured by the amount of affection in the family circle, and judging from this standpoint, it will not be any great hardship, considering the ultimate amount of good, for these people to be forced to either educate their children or that it should be done by the State from a central position.

These people neglect every duty of parents. My idea is that all children aged five or six should be placed in an institution devoted to them and my reason for this is, in rural districts, the parents of ordinary children would not consent to allow their children to sit side by side with those coming from tents who, in nine out of ten cases, would be covered in vermin. I know it is said this plan would never answer, and that on dismissal from a State institution the people would drift back into their original state. But I have better hopes of the results of education than this.

For the elder branches of the tribe I fear there is no hope, and the only thing I can see is to make it an offence for any person to allow another to fix a tent on their land without the proprietor of the tent having first obtained a certificate from the Sanitary Officer for the District or, failing one, from the police, that it is a habitable dwelling for the season of the year in which it is proposed to use it. Where a certificate could not be obtained, they should be passed on as casual paupers and treated as such. I am afraid I appear rather hard-hearted and callous in the few remarks I have had the honour of addressing you, but I am firmly convinced that the only effectual treatment is ERADICATION!

For the children I have only pity. For the grown-up members, knowing them as I do, I feel sure that all efforts based on sentimentality are useless.'

The evidence from here on seems to step up a gear in favour of removing the children, burning tents and eradicating the lifestyle, and at this point I feel I have transcribed enough of the report so far to allow readers to see that the life of the wandering tinsmith was rapidly approaching the end of the line. A 'Reserve' similar to an American Indian reservation was favoured by a few members of the committee but the majority decided against this. Houses were the only way to tame the roving spirit of the Tinker, but the problem was how to obtain suitable dwellings and where to accommodate them without upsetting the settled population, who would definitely not appreciate Tinker neighbours.

I read a lot more into this loaded series of questions and answers than was openly stated by the witnesses and chairman. The underlying message is found in the repetition of words like neglect, immorality, drunkenness, defective, illegal, quarrel, vermin, beggars, filth, illegitimate and cruelty, a whole catalogue of negative nouns and adjectives. There is another crucial word which was repeated on every page over and over again: 'children'. This was the justification for all the measures that were taken, and the cover for what was really the hidden agenda – the 'ERADICATION' of Tinkers.

Most of the committee of the enquiry and the witnesses who appeared before it would have been aware of Scottish Tinkers, who had been part and parcel of the landscape for centuries, so why their apparent ignorance about the Tinkers' way of life? Colonel Williamson, I believe, would happily have listed the many jobs they did on his estate in Lawers between Crieff and Comrie. The Tinkers who returned annually were experts in the care of horse and hound, with skills of fence-mending, drystane dyking and vermin control. The Colonel would have looked to his Tinkers for help with jobs in his sprawling outhouses and barns, the grouse-shooting, deer-stalking and countless other important tasks he'd have looked to his 'Tinkers' for help with.

I live a few miles from this place and have heard many personal recollections of the 'Guid Gentleman' who provided homes for elderly Tinkers and displaced cottar folk, and any who wished to settle, both from the Highlands and Lowlands. I wonder how many of his answers were omitted from the final report?

According to three very old Crieffites I was told that Colonel Williamson was amazed by the way Tinkers constructed their tents and had on many occasions watched the young men of a family he'd employed for the winter building their abode. This would take four large tarpaulins, twenty-four hazel wattles for the ribcage and a fourteen-foot length of strong alder spine with slots for the ribs to fit in. Before the tent was erected a ditch was dug with several drain-off points for rain and melting snow. Once the ribcage had been assembled the covers were carefully overlapped, leaving only an opening at the front to serve as the door. The bottom of the canvas went into the ditch and was anchored down by large boulders. Inside, at the far end of the tent, went either a straw-filled or horse-hair mattress. This was usually where the parents and smaller children slept. There were two other beds at the sides of the tent which were rolled up during the day and used as seats. Near the entrance was an oil drum, with a small circular opening cut in the side so it could be fed with sticks and coal. Several pieces of cut tin, soldered together, protruded from the tent roof and served as a chimney. A wire guard kept the little ones safely away from the fire. At the mouth of the tent cooking utensils etc were kept. As with all who live migratory lives, whether Bedouin tribesmen of the desert, nomads in Tibet, on the North American plains or in northern Asia, the proper construction of their homes is a matter of life and death. Tinkers are expert builders and know that if their home is weakly constructed the entire family can find themselves at the mercy of the elements.

When I read in the government report of the tiny 'umbrella' homes that witnesses stated was where the Tinkers lived, I know that what was being described was probably the camps of cottar folk and other miserable souls who'd been forced from their homes and onto the road. These sorry people, many of whom would speak Gaelic, only needed help to find permanent places to settle but had been so badly treated by their previous landlords that they refused to trust authority. These refugees would not have been aware that Tinkers didn't camp in full view of the world; instead they moved far away from civilisation, living on ancient no man's land or in secluded places, with heavy woods around them where possible.

37

ERADICATING THE CULTURE

I'm certain the planned eradication of Scottish Tinkers was a lazy attempt to rid the countryside not just of those small bands of travellers but of everybody who was displaced and homeless. The elimination of Tinkers and Gypsies was acceptable to most people; after all, who had had the worst press, no roots, no respectable religious status apart from those who held to the Catholic faith, which at the time was deemed an inferior one? I believe that the use of the words Tinker and Gypsy to describe all these people of different origins was a convenient way of dealing with a massive rural problem, and the policy of compulsory education for their children was a pretext to monitor and control migratory and homeless people of all kinds. Not just one group was targeted but many: Perthshire Tinkers, Irish Catholic Tinkers, cottar folk and displaced Highlanders. So began a 'Big Brother' approach to the problem of Travellers.

Around the time of the report hundreds of Irish (Pavee) Tinkers had been filtering into Perthshire and other places around Scotland, driven from their homeland by the Angel of Death. The Potato Famine was raging through the land, and great numbers of people were dying of starvation. Ships loaded down with emigrants fleeing the Famine sailed weekly from Ireland to America and Canada.

Coastal ports in Britain such as Liverpool, Glasgow and Dundee also saw a large influx of Irish migrants. My own family came to Scotland that way, looking for an escape from the Great Hunger. Many of them, used to living in areas of moorland, forests and mountains, saw a home from home in Perthshire, Scotland's sprawling rural county. It had so much to offer.

I notice that in the government report on Travellers there is no contribution from Catholic priests, who would have been able to speak in favour (or not, as the case may be) of the Irish and Highland Tinkers that the report noticeably omits. I know for certain from the census information I have at my disposal from the second half of the nineteenth century that there were as many Irish Tinkers as Scottish ones in the county of Perthshire. They had intermarried with each other in a series of enduring unions. My own great-grandparents of McArthur and McAllister families joined with McManuses, Mackays, Malloys and Powers to create my Mother's proud line. They weren't drunkards but were honest, hard-working, staunchly practising Catholics. Their religion certainly wouldn't have gone down too well with the Reverends who spoke with such authority in the report about the so-called 'sorry state of Tinkers'. The majority of my father's family who were related to Burns, Riley, O'Connor and Johnstone stock, to name a few, weren't alcoholic soaks by any means, and only partook of the stuff during Hogmanay and at weddings and funerals. So it seems clear that the leading witnesses in the report, apart from a few who spoke in favour of Tinkers, had never met my Pitlochry, Crieff and Perth relatives, who were resident winter campers around Perthshire.

The main witnesses to the committee were of the Protestant religion and as I say I think at that time Presbyterian Scotland was prejudiced against Irish Catholics. Combine this foreign religion with the wandering habits of the rural poor and Irish and Scottish Tinkers and you have a large social problem, according to the establishment. I believe it was this kind of thinking which lay behind the report and its recommendations.

The report distorts many truths and one way it did this was to exaggerate the antics of a few unfortunates, so-called drunkards who neglected their children, left them sitting by the roadside for the police to find, smothered babies while drunk and put those lucky enough to survive out to beg while they waited in some secluded place for the proceeds which they would then proceed to drink. These were the individuals who were highlighted in the report. These stories reprinted in the newspapers would reach an ignorant city-dwelling public and so deepen distrust and hatred towards Tinkers once again.

In my search for the truth I have spoken at great length to descendants of these so-called vermin-infested subhuman tribes. Yes, of course there were some who got drunk and quarrelled with others, but the silent majority gave them a wide berth. In hindsight perhaps it would have been better for the sober Tinkers to try to stop the minority making spectacles of themselves, because they let the side down; but it seems they were tolerated and their behaviour overlooked because they were someone's brothers and sisters, mothers and fathers. Despite their weakness they were loved, and as in all societies the unfortunate and weak live alongside the strong and the fortunate. But as far as outsiders are concerned, as we know to our cost, a noisy drunk is always the member of a group who is remembered and pointed at. I see an alcoholic as someone who drinks to hide from some misery in the past or who simply has an illness associated with physical dependency on a drug. Sadly it remains one of modern society's biggest problems. Society on the whole has always had alcoholics and addicts. Tinkers were a tiny part of this, but seemed to have served as society's scapegoat for this kind of problem. There are worse criminals who sit in high places lording it over the rest of us who are never blamed or criticised.

The witness who was horrified at the 'immorality' of three generations of a family sleeping under canvas all huddled together made me cringe. I'm thinking that surely one of the witnesses should have pointed out that in Scotland it can get pretty darned cold in the dead of winter, and all across the land families slept huddled closely together for warmth. Glaswegian comic Billy Connolly tells a story of when the priest came to call in the tenement where his family lived, to find all the children huddled under a coat that his mother regarded as a 'duvet with pockets'. As I've pointed out, the skills of tent building which the Tinkers possessed were essential for survival in Scotland's ferocious weather and determined whether the tent-dwellers lived or died. I myself can build a 'barricade' (bender tent) in which no draughts can enter.

A question asked at the enquiry was why couldn't the Scottish Tinker live in wagons like the Gypsy from the south? If they had brought in an expert from the Tinker culture itself this query would easily have been answered. Perthshire is very hilly, with twisty roads and precipitous drops, and is totally unsuitable for horse-drawn wagons. My father told me that my grandfather was nearly demented trying to work a horse up and down Perthshire's steep braes.

The recommendations of the report after it was presented to Parliament and the House of Lords would not all have been implemented, but legislation as an indirect result of it had a huge impact, the Children's Act 1908. Here is a letter from the Scottish Education Department to the Clerk of a local school board.

Sir,

I am directed to call attention of your board to the provisions of Section 118 of the Children's Act, 1908, dealing with the committal to Industrial Schools of the children of persons having no settled place of abode and habitually wandering from place to place through the district of various school boards. I am to state that prosecutions under this section of the Act fall to be conducted by the Procurator Fiscal, and instructions have been issued to the Procurator Fiscal for the institution of proceedings against persons contravening that section in any case where the necessary evidence is available. I am to request, therefore, in view of the importance of this matter, that your board will be careful to afford to the Procurators Fiscal all the facilities and information they are able to give in connection with cases which come under their notice, and generally do all in their power to render assistance in connection with such prosecutions.

I am to point out that it is provided by subsection (5) (e) of section 74 of the Children's Act, that the obligation imposed on school boards to provide for the reception and maintenance of children in a suitable Industrial School in certain cases does not apply to children of the class referred to. In order to meet the serious difficulty of dealing with such cases it has accordingly been provided by a minute of the Department, dated 2nd November, 1910, that –

'Where a child is brought before a Court for any cause upon which he may lawfully be sent to a certified Industrial School, and where the Court order the child to be sent to a certified Industrial School and declare him to have had no settled place of abode and to have wandered habitually from place to place through the districts of various school boards, it shall be lawful for the Scottish Education Department, if they think fit, upon intimation of any such case, and upon being satisfied of the facts, to make, under such regulations as the Department may from time to time prescribe, to the certified Industrial School to which the child is sent, or to any certified school to which he may be transferred, a contribution of an amount not exceeding that which would be payable by a school board in respect of the reception and maintenance in the certified school of a child for whom the school board is responsible, and such contributions shall be a charge upon the Education (Scotland) Fund in terms of Section 16 (10 (f) of the Education (Scotland) Act, 1908.

I have shared many of these reports and regulations with some of my Traveller friends. One told me, 'They wrote their laws on miles o' paper, and the auld yins lit their fires wi' it.' Another said, 'They chased us aff the common grun but couldnae pull us fae the fox's hole.' They referred to the authorities as, 'The stoorie boots and strippet mooths', 'wattery Wulls who'd been weaned aff a sow', 'shan gadjis and sookit manishis'. I'll let you imagine how blue the air got at times.

38
BERRY FIELDS O' BLAIR

The previous chapters were deep, painful and hard going. I have more tearful words to share with you of a more personal nature concerning my own family, but before we travel that difficult path, let's spend time in Blairgowrie, home of the berry fields and the famous Stewarts of Blair.

Every year, no matter what bullying and mishaps had befallen me during winter, I knew that when my father sat behind the steering wheel of the Bedford or whatever vehicle he decided to take us in, my summer madness was waiting for me at Blair. The Tinker kids mixed with Dundee juteys (workers from the jute mills on their well-earned holidays), Glesga tennies (what we called Glasgow tenement dwellers: places in the city like the famous Gorbals were full of tenements. During the Glasgow Fair Fortnight many came from there to make a few extra shillings at the berries), Perth scaldies (our name for non-tinker folk), caveys from Caithness (so-called because of folk-tales about the last of the Vikings hiding in caves at Caithness and keeping a look-out for the longboats coming back to find and take them home to Norseland), Gaels from the whispering isles (the Western Isles didn't have many inhabitants but there were always a few families came to the berries. They had lovely lilting voices and it was a joy to hear them singing in the berry-fields), and whoever else wished to join us. Life could not be better!

The green of Ponfaulds was where we headed. This was the favourite green for most berry-pickers, whether from the culture or not. It had clean toilets, fresh running water and there were no restrictions on campfires. The local farmer provided the amenities in return for work; strawberry-picking, pea-gathering and of course the raspberries.

Some rasps were as big as your fist, others were tiny; some were heavy, others light. When it was fruit for jam and eating we had to be careful not to bruise the fruit, so little baskets (punnets) were provided. If the fruit was for dye then we packed small pails (luggies) which we tied around our waists on belts. Some folks would add a few little stones and dirt to weigh down the contents and make more money, but I just gathered the fruit, and when I'd made enough money, headed home to wash out the red juices from my face and hair, then went to play with the other kids. Playtime was free and the farmer allowed us to wander all over his land.

My father told me all about the soil and what kind was best suited for growing rasps, strawberries and other fruit and vegetables. His mother, my Granny Riley, had green fingers – whatever she planted, it grew, in abundance. Born in a tent and not staying in one place for any length of time one wonders how she came by the knowledge she possessed, but it was vast. She passed it on to her son, but although he knew a great deal about the horticultural world he seldom grew things himself. I remember at the end of his life when he and Mammy retired to Glenrothes, they inherited several roses in a small front garden from the previous tenants. He took an immense pleasure tending them; even giving each one a name. A special one was a pinkie-red rose he named Jean, after Mammy.

It was at Ponfaulds one quiet Sunday afternoon I discovered that boys and girls were not actually made the same. As one of a family of eight girls, no one had informed me that there was a difference. My father was always acutely aware of his modesty and made doubly sure he was fully clothed at all times around his female family.

I was seven at the time, and playing happily with several other lassies, discussing things like why aeroplanes stay up in the sky and why ships don't sink – you know the kind of things kids talk about when they are only seven?

Well, another child of the same age was my cousin Joey, who was a right devil. He used to pull worms apart, rip feathers from crows' wings if he caught them and cut off mice tails. For this wanton cruelty I hated him and wouldn't trust him an inch. Well, when he appeared that day leading a troop of like-minded brainless lads I stood my ground, because as far as I could see, my cousin Joey was about to torture some innocent creature. He asked us girls if we wanted to see what he was holding in his hand, down the front of his trousers.

All the other girls stormed off, not wanting to witness the scene but I was not about to allow this brute to harm a tiny wee thing. He laughed and dropped his trousers. When I saw the small, wriggly, pale-coloured slow-worm protruding below his belly button I was left with only one option – to free it! Losing no time I grabbed and pulled it, and tried my utmost to free the worm, telling Joey he shouldn't have picked it out of the puddle because it had bored its way into his body and he'd now have to go to hospital and get it cut out! Needless to say I got a right battering from Mammy when the worm squirted water all over my auntie Maggie's freshly laundered sheets which she was just in the process of hanging out to dry! So I got a lesson in life and Joey got a swollen you-know-what.

———

It was at Ponfaulds we took possession of Tiny the stud, our terrier who travelled with us for years afterwards, from an old woman who was dying. She had a full set of pups that her old bitch was weaning when both she and the dog died. Mammy allowed me to take the smallest puppy and got homes for the rest.

It was around the same time that our family had another addition to the fold – my parents' first grandson was born. The whisky flowed in celebration as my second-oldest sister was toasted again and again.

One year we arrived to find that there was not an inch on the Ponfaulds green on which to erect our tent, so my father decided to move a few miles north and work for a rising star of fruit-fields, Mr Marshall. He had plenty of space on his green, toilets and running water. So for the remainder of our visits to the famous berries we, my father and I, spent our last summers on Marshall's meadows.

Belle Stewart's famous song sums up perfectly how lively the berries were for everybody involved.

The Berry Fields o' Blair

> When berry time comes roon each year,
> Blair's population's swellin'.
> There's every kind o' picker there,
> And every kind o dwelling.

There are tents and huts and caravans,
There's bothys and there's bivvies,
And shelters made o' tattie bags,
And dugouts made wi' divvies.

There's corner boys frae Glesgae,
Kettle-boilers frae Lochee,
There's miners frae the pits o' Fife,
Mill workers frae Dundee,

And fisher folk fae Peterheid,
And tramps fae everywhere,
All lookin for a living aff
The berryfields o' Blair.

There's trevellers fae the Western Isles,
Fae Arran, Mull and Skye;
Fae Harris, Lewis and Kyles o' Bute,
They come their luck tae try.

Fae Inverness and Aberdeen,
Fae Stornaway and Wick,
All flock tae Blair at the berry time,
The straws and rasps tae pick.

There's some wha earn a pound or twa,
Some cannae earn their keep,
There's some wid pick fae morn till nicht,
And some wid rather sleep.

There's some wha hae tae pick or stairve,
And some wha dinna care,
There's comedy and tragedy
Played on the fields o' Blair.

There's families pickin' for one purse,
And some wha pick alane,
There's men wha share and share alike,
Wi' wives that's nae their ain.

There's gladness and there's sadness tae,
There's happy herts and sair,
For there's some wha bless and some wha curse,
The berryfields o' Blair.

Before ah pit my pen awa,
It's this I would like to say;
You'll trevel far afore ye'll meet,
A kinder lot than they.

For I've mixed wi' them in field and pub,
And while I've breath to spare,
I'll bless the hand that led me to
The berryfields o' Blair.

In Sheila Stewart's poignant biography of her mother, *Queen amang the Heather*, she tells us that Belle wrote that song for a Hogmanay party. She recalls the first time it was sung. 'There were strangers in our house that year who said to my mother's face, "How can a tink write a song like that?" My Uncle Donald and my father weren't long in showing them the door with a couple of kicks up the arse, and you can guarantee they were never allowed in again.'

Sheila goes on to say that after her mother had written this famous song it was expected that each year she'd write a new one for the Hogmanay party. One year Belle wrote a beautiful song that has never been published. Sheila was happy to let me publish it for the first time, and has given me permission to share it with you now.

Glen Isla

Keen blaws the wind roond nooks o' the shielin',
His auld mallin promise is covered wi' sna,
Hoo changed fae the times since we went up Glen Isla,
Lookin for rags or a wee taste o' blaw.

We went up by Forter, or maybe the Linns,
Lookin for rags or a wee puckle skins,
Naebody kent on what we had to bear,
The hardships and cauld till we got back tae Blair.

But me and my mither we aye trauchled through,
And we aye got the price o' a wee taste o' brew,
And Donald and Jimmy, they aye did their share,
And that was the reason we never left Blair.

Times they have changed, but we cannae help that,
And mony's a nicht when we sit doon tae crack,
We think on wir mither wha noo is awa',
But it's grand tae hae memories that we can reca'.

39

The Undesirables

When I reveal the government's plans to eradicate Gypsies and Tinkers to others I am asked many questions. Did the authority really send children to Mars training ships based in Hull dockyards? Were the Industrial Schools inundated with Tinker children? Were children forced away from their parents? The answer to all these questions, sadly, is yes, and the most horrendous consequences were the result. Here are some personal stories.

Bridget's Story

It was snowing when Bridget heard the crunching of footsteps outside her tent. Gerald was there piling sticks on the fire and she could hear him talking to some strangers. As she peered from the tent to see who it was, two shovel-shaped hands grabbed her by the shoulders and hauled her from the tent. She landed on some logs and felt a sharp pain in her back. Gerald was lashing out with his fists all over the place and that was the last she saw before her body crumpled over and she lost consciousness.

Some minutes later, still in agony, Bridget opened her eyes to see people crowding round her with blankets. An elderly woman was washing blood from her face, but it was not her own blood.

'Gerald was fighting with the hornies and the cruelty man, lassie. They've taken him off with them.'

Bridget was filled with terror, and asked where were her two children, three-year-old Rachel and nine-months-old Johnnie.

'Oh, my puir soul, they've taken the bairns awa tae,' said the old woman, trying to wrap the blanket round Bridget's shaking shoulders.

The young mother was unable to control her grief; and with dead eyes staring from cold white sockets, she limped away from the bystanders and threw herself into the freezing waters of the River Tummel. No one was able save her.

Locals burned the family's tent and warned other Tinkers who were in the area about what had happened. The next day they were nowhere to be seen.

Bluebell McDonald

Bluebell McDonald was six months old when a policeman informed her mother, Margaret, that the child looked malnourished and insisted that she hand her over to him. Margaret McDonald warned him if he laid a hand on the bairn she'd eat off his cheeks. He laughed and reached out to take Bluebell. Margaret sank her teeth into his face, and for all his strength the policeman was unable to stop her ripping his flesh down to the bone. Bluebell was removed by the cruelty officer, who had her sent to Australia as happened to hundreds of other Tinker children and was never seen again by any of her dozens of relatives. Margaret was later certified and put in an institution for the criminally insane.

Jane Healy Burns

When Jane Healy Burns, aged five, was found wandering in the streets of Elgin, she refused to speak to anyone. The authorities held her in an orphanage until they decided what should become of her. Letters went back and forth, with no one from either the local children's services or the church offering to pay for her upkeep until such time as she was old enough to look after herself. Unable to come to a satisfactory conclusion, they unanimously decided that since she was probably a Tinker child she would be mentally defective and should be committed to an asylum. I have no documentation to say whether Jane ever left that establishment.

Janet's Story

Fifteen-year-old Janet's mother had died aged forty-one. Janet was pregnant and terrified to tell her father, so she ran away. Her older brothers went searching for her, found where she was and took her to Perth Industrial School. Because of her condition she was given light duties. When her son was born he was removed and given to a childless couple. Janet was heartbroken. One day she sneaked inside the office of the school and found information relating to the couple with their address. She ran off and watched their house for signs of a pram. Her waiting paid off; she saw the beautiful baby boy lying asleep in his pram outside the front door of the house. Janet only wanted to look at him but was seen by the baby's adoptive mother. The police were sent for and Janet was taken away. She was sent to London where she was to be taught to be a servant to rich families. Janet was judged to be unsuitable and so was put out on the streets. No one knows what became of her after that. Yet another casualty of the Tinker eradication programme.

Over the coming years numerous families who were born in Perthshire, and had seldom left the area, began showing up in Argyllshire, Aberdeenshire and the far north. On census forms I can trace an explosion of babies from Perthshire Tinkers, Hawkers, and Peddlers who were born in Inverary, Oban, Kingussie and other parts. Something had frightened them away from their traditional home area – was it changes in policy to Tinkers as a result of the 1895 report? I feel it had a great deal to do with it.

Only Crieff and Blairgowrie held onto a majority of their Irish Tinkers. Some were now third generation Scots, and although I'm not a hundred percent sure, to go by the Chapel records and my father's own tales about the area, these towns seem to have offered a hand of friendship to the Tinkers instead of the whip of authority. I find few instances of the breaking up of family units here.

Pitlochry and adjoining areas, on the other hand, didn't seem to allow for a gradual progression from tent to house. There was a mindset here which resulted in an ongoing disruption of the Traveller lifestyle, especially for those of Irish Catholic descent. I discovered that an infamous solution to the Tinker 'problem' was to stem from here. One day I received a large pile of Perth and Kinross documents relating to Tinkers from my source at the National Archives. Most of the documents were dated between 1900 and the 1930s.

Plainly there was still in place a policy of eradication, but this time it went by the name of an 'Experiment'. Certain families had been earmarked for a Tinker 'reservation' planned at Torwood, near Birnam, Dunkeld. The authorities had deemed that Tinkers with Perthshire connections who had travelled the area for many centuries and were well known to locals would be suitable tenants for the reservation. Funding was set aside, and trees had already been planted to shield the site from the main road. However, a problem arose. Several families of Irish and Highland descent living in a wood at Edradour near Pitlochry had not been included in this plan, therefore the question arose of how to deal with them and in what location. This presented a headache for the authorities. Imagine my horror to read in the very public documentation about this that the people concerned were my own relatives! Although the papers do not describe them as such, I know for a fact that my relatives included skilled woodmen, spotlessly clean, caring mothers, and well-mannered children who certainly did not suffer from infestation of vermin, as I've read in the anti-Tinker propaganda. However, the documents stated that the people at Edradour were unfit to be called Tinkers, and therefore their disposal posed a problem.

My parents used to speak fondly of the Edradour area and of how their own parents had arrived there before they were born. There they lived in Aldour Wood at a place known to the tinkers as the Black Spoot (Spout). Here, along with others, their families had set up their winter camping green. They had chosen a secluded area with running water from the burn and plenty of shelter, by an ancient Pictish burial ground. The thick woods around shielded them from harm and harsh winter chills. The menfolk found work in the nearby Atholl forests while the women wove baskets and hawked around the rural areas of highland Perthshire. In summer they wandered around the country, returning to the home ground for winter. For several years they changed winter grounds between a house in Crieff and the Black Spoot.

Meanwhile, the numbers of Perthshire Tinkers generally had dropped to a manageable level. Once an annual census had been taken, all was ready for the authorities to begin herding them into the reservation at Torwood. However, the plans were put on hold at the outbreak of World War I. All able-bodied men had to take up arms.

40

THE NEXT ATTACKS ON TINKERS

Twenty years later the reservation was again in the offing. This time, as the influx of Irish and Highland Tinkers had swelled the numbers, the previous level of funding was no longer sufficient to pay for the reservation as originally planned. Progress was halted and the plans revised. The 'problem' needed another approach. The church would take control of matters. A missionary called Lady Dorothea Maitland was assigned to be the 'Tinkers' friend'. And here are a few of her notes which were in the archives of Perthshire Council . . .

> I find that the word 'Tinker' is being more and more applied to vagrants who are not Tinkers. Failings are attributed to Tinkers which are not theirs, with the result that the magnitude of the Tinker problem is exaggerated. It appears to me to be important that public authorities should be aware of the differences between them: –
>
> (1) Tinkers of definitely nomadic habit and instincts.
>
> (2) Hawkers who have merged into Tinkers to such an extent as to be hardly distinguishable from them, although they were not originally the same and are still different in their ways.
>
> (3) Tramps, who are usually solitary and do not affect the education problem.
>
> (4) Show people and English Gypsies, who wander and half wander in Scotland.
>
> (5) Other families, sometimes of Irish origin, who have become vagrant in Scotland.

I think that, unless the differences between these types are kept in view, there is a risk of the circle of vagrancy in Scotland gradually widening far beyond the limits of native vagrancy. Those of Irish origin are of this type. They have multiplied exceedingly, are troublesome, a nuisance, they are squatters, rather than wanderers, and thoroughly undesirable!

She expresses her Christian views even more forcefully later in the document, describing a group of northern Tinkers as, in her opinion, 'retreating to the APES'. Where did this highly thought-of church member find her charitable sentiments, and where do Adam and Eve feature in the 'ape' ancestry of these Tinkers?

The Tinkers began to feel uneasy with their new friend, no matter how polite and plausible she was. For a short time there was a sustained assault by cruelty officers on the people in the woods at Aldour, but with little success. Many families who'd been raised in fear of the 1895 report and spent years hiding from these child stealers were not about to see their beloved offspring being taken away now, for no other reason than that their numbers had upset the Perthshire Council's plans for a reservation. They upped sticks and were never seen again.

In 1932, while residing in these woods, my parents were married in Strathtay Chapel and for the following year went on the road like a pair of hikers – a magical honeymoon, they called it. My father said he'd had a hard job fending off lads who fancied his bonny lassie. By the time they arrived back at Aldour, she was pregnant with their first baby.

Our paternal grandparents had found a lovely home called Lettochbeg above a Pitlochry suburb named Moulin. It was a heaven-sent low-roofed cottage with two large rooms. Although there was no plumbed water, a large well at the side of the house supplied them with plenty of fresh running water which came straight off the mountains. Granny put her green fingers to the best use in growing vegetables, rasps, rhubarb, strawberries, blackcurrants and flowers that filled the slopes of Ben Vrackie with the sweetest fragrance. The lighting was paraffin-filled Tilley lamps. The landowner allowed Granddad to keep horses, which he used for his work in the Atholl forests. Latterly he pulled a cart and gathered scrap and rags in and around Pitlochry, and also bought a grand funeral carriage which he hired out. Granny had a roof over her head and this meant protection for her family. Even allowing for the lapse of almost forty years since the infamous report they still had a fear of burning tents and removing children.

The remainder of my family and many others had had enough – they were searching for a home; nothing else, just some place where they could feel part of a community. The travelling lifestyle was drawing to a close; they knew it, and only wanted a chance to prove they could be worthy citizens. They were going nowhere. The faced the white-collared wolf at the tent door, stood their ground and fought for respect.

Let's read some more of Lady Dorothea's notes.

In my experience tinkers are passionately fond of their children in an almost wild-animal kind of way; if their children are forcibly removed from them, the parents become frantic in behaviour. They neither eat nor sleep, and they travel fast and aimlessly until this phase wears off. I do not know what the corresponding happening within the child's mind may be. I find that Tinkers wish to educate their children; they call it, 'coming out of the dark,' but the difficulties and the hardships arising from compulsory attendance at school are very real and very severe. The following are only a few of them: –

1. Some Tinkers have houses in the meaner parts of towns, as in the Overgate, Dundee; Manse Street, Fraserburgh; Merkinch, Inverness; or in dilapidated cottages in small towns or villages. These houses are invariably poor; they are less harmful if they are cottages and not tenements. As a rule they are thoroughly unwholesome, and Tinkers neither thrive in them physically or normally. It is virtually impossible for a homeless Tinker to get one of these houses, because when one becomes vacant, it is either taken at once by a very poor settled person, or it is condemned or pulled down by the Health Authority. I know that these houses which the Tinker is forever seeking are castles in Spain. I have sought for them myself, and I know they don't exist.

2. Every month sees another camping ground closed against Tinkers. Some are only available for twenty-four hours and so, between the want of a house and the lack of camping

grounds, the Tinkers are living in a perpetual state of fear that their children may be taken from them for failing to 'educate.' The consequence of this state of affairs are that the Tinkers are feeling bitter and badgered and they are suffering. During the war (1914–1918), Tinker women got themselves stowed away in the poorest kind of houses, for they will never camp outside without their men. When the men returned, these houses were pretty much in ruins, and the Health Authority condemned them often as even dangerous. This meant that the Tinker men had to go back to their wandering when they returned from the war, often very much damaged in health as, for instance, Alexander White, who contracted malaria in Egypt and is at this moment in frightful difficulties over his camp.

3. While this acute distress over want of camps and houses exists, greater pressure in the matter of schooling would mean cruel repression, and there would be nothing left but the Poorhouse.

4. Even if a Tinker does find a camping ground near a school it may not satisfy the authorities, who are used to conditions of other children and do not understand how a Tinker manages in his tent. This, in fact, often does happen. Besides, sometimes a keeper objects to Tinkers being in school with his child, and uses the simple expedient of ejecting them from their camp.

5. One hundred days is too long for a Tinker to be away from his trading rounds and it is too long to trade in one place, which gets 'bettered', that is played out, for peddling and other small commercial enterprises. At the end of 200 attendances the financial position is bad, and sometimes the Tinker breaks away. 'Settlement by birth' leads to a discouragement of families becoming dependent on public funds in case of the birth of a child, which will be forever chargeable to the place of its birth.

The Church of Scotland is prepared to make an endeavour to intervene in the matter of camping grounds and it hopes to be able to assist the Tinker. But the amelioration of the position of Tinkers is always a slow, cumbrous business and it will take time to bring about any welfare scheme. In the meantime, things are oppressive and hard on these people and rather unsatisfactory to all concerned.

As there is a definite movement to take a more kindly interest in the Tinkers, I suggest that it would be a very good thing to call a truce for the moment and remove no Tinker's child for failure to educate or because of a poor camp near a school until each case has been thoroughly examined by a Tinker's Friend. Exception from this policy would naturally be made in cases of cruelty or neglect arising from drunkenness, but such cases of cruelty are rare among 'real' Tinkers. Unfortunately Tinkers fear no one as much as they fear the 'Cruelty Inspectors', and the Society has quite lost the confidence of the Tinkers because its inspectors are the agents who carry out what proves in practice to be a repressive law against them. The Tinker's mistrust of the 'Cruelty' is deep-seated and it will take generations to live it down.

Tinkers are most amenable to kindness. They would soon understand sympathetic action on the part of a governing body, and it would have a very good moral effect among them if they realised that the Education Department appreciated their trouble over the dilemma of no camping grounds or houses and schooling.

If I had any doubts as to the reality of the plans for a reservation to be run by the Church of Scotland, this next piece in the *Scotsman* put paid to them. This wasn't just a few typed notes from the archives by the Tinkers' 'Friend' and her colleagues, addressed to the Perthshire councillors. No, this was a statement given to the press for the world to read. The Church certainly meant business. The measures that had been planned in the 1895 report, although delayed by the outbreak of war and by lack of funding, were still in favour. The knives were out – Tinkers were a blot on the landscape and had to be got rid off. The unanimous decision of the authorities was to achieve this by forcing children into education, as the 1895 report had recommended. As you will see, Lady Maitland, who had so much respect for Tinkers, included her thoughts about the nasty Rileys and others camped in Aldour in her press release, though thankfully the thoughts she expressed in her notes to the council were watered down. Still, she was determined get rid of us and to push all her pet Tinkers into the reservation, where God alone knew what enforced lifestyle was awaiting them.

SCHEME FOR TINKERS

—

CHURCH LENDS A HAND

—

WINTER CAMPING GROUNDS

4 February 1933

A scheme for the welfare of tinkers in Perthshire is being developed by the Home Mission Committee of the Church of Scotland. The scheme, which is founded on a successful experiment in Surrey of allowing gypsies to camp by permit only and under the close supervision of the Hurtwood Control Committee, has been adapted to suit Scottish conditions.

Under it the supervision of camps in Perthshire will apply only to Tinker families with a definite connection with Perthshire by birth or habit. No Tinkers from other counties without a Perthshire connection will be admitted on supervised camping grounds. Thus there will be no increase in the number of Tinker or vagrant families should this scheme be put into force.

The selection of families for admission to special camping grounds will be referred to people with local knowledge and experience of Tinkers in Perthshire, and care will be taken that no more Tinker families will be camping under supervision in one district than are normally either wandering to and fro in that district or resident in it.

SCARCITY OF SUITABLE HOUSES

In a memorandum which has been drawn up by the Home Mission Committee for circulation among presbyteries and those interested in the scheme it is stated that some Tinkers are now living in houses for the whole or part of the year; that they can only afford to live in old and dilapidated houses at rents from £6 a year to 3s a week or 6s a month, or other small amounts, and that they can only pay low rents and support themselves without recourse to public assistance. It is pointed out that houses of this type are very scarce and in great demand.

The memorandum also states that unemployed families sometimes sub-let rooms to tinkers, but adds that the means test will take into account the revenue of these rooms.

One of the main points made is that camping grounds all over Scotland have been closed against Tinkers in rapid succession without provision being made for them elsewhere. There are now not enough to go round, and if ground is available it becomes overcrowded. To comply with the law as regards education of their children, Tinkers must find a house or camping ground near a school during the winter months. It is with the utmost difficulty that a winter camp can be found.

It is therefore proposed to start a scheme for a winter camping ground on an experimental basis, and to attempt nothing on a permanent footing until experience has been gained. In its first season the period of time covered will be from about the middle of September until about the middle of May. The intention is to lengthen the time of control gradually.

BETWEEN BIRNAM AND KILLIECRANKIE

In its first season the area it is supposed to cover is roughly from about two miles south of Birnam to about a mile south of Killiecrankie, and east and westwards following roughly the outline of the side roads to Blairgowrie and Aberfeldy.

There will be no massing of Tinkers together, and what is asked for is that small patches of ground may be placed at the disposal of the Home Mission Committee, where one Tinker family may camp to one piece of ground, or, in exceptional cases, as for example, where a grandparent habitually camps alongside relations, two camps together.

A Tinker's tent, says the memorandum, can be comfortably placed on a piece of ground, from about 12 to 14 ft square, preferably where there is a screen of rough or wooded ground round it, and where water is not far off. If patches of ground of this description are placed at its disposal the Home Mission undertakes to supervise Tinker camps sprinkled sparsely over the area mentioned. Every small patch of ground allowed for this purpose will have a notice board with some such inscription as 'Church Private Camping Ground,' so that it may be under-stood that the ground is private and camping on sufferance. A male ranger will be employed, whose duty it will be to issue and check permits, supervise camping grounds, see that all rules are kept, inspect water, attend to the wellbeing of the Tinkers under his charge, help them if possible to get work, deal with them in sickness, and in general carry out the intention of the Home Mission. A small local committee will also be formed.

TINKER FAMILIES

Tinkers with a Perthshire connection are among others, Reids, Stewarts, Whytes and Johnstones, but there are vagrant fami-lies in Perthshire not of Tinker origin, Rileys among others. The Rileys are a large connection, some settled and some half settled, and says the memorandum, it may be to the advantage of the community if some or all of these families are brought under the scheme.

[Despite my family being described as vagrants rather than Tinkers, you will find as we go further into this chapter that we revert back to our Tinker label.]

Special regard will be paid to the well-being of Tinker children camped on supervised ground and Tinker ex-servicemen will be encouraged to regain something of their army bearing and self respect. Particular stress is laid upon the welfare of the children and the Home Mission proposes, in co-operation with the Perthshire Education Committee, to seek to secure special instruction for children camped under its care. It is prepared to provide a wooden classroom, to provide its heating and lighting, and erect and take it down again, for this purpose, should this be acceptable and should the committee not prefer to use a classroom in one of its own schools. Inducement will be offered to children to take up regular occupation when their education has been completed.

It is also pointed out that, in the event of the Education committee being unable to offer a 'special' teacher for chil-dren on supervised camping grounds, the Home mission is prepared to guarantee a teacher's salary for the first season of 200 attendances, and a teacher whose time may be devoted to children not camped under its care.

The Home Mission has been advised to leave the Tinkers free to disperse after school time, keeping the aim always in view of a very gradual settling down of tinker families. Such are the outlines of the scheme, which is frankly tentative. The Home Mission Committee is in touch with the Perthshire County Council, which administers education in the county through its committee, and it is hoped that, when the details of the scheme are more widely known interest in it will expand.

Miss Dorothea Maitland is acting as honorary investigator for the work and the whole situation with regard to vagrancy, as it is being studied by the Church of Scotland.

Tinkers who didn't have the names mentioned in the article were warned to leave the area. So what happened to the welfare of their children – why was there no intervention to save them, no outcry?

I can tell you, reader, that the panic that all Tinkers living in the designated area were thrown in, when they heard of the plans to control them, was like when a burning rag soaked in petrol is hurled into a barn to burn out mice. Many deserted their camp sites, often during the night so they would not be seen. Even 'safe' names who had married into other families, upped sticks and left. Men and women filled the old A9 carrying all they owned in large bundles tied to their backs. Little children were strung together on a rope which their mother had tied around her waist. My father often spoke of how the exodus of Tinkers, Gypsies and Johnnies of the road was like a procession out of the area. It was at that time many took to the ancient drove roads, going far into moorland to find the old paths of their ancestors. Some managed a few nights' sleep by setting up their camps in boggy ground, thinking that cars wouldn't reach them. It was a new time of fear brought about by the Church of Scotland.

In some small areas in and around Perthshire, where farmers and landowners thumped the tables of and demanded the continued use of their Tinkers' skills, families were allowed to stay on without much interference, and this helped put food in bellies and allowed a form of normality. Until the work to be done was finished, of course, then it was on the road again.

41

Apartheid Education

By 1938 my two oldest sisters had been born and my people had already decided that Aldour in Pitlochry with its ancient graveyard and Black Spout waterfall was their favoured winter ground. Fortunately it seems that the authorities and Home Missionaries eventually saw that interference was not beneficial to anyone, so they left them alone. All the same, the government's Education Act had to be strictly adhered to; children between 5 and 14 had to attend school, it was non-negotiable. But for my family and other Tinkers who decided to put down winter roots in the area, there was a problem, and for once, according to the authorities, it wasn't their fault. Mr Brydon, headmaster of Pitlochry High School, was warned by a large number of the parents of his pupils that if the Tinkers were allowed into his school then they would remove their own children. So it was back to the Home Mission to see if they had a solution.

Well, as it turned out there already was a plan to deal with this situation – a separate school, one for Tinker children only. In Aldour, where the wood and the railway diverge, a good solid piece of ground was chosen. Here the church would build, for those dreadful Rileys, along with a few others, a single-classroom school.

My father never told me about this school, but I think he would have mentioned it in his autobiography that he wrote all those years later. I did hear stories in which Tinkers were taught separately in a small shed by a teacher who sprayed them with DDT to kill vermin, but I didn't believe for a moment it really existed.

I discovered that this special establishment was real one evening after I'd spoken at an event in Cupar, Fife. A lady approached me and asked, 'Where was the Tinker school?' She smiled and added, 'I'm from Pitlochry, but we never went near the woods nor ever discovered where the school was.' At that time I hadn't a clue about the place and wondered if she'd heard the same tale I had, and was quick to say so, but she was adamant that there really was such a school. Her next statement was jaw-dropping. She even remembered one day, as a young girl sitting in her classroom in Pitlochry School, my Granny Riley came charging in with a boy and a girl. She marched up to the teacher and said, 'These are my children, get them learnt!' The teacher told her to take them to take to the Tinkers school. Granny refused and left without them, saying, 'My kinchin are as good as any in here.' The Cupar lady was proud to say that the reason she never forgot that incident was that the little girl, Margaret, and she remained friends throughout their time together in Pitlochry School. Margaret was my auntie and the little boy, Edward, was my uncle.

Driving home from Cupar after my encounter I was, in my imagination, floating like a feather above a school from the past with Tinker kids in it. My God, I thought, they had actually done it – corralled up my wandering relatives in a separate education system.

Next day I phoned the A.K. Bell Library in Perth and asked about their archives to do with education. 'Yes,' the sweet-voiced lass informed me, 'we have a small collection of Tinker education papers, would you like to view them?' What a question! I must have damaged the poor soul's eardrums with the loudness of my reply. We chatted for ages as I told her all about the conversation with the Cupar lady, and gave her some family names in the hope that perhaps she'd unearth a line or two in the archives about them. I really still didn't think there could be much truth in the idea of a 'Tinker' school. This is Scotland, surely we don't do apartheid here?

Next morning I was in the foyer of the library to meet the librarian with her bunch of keys. I followed her like a puppy dog expecting a bone. I should have taken my time, I should have been prepared for something traumatic, but I wasn't. The magnolia-coloured folder, tied up in soft brown ribbons, was laid on the desk before me. I slipped on white cotton gloves and opened the doors of Aldour special school. The very first papers I saw told the story. Yes, they had really done it. They had separated children from one another as if they were from different species – children, the very future of the country, the babies who would grow into adults, into the decision-makers of the future. What an idiotic thing to do.

As my eyes found the names of my relatives and read the language used to describe them I had no control over the pools of tears welling in my eyes. In these pages were Mother's beautiful sister, her blessed brother, her cousins and other children, all my relatives. The librarian laid a box of tissues beside me and left; she'd obviously read the documents before I came in and knew that the people described were my relatives. I'd be upset, that went without saying, and she left me to my grief.

However strongly the waves of pity and anger overwhelmed my emotions, I had to stop and think rationally. However personal these documents were, the contents of the folder had to be viewed objectively as social history; if not, my planned book would never be completed. So I took lots of notes before visiting the washroom to clean my face. After a warm cup of coffee I went back. Somehow I felt guilty leaving my family hidden in a box on a shelf; I wanted to gather them in my arms and take them home with me. How dare the authorities write things about my mother and father then leave them in a public place for all the world to read and ridicule. Regardless of my attempt to be objective, I was deeply angry, and I'd challenge anyone not to feel the same if it was their loved ones whose private lives were being paraded in a public archive.

One Scottish Education Department document dated 21 October 1938, had all the information I needed.

Educating the 'Tent Dwellers'

The special part-time school for the education of the children of Tinkers which has been erected by the Church of Scotland Home Board with money provided by the Girls Association was formally opened last week by Miss Eva Robertson, Edinburgh. The school, a corrugated iron building on a brick foundation, with a large classroom, a teacher's room, and other accommodation, is a well-designed little building on the Pitlochry-Ballinluig Road. It is invisible from the road, and is reached by a rough track which passes by the Aldour Burn and under the railway. There is accommodation for from twenty to twenty-five children. In some subjects – particularly, of course, nature study – these children display a much wider knowledge than ordinary children, and their colour sense is usually very lively. Their school 'session' begins in the autumn and ends at Easter.

Welcoming the guests, Dr White who presided, said that for many years the church has been deeply interested in the 'tent dwellers.' As a type, they had suffered much through many generations in all nations, especially among so-called more civilised communities, who were always saying 'No camping here: Move on.' But Scotland had been more kind and merciful than other nations. Gypsies had danced at Holyrood before kings in the sixteenth century, and Johnny Faa had been recognised as the Lord and Earl of Little Egypt by James V. On the other hand, four Faas were executed in Edinburgh for the crime of 'being within the realm, they being Egyptians.'

To-day, they were taking an important step, said Dr White. They were giving these tent dwellers a fixed centre, and that would tend to alter their nomadic mode of existence into a settled family life.

Civilisation always proceeded first from the tent to the home, from the home to the city, from city to civilisation. So long as the Israelites dwelt in tents they were a wandering tribe. It was when they came into a settled land, a land of homes that their history began.

Dr G. F. Barbour, expressing acceptance of the school on behalf of the Education Committee, remarked that for a number of years the Inverness Education Committee had carried on a school of this kind of the banks of the Ness. There had also been a class carried on by Perthshire Committee for a number of winters, first at Dull and since then at Pitlochry High School. From the experience in Inverness, it had been found that the children made more progress in a building of their own. He trusted that the number of children coming to the school would grow, and the Education Committee might find they could provide transport facilities to bring children from encampments outwith walking distance.

Another document gives more details:

Perth and Kinross Joint County Council (16th November 1938). Intimation has now been received from the Department that the Tinker School at Pitlochry is to be known as Aldour School and not Aldour Special School as was originally proposed. The school has been placed on the list of schools conducted under the Day School Code and its official number is 6934.

On my next visit the librarian had some further revelations for me. She ushered me to my seat, handed me the gloves and said, 'I've uncovered something else – the log book! Here, sit down and take a look.'

I was amazed – they had actually written a daily log book! This time there were no tears. In my eagerness to read I forgot to pop on the gloves. The librarian didn't stop me, though, she simply left the room. I spent the next three hours going over page after page, reading everything and packing my head with every tiny detail. Later I left the archive department, but not before I'd ordered a photocopy of the entire folder, including the log book. This privilege is one that is afforded to published authors (praise be!).

Here are some extracts from the journal. On the first page, dated 26th October 1938, Mrs Flora Brown, the teacher, begins:

I took up duty at this school today. Dr Brydon Rector of Pitlochry High School interviewed two parents who came with their children, and helped me to work the six pupils – three boys and three girls. I divided the children into three groups; infant, senior and junior, with two children in each group. The children were very pleased with their new school and expressed their admiration of their new desks and furniture. The chimney smokes very badly.

28th Oct. The school was visited by Rev. Dr Macdonald and Mrs Macdonald.

A photographer came from Glasgow to take photographs of the school and scholars for the 'Daily Record.'

As I read this, I was thinking, it gets better. I will now have an opportunity to see my people's faces and the inside and outside of the school. But at the same time I gave a deep sigh of anxiety. Were the photos still in the newspaper's archives? Could I find them, and could I purchase them?

The staff of the archive department of the *Daily Record* were nothing short of brilliant. Not just one photo but six came, reproduced in sepia and enlarged. There he was, my beautiful uncle Nicky, who was one of the older boys. There were pictures of several others and of the teacher. I counted ten pupils, all wearing their uniforms which featured a tie with a thin stripe.

The newspaper piece was as follows.

SCHOOL FOR BAIRNS OF WANDERING FOLK

In the spring of the year Scotland's wandering folk take to the road, with their jingling carts. You see the sun-tanned children round nomad fires near the main roads. Where do these youngsters go in the winter time? The pictures supply the answers. The first school for the education of these young wanderers has been opened near Pitlochry. The pupils come from their winter camps, pitched in sheltered places around Pitlochry, and struggle with the three 'R's. You see them at lessons in the newly opened Aldour Special School, where between 1st October and 31st March, they must register at least half the number of attendances required from children who go to school all the year round. According to their teacher, 'They are smart pupils – quick on the uptake. They are particularly interested in nature study and art, subjects which require the observant eye developed in their mode of life. Note the ear-rings of the girl on the right.

(What isn't mentioned is that the girls had their long hair shorn to the nape of their neck, and before entering the school they'd been sprayed with DDT.)

Logbook entry for 2nd November. Chimney continues to smoke very badly. Miss Robertson, supervisor of needlework, visited the school and made arrangements for supplying material and wool.

Attendance 100%

4th Nov. Mr Duff, Strathtay, came with two men to attend defective chimney. Dr Sellars and Mr Stocks (cruelty inspector) visited the school. Closed school at 3.25 pm; workmen were busy in classroom.

Attendance 100%

8th Nov. Dr Dawson and Dr Brydon visited. Supply of wool and material arrived. Map of Scotland was supplied.

10th Nov. Supply of apparatus for individual work arrived

11th Nov. Two minutes silence observed

Perfect attendance for the week.

14th Nov. Two new pupils were enrolled this morning making a total of eight

18th Nov. Attendance 98.75%

23rd Dec. School closes today for Christmas holidays. Weather has been exceptionally cold. Temperature in schoolroom has seldom been above 50 F.

From the logbook it appears there were more visitors than pupils. Many were doctors, inspectors from various Government departments etc, but who would have imagined that the Moderator of the Church of Scotland would visit? Well, according to the logbook, on 21 Nov 1939, the Right Rev. A. Main did indeed pay the tiny school a visit.

4th January 1939. School opened today. Two new pupils; makes 10, telephone installed.

16th Jan. No water in school – pipe is frozen. Used telephone for the first time to contact Mr Menzies plumber, Pitlochry. The pipe was frozen near the bridge on the main road. It took a considerable time to thaw it.

On 23 January 1940, the logbook notes that two of my relatives had gone to Fort William School.

3rd Feb. Temperature in classroom at 9.30am – 31F. Very inadequate heating. Children complaining of being very cold – allowed home half an hour early.

The logbook continues to mention children coming and going, with the roll never exceeding 16 pupils. One poignant entry notes that because the children had no time pieces in their tents, they came to school on the first whistle of the passing train. One day the train added an earlier run to the timetable and the kids found themselves waiting a whole hour for the teacher to arrive. It is recorded that my Riley clan took to the road on 22 March 1939 for the season, but were forced back. This time the education vultures, the cruelty men or ministers of any church were not to blame. A new enemy had appeared, and not just of the Tinkers but of the entire country – Adolf Hitler.

My father and dozens of male relatives had already said their farewells and gone to fight for their country. The women were left behind. My Mammy was pregnant with her third child, but was terrified to send her five-year-old to the Special School. For a start, it had no air-raid shelter, there was no protection on the windows in case of an attack, and she hated the thought of sending her delicate child to a place she was convinced would carry out experiments on the children. I have unearthed letters which show what her concerns were, and that she visited the headmaster of Pitlochry High School to complain.

The first verifies what my Cupar friend had told me. It's a letter from Mr Brydon, the Pitlochry headmaster, who was having trouble with a tinker woman; none other than my wee warrior queen, Granny Riley. He wrote to Dr Dawson, Director of Education.

Dear Mr Dawson,

Special School.

I have reason to believe that I may expect a little trouble with Tinker parents in connection with the new school. One woman is saying she is determined to send her children to this school and that she will have nothing to do with the special school.

It would make things easier for me if I could have from you definite instructions to the effect that I am not to enrol any of the Tinker children in my school. It is just possible that some of them may want to enrol in my school on Thursday first, and I would like to know what I am to say.

The Master of Works is sending me forms etc. in connection with the special school, and I would like to know what my position is with regard to it.

Yours faithfully,
R.S. Brydon.

Another letter in a similar vein describes how another warrior queen, my mother this time, is causing trouble for the so-called education system.

Dear Mr Bates,
5th November 1940
Aldour School.

This morning another Mrs Riley came to enrol her child. (Pitlochry High School.) She is living with her mother in a hut. I told her to take her child to Aldour School. She refused, saying that she was looking for a house, and if she did not succeed she would live with her father-in-law, a householder whose children attend this school (Pitlochry High School). From what she said I began to think that one reason for this Tinker revolt may be the absence of any kind of Air raid protection at Aldour. Adhesive fabric on the windows might help,

Yours faithfully,
R. S. Brydon.

Mr Bates answered on 6 November, 1940.

Dear Mr Brydon,
Aldour School.

Regards your letter – I think we had similar trouble last year about Tinkers wanting to attend your school, and the ruling we gave was that, if Tinker children are to attend the ordinary school, they must comply with the regulations there and attend for the full session.

Your letter raises the interesting query, 'when does a Tinker cease to be a Tinker?' If they change their mode of life to the extent of taking up permanent residence in a house, and are prepared to attend school like other children, I doubt if we can exclude them.

I have arranged for fabric to protect the windows being sent to Aldour School.

Yours faithfully,
Clerk to Education Committee.

In 1941, after a second immunisation for Diphtheria, the entry in the logbook reads:

April 4th. Today the school closes. Owing to the results of inoculation several children were absent with stiff sore arms.

A tiny Tinker child had suffered a terrible accident. Aged only eighteen months, she burned her feet so badly it was decided to amputate. By sheer chance a surgeon was visiting the hospital when she was rushed in. He was a pioneer in skin grafting. For the next eighteen months he worked on her small feet, grafting skin from her thigh, and in the end he saved her feet. In the Aldour logbook an entry describes a small girl coming into school with badly fitting shoes. A later entry mentions that the same little girl now has a better pair of boots, and the teacher is thankful for this. This tells me two things: one, the reason that the teacher thought the child was not wearing proper footwear was because she was unaware of her painful struggle to walk again. And secondly, the mother had failed in her attempt to get her child into the 'normal' school.

—

This poem by Athole Cameron, a teacher who taught in Perthshire schools and later was a headmistress in Midlothian, beautifully captures the experience of Tinker children when they were taken into a mainstream school:

The Gaun-Aboot Bairn

His little brown face was elfin sharp,
As he gazed at the classroom floor;
At the high prim walls with their gaudy maps,
And the tight-shut prisoning door.

He watched the alien children,
With their barriers of paper and ink,
And he heard the whisper that rustled round,
'Dinny speak til him. He's a tink.'

Doon whaur they camped at the burnside,
There were things that a laddie micht dread,

When the eerie shadows o' dawnin'
Cam' aroon' his bracken bed.

He minded the gaist o' the pine trees,
An' the kelpie that bides in the pool,
But he kent that he never was feart afore,
Till the day whan they shut him in schule.

42

No Life for Riley

When my father came home from the war on compassionate leave after the birth of my older sister Charlotte (Shirley) on 24 January 1940, he wrapped the newborn infant in a shawl and walked a few yards to where a refuse lorry was dumping Pitlochry's rubbish in the tip. 'See my bonny wee queen,' he said, 'you were born on the edge o' a midden.' He walked back to the tiny hut that he, my mother and the girls shared with his in-laws and declared, 'This is no life for Riley.'

He returned to the battlefields of Europe and painted Shirley's name on the front of his tank. We knew what he meant when he said, 'The first and last thing the enemy saw was our wee Shirley heading towards them!'

My father had entered the army as a Tinker soldier in the Black Watch. He showed a flair for mechanics, so was sent on a crash course in engineering. He was then transferred to the REME (Royal Electrical Mechanical Engineers). In the latter stages of the war he was again transferred to the Tank Corps. He was awarded several medals but refused to accept any of them.

Although baptised a Catholic, he had his own singular philosophy, and never, as long as he lived, could be swayed from it. He believed the Bible to be the most contradictory of any written work and never missed an opportunity to get at religious people by saying that bibles were instruments for spreading fear among the populace. 'That book is a truly brilliant piece of age-old propaganda,' he'd remind me many times. It still is, and was written to control the ignorant peoples of the world by instilling fear into them. 'Whoever thought the whole thing up certainly knew a thing or two about human nature,' he said. He would shake his head and add, 'To think the bible is handed to everyone who gives evidence in a court of law for them to say, "the evidence I give shall be the truth and nothing but the truth." Innocent people have dangled from ropes, others been locked away indefinitely because a liar laid his hand upon a book of myths and legends to demonstrate to juries that he or she was telling the truth.

The Church of Scotland had put his wife through hell with their separate school, and her hatred for the instigators of that school grew wings when her youngest brother Nicky was killed by a sniper on 4 September 1944. She never forgot how happy he was at the thought that he would be joining his relatives on the battlefield. To think that about five years before, he was lining up with his sister and the other Tinker children for admittance into Aldour Special School while at the same time his army mates, the ones from Pitlochry who he played football with, were lining up to enter the 'normal' school. He was never given a pen while he was in the wee school, but there was no lack of guns given to him when he was admitted as Rifleman 14709162, 9th Battalion, Cameronians. The hardest part from my mother's point of view was that Nicky had lied about his age when enlisting – he was not the stated lawful age of 18 but 17. If the MoD had checked his birth details he would have been refused entry into the army, and been safely at home when the war ended several months later.

I'm pleased to add that Nicky's name is proudly displayed on the Pitlochry war memorial. I'd further like to add that since I began my research into Pitlochry schools, many elderly inhabitants have offered to help me piece together the history of Aldour. One lady found an inkwell in the burn by the school and made certain it found its way to my door. Bless you all, and in particular the late Bob Smith, the plumber who guided me through the plumbing disasters that afflicted the school.

I have no knowledge of what committee meetings followed the closure of Aldour School, and what was said about yet another failure to eradicate the Tinker lifestyle through education. You would think that a country burdened with war and a heavy death toll should have realised that the Tinkers should be asked what they wanted. I am sorry if I am harping on and repeating myself, but if homes for Tinkers had been found, and talks between Tinkers and the authorities had taken place on a regular basis, an answer and a way forward would have been reached. One culture cannot live inside the mind of another, but we have to understand each other and the only way is through dialogue. The state sometimes got things wrong. They could have avoided their ongoing war with the nomadic peoples of Scotland if they'd taken a more collaborative approach. A narrow-minded government and a bigoted church did so much damage that it has never been repaired.

Before we close this book I'd like to take you on one last journey. It's not my father's nor is it mine; it is the road that Perth and Kinross Council took as they tried for the very last time to trap the Tinkers and herd them into a reservation.

43
No Room Here, Thank You

The holy book teaches that our Lord Jesus Christ was born in a stable. It wasn't for the want of his parents begging for a shelter. We are told that no one would take the heavily pregnant Mary in, warm her or give her a bed in which to give birth to her first child. Instead, the divine revelation was brought forth into the world in a stable, and she laid her infant, the precious gift from God himself, in a manger, from which the cattle ate, for his bed. I remember being told that story on a cold Christmas Eve in my bus home, and thinking what a terrible lot the inn-keepers and house dwellers were to turn away a poor mother-to-be. But then it wasn't the first time I'd heard that story . . .

Aldour woods and the Black Spout provided a good home for my people. They stayed put, made sacrifices and the children went to school. Other Tinker folk spread to different places in the district, settled and gained the respect of everyone whom they chose to call neighbours. The church still had its spoon in the porridge, however, and this time we were prepared to believe that they meant well. Granny and Grandad Power had now become Pitlochry-ites, as had Granny and Grandad Riley. Letochbeg was now known as Wullie Riley's place and Granny was happy to have her wonderful garden. The family were all settled now, and with the war over my parents with the four girls they had then headed to Weem, in an episode we have already covered.

1947 saw the offer of a home from the Perth County Council to the static Pitlochry Tinkers; one with a permanent position and a rent-paying house, and Mr and Mrs Power were included in this.

The Church had provided another helper to serve as the voice of the Tinkers, Reverend Webb. I have no idea of where Miss Dorothea Maitland had gone. Maybe her inability to communicate with the Tinkers arose from ignorance on her part as to what the Tinkers needed rather than want she wanted to give them. As I'm often reminded, 'It was how people thought in those days.'

Here is the news from the *Courier* on the day my mother's parents and three other families were given their keys to so-called respectability.

PERTHSHIRE HOMES FOR TINKERS

Monday was red-letter day for members of the Tinker fraternity at Pitlochry, when four families were each presented with the key of a two apartment house provided by Perth County Council.

Standing in a wood near the former Bobbin Mill, the houses are in one block built from a converted army hut, with brick partitions. Each has a living room, bedroom, scullery with a cold water tap, and inside lavatory. They are said to be the first new buildings to be erected for Tinkers in Scotland by any authority.

Rev. W. Alexander Ross, county council member for Pitlochry, presided at the inauguration ceremony and was accompanied by the Rev. D. F. Findlay, minister of Moulin and Pitlochry West Church and Mr William Webb, Church of Scotland Tinkers' chaplain, Perth.

The conditions of let having been read over, each tenant signed the missive and was handed the key. The successful tenants are Mrs Margaret Queen, Mrs Nell (granny) Johnstone, Mrs Margaret Power, and Mrs Agnes Johnstone. Rents are fixed at £1/12/6d per month; plus occupier's rates.

The formalities over, Rev. W.A. Ross congratulated the new tenants on their good fortune in having secured a substantial dwelling house. After a lifetime of homeless wandering and living in tents they had every reason to believe that they had been neglected and forgotten. But God had been remembering them. Now they had a place they could call home. He wished them many years of life to enjoy it.

Both ministers and Mr Webb conducted a simple ceremony service, after which 'Granny' Johnstone invoked a Tinker's blessing on the gentlemen.

Here is the letter from architect Mr Ian Moodie to Mr Bushell, Joint County Clerk, with the cost of the houses.

Dear Sir,
12/4/1946

I enclose herewith the schedules and tenders submitted for the removal of a sectional wooden hut at Auchterarder and its erection on a site at Pitlochry, together with additional works to make the building suitable for the housing of four Tinker families. The tenders are as follows.

Mr Robert Gow – £823

A. B. Kennedy & sons –£850/6/5d

M. H.Young – £877/5/8d

Wm. Duff & Son, Strathtay – £924/1/11d

The committee directed that the tenders be submitted for the approval of the Department of health.

Ian Moodie, County Architect.

Well, dear reader, there you have it – fame for my family! We were among the first Tinkers to receive keys to a rented army hut with a cold water tap and a lavvy. My mother's folks were getting old, and it's no joy plodding along the old bridle paths when the bones are rickety and sore.

Grandad Power, although he spent a while in the place, was never happy in it. One day Granny rose from her bed to find he was gone. He came back periodically, but for the rest of the time joined the tramps of the road and returned to his wandering ways. Sometimes people would trail into her Bobbin Mill house saying they'd seen him at the Pass of Killiecrankie or heard him playing his squeezebox in the Kingshouse, Glencoe. Sometimes she was told stories of how he'd not looked too good when they last saw him tramping on a lonely glen road and afterwards no one had seen hide nor hair of him for ages. But he usually turned up before the hounds were sent out to search for him. Grandad Power was a lonely old man who seemed to miss having his children around him, and when the youngest got married it was then he decided to join the dwindling band of tramps.

> Come all ye tramps and hawker lads,
> That gi'ed the way a blaw,
> That tramped the country roon an' roon,
> Come listen yin an' a',
>
> I'll tell tae ye o' roving tales,
> Of sights that I hae seen,
> Far up unto the snowy north,
> And doon by Gretna Green.

Way to go, Granda . . .

44

THE END OF THE ROAD

These first houses for Tinker families were just the beginning of a long hard attempt by the Council to herd Perthshire Tinkers once and for all into places where they could be counted and monitored. The wish to do so seemed like a ghost that leapt invisibly from one generation of officialdom to the next. Would they ever achieve this mighty undertaking? Perth County Council had hundreds of wandering Tinkers to deal with. Every other planned reservation had fallen by the wayside; kicked aside by horses' hooves and tackity boots, or in our case escaped on bus wheels.

Other measures were implemented. Signs saying definitely no camping did make a difference – police powers were used to enforce them. More and more the Pictish standing stones and barrows were lost as camping grounds as monster boulders were placed in their entrances. Up until the late sixties farmers opened their fields to the tattie-howkers but closed them again when the tatties were all gathered in. Some folk were allowed to stay longer to work at other jobs. Usually these were families with hardy lads who would work all hours and lift heavily loaded bags. The way of the Tinker was fast becoming a daydream rather than a real true path; everywhere the Travellers went the barriers were up. It was easier to phone for police assistance to remove them from one's land rather than to say, 'Tomorrow I want you off.'

For about twenty years after the conversion of the Bobbin Mill houses, county officials sent letter after letter to landowners suggesting that they sell a piece of ground suitable for houses or as stances for caravans. But everything that was proposed turned out to be unsuitable. Many Tinkers, faced with losing their children under the education laws, were forced off the road and into permanent houses. Others were not for living in prisons and continued to travel their natural paths. It should have been time to draw a line underneath the authorities' harassment of Tinkers, but Perth Council still had the ambition to control them, so after several long and intense meetings it was decided to have another crack at the reservation idea. Here is some of the correspondence relating to this new attempt:

From the County Architect to the County Clerk. 20th May 1963.
Re – HOUSING ACCOMMODATION OF TINKERS AT TORWOOD, BIRNAM, ON THE SOUTH SIDE OF THE MAIN PERTH-INVERNESS ROAD.

I refer to your memo of the 17th April.

The Town and County Planning Committee Minute (15th March) item 3, states with regard to the above proposal – 'the committee did not favour the Housing Committee's proposal as Torwood occupies a prominent site on a trunk road which is also a main tourist route, and is at the entrance to the Highland District and in an attractive area adjacent to an area of great landscape value.'

It would appear the Planning Committee take general exception in principle to the use of this site rather than exceptions to the details of the lay-out.

Information now obtained from the feu charter shows the site available with the Torwood property to have frontage limited to 80 feet which does not include the field to the south east as appeared likely from examination of the ground and fences.

The County Surveyor has sent me a plan showing his proposals for the future road widening and advised on the sight line clearance, which would require to be observed in siting new buildings on this ground, from which it is established that the future building line will require to be set back from the line of the front of the present buildings by approximately 37 feet.

The area available for development is, therefore, considerably restricted and to make full use of it a two storied block accommodating four 3 apartment flatted houses would appear more appropriate than houses of single storied construction such as the type plan provisionally approved by the Committee for the housing of Tinkers before a particular site was under consideration.

I would recommend that the block be of normal traditional construction and to byelaw standards so that if the 'experiment' of housing Tinker families here prove unsatisfactory the accommodation may be made use of for the general housing needs. To suit Tinker families, however, I suggest the external doors to be to the rear only, which may avoid the occupants congregating on the footpaths of the main road and I suggest that entry to lock-ups or stores at the rear be screened and that tenants would be discouraged from depositing collections of old iron and similar materials on the open space at the rear and in view from the living room windows.

I hope to have a sketch plan illustrating the general lines of these proposals available for the Housing Committee meeting on the 24th inst.

I am hardly exaggerating to say that the backlash this proposal provoked was so severe that tongues, pens and tempers were on fire! The saying, 'not in my backyard' could have been born from this plan. Needless to say the proposal never even passed the first planning stage. I'm sure that those who look after the Perth and Kinross archives on housing would be happy to allow you to read more about this sorry saga. Make sure you have plenty of time to devote to it, because it is a huge pile of paperwork and all negative in tone.

Long centuries of unmitigated abuse and neglect had taken their toll. Tinkers had had enough – they wanted change but it would be on their terms. Sheila Stewart MBE was their voice, and she, with a like-minded group of highly respected folks, and with Big Wullie Macphee, the last o' the pipers, in their midst, visited the Council and laid their cards on the table.

The Tinkers, who now referred to themselves as 'the Travelling folk of Perthshire', at that time were scattered in a shanty town of tents and huts along the Almond outside Perth in a place called the Double Dykes. (The River Almond was where an excavation had unearthed a large hoard of Roman armoury not that long ago.) They had been ordered off the area many times, but they put their feet down and refused to budge. After many consultations with the Council, at long last the Traveller deputation was asked, 'What do you need?'

'Give us a proper site with a washing area, toilets plus wash-hand basins, and enough space between the caravans to allow for privacy. We'll pay the rent on time and cause you no bother!'

At long last the ears of officialdom opened, and for the first time the wanderers dictated to the councillors. They listened and agreed. As my father always said, 'A wee bit of eye tae eye is all it takes.'

Recently the site has been upgraded and to date it is one of the most modern and well-appointed places within Perth and Kinross's jurisdiction. So where the Roman Agricola first set foot on Scottish soil, and set up his slave blacksmiths to forge weapons to maintain his army against the Picts, 2000 years later the self-same people have come home, thrown off their shackles and resumed a life as free Scottish Travellers.

In Scotland there are only two monuments to my culture. One of them is Kirk Yetholm. This lovely village lies about a mile over the Border in the beautiful valley of Bowmont, and is known as the gathering place of the Scottish Gypsy. Yet means gate, and holm or ham is Hebrew for road – or more specifically, as older Gypsies tell me, the road to heaven.

This bonny place was where, for centuries, Gypsies gathered, married and crowned their kings and queens.

There is a peaceful atmosphere about the place I can't put my finger on, but I'd have to define it as spiritual. The village has only one street and I'm told its rows of little cottages once had thatched roofs. At the western end of the street there stands a manse and on the opposite side of the road a church which was known as the 'Black Kirk', so named because it was built on black rock. At the other end the street opens onto a green, where once a row of little thatched cabins stood. One of these houses, the tallest in the row, was called 'The Old Palace' and was the homely seat of the true lineage of Gypsy monarchs who all were related by blood to Johnnie Faa. Johnnie was the famous Gypsy king who had been given leave to rule his people under the protection of James V.

The link to Kirk Yetholm, however, is attributed to Wull Faa, the most genial of the long royal lineage who died in 1784. The story goes that he was given the Old Palace after retrieving a stolen horse from a thief who had stolen the valuable steed from Sir William Bennet of Marlfield. Around the time of the first Jacobite uprising in 1715 horses were being stolen all over the land to help advance the cause of the rebels. Wull knew how much the horse meant to Bennet and that it was irreplaceable, so stole it back. The result was the gift of the dwelling in Yetholm.

The Gypsies believe that their protectors are the black-headed laughing gulls, whose Romany name is the Wetheris. Although Kirk Yetholm is quite a distance from the sea, thousands of black-headed gulls swarm in the area, following the plough. The Gypsies have a saying, if the rooks who fly with the Wetheris disappear, so will the Gypsy. They have always believed that rooks have the eyes of their ancestors and say that 'When the Wetheris and the rook no more couple the Bowmount Water, disaster looms on Northumberland's border.'

In his book *The Kirk Yetholm Gypsies* by Joseph Lucas, the author writes nostalgically about one of the monarchs of the Gypsy kingdom, Queen Ester Faa Blythe.

The Queen is a tidy and temperate woman, has a thorough knowledge of human character and can read the faces of all who she comes in contact with. From her I took 100 'Cant' words. I was shown the sword brought by her ancestors from Flodden field; she showed me a pink card with these words printed in letters of gold:

TO KIRK YETHOLM, THE HEADQUARTERS OF THE SCOTTISH GYPSIES.

Farewell to Kirk Yetholm, and Cheviot's green hills,
Where gentle Queen Ester the Gypsy throne fills,
Farewell to sweet Bowmont, whose bright water glides,
Through thy dark glen where nature's wild beauty resides.
The spell is now broken, thy glory is past,
Thy course, like the sun, disappears in the west,
Thy swart Eastern sons now no longer can rove
In freedom to plunder, to fight and to love.

Thy daughters who once, like the Fairies of yore,
Danced round the green knolls, now gambol no more,
Those dark eyes, whose glance set the heart all on flame
No longer in Yetholm their empire proclaim.

The other significant monument to Scotland's Travellers and Gypsies is a number of white quartz stones arranged in the shape of a heart. Known as the Tinkers' Heart, this poignant memorial lies just off the A815 Argyllshire road to Struchar, at the head of Loch Fyne, opposite the entrance to Hell's Glen. This is a narrow winding road which leads onto the famous Rest and Be Thankful.

There are different stories surrounding this profoundly spiritual emblem from ancient times and I feel each is important in its own way. Remember that the history of my people was held in the head and shared on the tongue, and so I must include each tradition that has significance.

The commonest explanation of the origin of the Heart tells of the time when the lads of the Cowal Peninsula took up arms for Charles Edward Stuart before his final battle at Culloden Moor, Inverness. The stones represent sons and husbands who failed to return from that fateful conflict. Some died on the battlefield, others were imprisoned and a few were sent as slaves to the Americas. In memory of those lost souls, marriages took place and babies were christened at the Tinkers' Heart.

Another explanation which I find just as intriguing is that this place had been used by couples to marry in secret. In the days of Wallace and Bruce, when English lords demanded the right to spend the first night with every newly married lass, this spot among the hills and heather was a sacred place where marriage could be celebrated but the bride kept out of the grasping hands of the rulers of the land.

The final explanation given for the Heart was that before Caird and master set off to the Holy Lands on the Crusades they were blessed there. This may even have been the place where a chastity belt was placed upon a fair maid by her departing husband. These were staunchly Christian times and who knows what form of religious ceremony took place here.

Regardless of the history, the Heart has survived through the generations. In 1929, when the roads in the area were being surfaced with tar, Lady Campbell of Inveraray Castle insisted that the Heart be protected. The tarred road was diverted around the sacred place and a chain set in the ground to protect it. Travelling people continue to visit, and take comfort in the spiritual power that it holds. The scattering of coins in the middle of the Heart clearly testifies to beliefs which are held to this day. Astonishingly, as with the words of doom repeated about the rook and the Wetheris at Kirk Yetholm, a curse lies on the Heart: 'The Rest and Be Thankful will be no more, when the stones of the Cowal are trampled ower.' For the last few years I have been involved with Travellers and other dedicated supporters in a campaign to have the Heart officially listed as an ancient monument. After much work and many setbacks our Heart of the Travellers (HOTT) group met with success, and on 18 June 2015 Historic Scotland scheduled the Heart as a Monument of National Importance, with these words: 'It gives us a great understanding of the traditions and material heritage of Scottish Travellers . . . It is a rare example of a permanent physical monument of Scottish Travellers . . . and it holds a high significance in the consciousness of Gypsy Travellers and the people of Argyll as a symbol of Scottish Travellers and their heritage.'

These two monuments, small but of great spiritual significance to the Gypsy and Travelling people, proclaim an undeniable fact: we have been here a long time and seen a lot of history. As Joseph Lucas writes, the Gypsy Travellers are one of the most important links between peoples of the East and West. Making a bridge between the two is acknowledged to be the greatest challenge of the age. It is my belief that this connection, represented by language, will increasingly be confirmed when the true history of the Gypsies, which has still to be written, emerges. Scotland and Europe will then be joined to India through Egypt.

—

Alas, progress brings changes. Within a generation the cant language has fallen into disuse in many families and been forgotten. People are no longer entertained by the old stories and songs; televisions, computers and new technology offer much more fun. Scottie dogs and pug-faced Pekinese have replaced the working dogs of before, and the hunting hawks once used for hunting on wrist and fist have been downsized to budgies that sit in cages dreaming of the open air as their masters once did. A lifestyle that had stood the test of time and withstood war after war against it is fast disappearing.

Tinker time is dying; even the the name Tinker itself is considered derogatory. In the mid-sixties a delegation approached Parliament and asked that Tinker be made a racist term. Traveller was considered much more acceptable – after all, that was what we called ourselves.

For my part, however, I can't help but be sad that my old mate, he of Lochgilphead who was as proud as a stallion of his trade, should be made to feel ashamed of a craft that had been handed down from one generation to the next. His stubby-handled tools, his soldering iron, his tales of bygone eras that were told in time to the clinking of his hammer, these were to him what made us different, not travelling. Dogs travel and so do birds. I hope he and his like were no longer around by the time we disowned the name Tinker and were officially known as Travellers. So here we are, reader – the same as everyone else. Is the doctor who travels about the district to attend to our health needs from the way of the road? Perhaps every councillor has the seeds in him, the dentist, the lawyer, Uncle Tom Cobley and all Jock Tamson's bairns – do they all have that wee germ of wanderlust?

We were known as Cairds and then for centuries we had been known as Tinkers – how long would our new title last? Well, to be honest, not very long. Today if you go into an airport, everyone is described on signs and in announcements as Travellers; it is the same in train stations too, the name simply refers to people taking a journey. Traveller representatives hurried through an amendment to the legislation; the word Gypsy should be put before Traveller, as in Gypsy/Travellers, and in that way the culture would be properly recognised.

For me, something has been lost. I would love to think that if I happened one day to be in some lonely wooded glen I might just catch a glimpse of a thin spiral of smoke and say to myself, is that a Tinker at his fire hidden in the wood?

I remember reading this piece by a retired gardener, Thomas Harper, on the loss of Tinkers in an area in the north, who reminisced:

'I never see a Tink on the road. What has happened to them? I mind my grandmother once told me how a Tinker lass came to her door early one morning with an empty pail and begged her for a couple o' peats. "Mistress," she said, "I canna get a fire gyan the day, the bairn pished in the tinder box." Ma granny geen her a couple o' peats. Fires were never allowed to go out because it was unlucky – so there was always peat, and in the evening the fire reestit with smouldering dross.

They were hated by the gamekeeper for poaching rabbits or pheasants. In winter it was worst because they snared his grouse wi' horsehair snares. Sometimes they kept a lurcher dog that could run down a hare. Then on a dark night a lonely hen roosting on a "cairt" shed might find her windpipe gripped and wings wrapped in a jacket, quite unable to utter a squawk or make a single flutter. Oh aye, the Tinks never died o' the hunger in the old days.' He went on: 'Young Tinks, who were physically fit, enlisted in the Militia, a third battalion of the local regiment, for home service only, and were called on to do at least 21 days training. They were housed in barracks in Aberdeen. Lord Haldane abolished the Militia in 1908 and founded in its place the Territorial Army. There were many Tinkers in the Militia who played the pipes.'

As we near the end of our journey, I'd like to remind you of one of the reasons why I put pen to paper in the first place – the silence in Glencoe left by the absence of the pipers who carried within them the soul music of our race. I have so many memories of growing up with these instruments. They were a permanent feature on the carts, rolled up in tartan rugs in caravans, kept as precious objects in boxes under beds and in cupboards. Almost all Tinker families had a set.

Fragments of piping history come from all over the world. Bagpipes are found in Egyptian mummy cases. Nero, the Roman Emperor, was a skilled bagpipe player, although he fiddled while Rome burned. Some musical historians say that the Scottish instrument can be traced back to 100 AD and was brought to Scotland by Irish colonists who came to Scotland in 120 AD and later.

Scotland and Ireland gave the pride of the pipes to the world. The old Scottish pipers held a very special position in society, they were closely attached to the chieftains and would share their food and drink. This might be why a lot of my piper relatives enjoy a good dram, the best of whisky.

The Macleods, who have lived at Dunvegan Castle on Skye since the thirteenth century, had as their hereditary pipers, the renowned MacCrimmons. Lands at Boreraig were given to the MacCrimmons about the end of the fifteenth century. It was here they established the first College of Piping. They lived in a long two-storied farmhouse at one end with the Piping School at the other. In this building and the surrounding caves some of the greatest pipe music ever was composed. The most revealing test of any tune is the test of time, and few types of music have withstood the ravages of time as well as the Pibroch. Some of the most popular pieces of today are centuries old and can be traced to the old hereditary pipers who could not write a note of music and used only the mouth to hand down their music. The Canntaireachd is a form of music taught in syllables, then converted to musical notes for the pipes; nowhere in the world is there anything like it. It is a language all on its own and quite unintelligible to the uninitiated.

As Thomas Harper says, Tinkers and pipes go hand in hand – they are never apart. Who has not felt the tears well up at the sound of the pipes, especially on Remembrance Sunday standing by the war memorial? The same sound could be heard by tourists who visited the Pass of Glencoe and the Rest and Be Thankful, the car park at Ben Lomond, along the shores of dozens of lochs like Loch Ness, Lomond, Tay, Long, Awe and Etive; in the Great Glen, Nevis Glen, at Killiecrankie, at the Queen's View at Pitlochry, at Gretna Green and John o' Groats, Culloden Moor and all the other beautiful places in Scotland where there are natural stopping points where tourists can take photos. At one time the Tinker piper played for tourists at all these places and made a wonderful addition to their memories of a Scottish trip. These days an official ban has reduced all these pipers to silence. Only a handful of pipers are authorised now, and they are usually only to be found at the entrances to castles and stately homes. To the tourist chiefs I say, bring back the pipes to Scotland's glens and lochs; they have lain silent too long.

Traveller Belle Stewart was once asked what was the future for our kind. With her husband Alex, the renowned piper, by her side and members of her family nearby, she smiled wryly and answered, 'There will be Travellers until Doomsday in the afternoon.'

And from some mysterious heather-covered braeside the ghost of Charlie Riley says, 'From me and the White Nigger, many thanks for sharing the road.'

Books Consulted

Robert Dawson, *Empty Lands*

Robert Chambers, *Domestic Annals of Scotland from the Reformation to the Rebellion*

Andrew Sinclair, *Rosslyn: The Story of Rosslyn Chapel and the True Story Behind the Da Vinci Code*

Walter and James Simson, *A History of the Gipsies*

David Macritchie, *Scottish Gypsies under the Stewarts*

Robert Chambers, *Exploits, Curious Anecdotes, and Sketches, of the Most Remarkable Scottish Gypsies, or Tinklers*

F.W. Robbins, *The Smith: Traditions and Lore of an Ancient Craft*

Mary Mackay, *Famine's Harvest*

Douglas Fraser, *Highland Perthshire*

Colin Mayall, *History of Strathearn*

William A. Gillies, *In Famed Breadalbane*

John Dixon, *Pitlochry Past and Present*

John Mackay Wilson, *Wilson's Tales of the Borders and of Scotland*

Andrew Mccormick, *The Tinkler-Gypsies*

David Webster, *Scottish Highland Games*

Adam and Charles Black, *Black's Guide to the Trossachs*